THE
ABOLITION
OF MARRIAGE

THE ABOLITION OF MARRIAGE

HOW WE DESTROY LASTING LOVE

By Maggie Gallagher

Regnery Publishing, Inc.
Washington, D.C.

Copyright © 1996 by Maggie Gallagher

Manufactured in the United States of America

Library of Congress Cataloging-in-Publication Data

Gallagher, Maggie, 1960–
       The abolition of marriage : how we destroy lasting love / Maggie Gallagher.
         p.   cm.
       Includes bibliographical references and index.
       ISBN 0-89526-464-1 (alk. paper)
       1. Marriage—United States. 2. Married people—United States.
3. Domestic relations—United States. 4. Divorce—United States.
5. Divorced people—United States. 6. Sexual ethics—United States.
7. United States—Social conditions—1980–   8. United States—Social policy.   I. Title.
HQ536.G345   1996
306.81'0973—dc20

                                95-42998
                                    CIP

Published in the United States of America by
Regnery Publishing, Inc.
An Eagle Publishing Company
422 First Street, S.E.
Washington, DC 20003

Distributed to the trade by
National Book Network
4720-A Boston Way
Lanham, MD 20706

Design by Marja Walker
Set in Minion

10 9 8 7 6 5 4 3 2 1

Books are available in quantity for promotional or premium use. Write to Director of Special Sales, Regnery Publishing, Inc., 422 First Street, S.E. Washington, DC 20003, for information on discounts and terms or call (202) 546-5005.

TABLE *of* CONTENTS

To my mother, Darrilyn Gallagher,
who taught me more than she knows
and more than I can ever thank her for.

Acknowledgments

I AM INDEBTED TO MANY PEOPLE for making this book a reality, especially my editor Richard Vigilante, without whose relentless confidence and equally relentless intellect this book would not have been written.

David Blankenhorn of the Institute for American Values gave me an institutional home and intellectual support when it was most needed. David Popenoe gave me the benefit of his inestimable expert opinion. David Dortman's Sisyphean editorial labors did not go unnoticed or unappreciated. I should acknowledge a large intellectual debt to Alan Carlson and the Rockford Institute, whose newsletter, *The Family in America*, pointed me toward many fruitful avenues of research.

My warmest thanks to Michael Joyce, Heather Higgins, Richard Gilder, and Gary Bauer for their indispensable vote of confidence in my work.

The virtues of this book owe much to the people named above; any vices that remain are, of course, my own responsibility.

PART ONE

※

THE
COLLAPSE
of
MARRIAGE

1

THE ABOLITION
of MARRIAGE

OPTIMISM IS AMERICA'S BIRTHRIGHT. There is no age-old problem we do not insist on trying to cure, rather than endure: slavery, prostitution, drunkenness in the nineteenth century; poverty, domestic violence, and inequality in the twentieth century. Total victory often eludes reformers. Still, Americans have an impressive record of refusing to bow to historical inevitabilities, of taking active responsibility for forming the society in which we live. There is no social problem Americans dare not attack, except one: about marriage, and marriage alone, we despair.

"[T]he changes in the structure of the family are probably the result of some sizeable and largely unstoppable changes in social and economic patterns," concludes David Ellwood, one of America's leading social scientists, in his study of single parents and poverty.[1] "[T]here is no way of going back to where we were before," agrees famous family scholar Arlene Skolnick.[2]

And yet as the twenty-first century looms, concern about family breakdown has moved to the very center of American life. A large and growing body of social science research has confirmed that, as Barbara Dafoe Whitehead put it in her now famous 1993 *Atlantic* article "Dan Quayle Was Right," "The dissolution of intact two-parent families is harmful to large numbers of children." The overthrow of the marriage culture and its replacement by a postmarital culture is the driving force behind almost all of the gravest problems facing America— crime, poverty, welfare dependence, homelessness, educational stagnation, even child abuse. Above all, the decline of marriage is behind the precarious sense of economic instability haunting so many Americans in this time of statistical economic abundance, low unemployment and inflation, and rising GNP and personal income. Even in sheer economic terms, the greatest threat to the American dream comes not from the productivity of the Japanese but from the instability of our marriages.

We have begun to realize all this and more. Yet we have refused to act, taking, as it seems, bizarre comfort in the belief that family, or rather marriage, is ultimately a private matter, and therefore we can do nothing as a society to prevent its collapse. Even the political Right, though willing to fiddle with welfare formulas to discourage, however moderately, illegitimacy among the underclass, refuses to take on the decline of marriage more directly. Welfare, which requires taxpayers' money, is deemed a legitimate area of Republican concern. But marriage must shift for itself.

Not every child will slip into poverty as a result of his parents' divorce or failure to marry. But almost every child will become poorer as a result. The great rallying cry of the American people has always been: Each generation better off than the last. By contrast, the hallmark of the postmarital culture is downward mobility. Affluent kids slip into the middle class. Middle-class children experience the strains of blue-collar life. Working-class children slide into poverty, and the poor become trapped in a permanent underclass.

When divorce and illegitimacy become normal, when single parenthood begins first to compete with and then to displace marriage, when not just a few, but many or most parents adopt a risky pattern of child rearing, the result is not just a bit more suffering for a few more children, but the impoverishment of the society and the none-too-slow erosion of American civilization.

The collapse of marriage can be summed up in just two statistics.

- Almost one-third of all American children (and two-thirds of African American children) are now born out of wedlock.
- Demographers estimate that up to 65 percent of all new marriages now fail.[3]

The result? "About half of today's young children will spend some time in a single-parent family," writes demographer Larry Bumpass. "The majority [who do so] will reside in a mother-only family for the remainder of their childhood."[4]

The suddenness with which marriage has been overthrown is breathtaking. Just 14 percent of white women who married in the forties eventually divorced. A single generation later, almost 50 percent of those married in the late sixties and early seventies have already divorced.[5] This explosion in divorce was followed in quick succession by an unexpected surge in out-of-wedlock births. Between 1970 and 1992, the proportion of babies born outside of marriage leaped from 11 percent to 30 percent.[6]

Even since 1970, the marriage rate has fallen almost 30 percent, while the divorce rate has jumped nearly another 40 percent. Cohabitation, the great historic competitor of marriage, increased sixfold.[7] By 1994, 40 percent of never-married women in their thirties had had an illegitimate child.[8]

Dan Quayle may have been right, but Murphy Brown is winning. Marriage, from the child's point of view, has become a risky, unreliable business. The optimistic view by divorce advocates, that, as the title of one divorce self-help book proclaims, Kids Are Non-Divorceable, has turned out to be heartbreakingly false.[9] For all the noise made about the new fathering, most children raised outside of intact marriages see little of their fathers; almost all experience profound grief, longing, and loss as a result of their parents' divorce.

In 1927 John B. Watson, an eminent American psychologist, made an ominous prediction: "In fifty years, unless there is some change, the tribal custom of marriage will no longer exist." Ten years later Pitirim Sorokin, a prominent sociologist, prophesied that "…divorces and separations will increase until any profound difference between socially sanctioned marriages and illicit sex-relationships will disappear."[10]

Today, experts who resurrect quotes like these generally do so to ridicule them. Or, more precisely, to reassure men and women currently troubled about the state of marriage that they too are misinformed.

"What about the supposed eclipse of marriage?" concurs sociologist Stephanie Coontz in her 1992 book, *The Way We Never Were.* "Neither the rising age of those who marry nor the frequency of divorce necessarily means that marriage is becoming a less prominent institution…. Ninety percent of men and women eventually marry, more than 70 percent of divorced men and women remarry, and fewer people remain single for their entire lives today than at the turn of the century."[11]

"High rates of remarriage could mean that people are giving up not on marriage but on unsatisfactory relationships," chimes in a college textbook, "…is the rise of illegitimacy a sign of moral breakdown? Or does it simply reflect a different, more enlightened set of moral norms…?"[12]

Here are just a few of the founding myths of the postmarital culture: Marriage and the family aren't declining, merely changing, and for the better. Marriages are healthier and happier; children are better off; and people have more freedom, now that the stultifying taboos against divorce and unwed motherhood have been overthrown. Wielding these myths, the voices of intellectual and moral authority have insisted for more than a generation that there is no cause for alarm. Psychologists, marriage counselors, ministers, college professors, and lawyers united in insisting that divorce was better for kids and society than what they saw as the necessary alternative: a grim and hate-filled marriage.

So one sociologist, Martin King Whyte, was only repeating an intellectuals' cliché when he wrote in a 1990 book, "Clearly these dire predictions [of the end of marriage] have not been fulfilled in American society and perhaps this fact should warn us to be skeptical of such prophecies."[13]

Lately a few intellectuals have broken ranks, timidly conceding that divorce or nonmarriage may cause some children harm and that today more children are exposed to this risk. This argues a far more radical thesis: Not only is marriage in danger of disappearing, but though we do not fully recognize it yet, *it already has*. The law no longer permits men and women to make permanent commitments to each other. Marriage did not collapse from its own weight. It was ruthlessly dismantled, piece by piece, under the influence of those who (though they do not say it and may not realize it) believed that the abolition of marriage was necessary to advance human freedom.

From a formal, legal standpoint, marriage is no longer an enforceable commitment. Children born in wedlock are accorded no special protections by law or public policy. Spouses who wish to keep their marriage together and hold their spouses to their marital commitment are given no official support. Culturally and morally, marriage has been demoted from foundation stone to just another lifestyle, about which neighbors, therapists, grandparents, priests, and policymakers are supposed to remain conveniently neutral in comparison to other lifestyles. A husband for oneself, or a father for one's child, has been redefined as discretionary items: nice, if you happen to like one, but certainly not necessary. The legal, social, and economic supports that sustained marriage over centuries have dispatched with astonishing speed, and marriage has been reconceived as a purely private act, not a social institution but one possible scenario, sustained entirely by and for two individuals for their own mutual pleasure. Thanks to no-fault divorce and the attitudes, norms, and policies that support it, getting married now more closely resembles taking a concubine than taking a wife.

Under these circumstances, while individuals' aspirations to marriage remain strong, their ability to attain marriage is severely compromised. The spirit is willing, but the body has been dismembered. Over the past generation, we Americans gained the right to unilateral divorce but in the process lost the right to give ourselves in a lifelong commitment to another human being.

The longing for marriage has not subsided. Despite easy divorce, easy cohabitation, casual sex, and even relatively easy unwed mother-hood, marriage remains an all but universal aspiration: Over the past thirty years a consistent 96 percent of the American public has expressed a personal desire for marriage. Only 8 percent of American women consider remaining single an ideal, a proportion that has not changed over the past twenty years. Almost three-quarters of adult Americans believe that "marriage is a lifelong commitment that should not be ended except under extreme circumstances." Even 81 percent of divorced and separated Americans still believe that mar-riage should be for life.[14]

As if in desperate affirmation of these aspirations, weddings have gotten more extravagant as marriage has become more fragile. One study of Detroit women found that, though only 39 percent of the women who married in the relatively stable years before World War II had bridal showers, 68 percent of recent brides had a party in their honor. Weddings have gotten bigger: an average of 50 guests in prewar wedding receptions has ballooned to 150 champagne-sippers today.[15] The diamonds and the receptions grow bigger as the thing they sym-bolize, a permanent union of lovers, grows increasingly elusive.

Coming of age in the age of divorce, schooled in a culture of courtship increasingly disconnected from and hostile to marriage, young Americans still aspire to attain enduring love, but increasingly fear they will never achieve it. Eighty-six percent of male high school seniors queried in the mid-eighties said that "having a good marriage and family life" was either "extremely" or "quite" important (girls were even more enthusiastic). But only slightly more than half retained enough of their youthful illusions to believe that it was "very likely" they "would stay married to the same person for life."[16]

The gap between the word and the thing, between the aspiration and the institution, has grown from a private nightmare into a public catastrophe. Yet growing recognition of the disastrous collapse of marriage has not yet translated into any active political movement to restore it. "Family values" is a slogan without content, a perfect politicians' phrase, committing no one to anything, least of all a serious agenda to restore marriage. Liberals and conservatives alike have been paralyzed by ambivalence and despair.

The ambivalence stems in large part from the false framing of the debate as one between choice and coercion, individual liberty and state control. "You can't force two people to stay married," we tell ourselves, and turn the page. Divorce, however, is not usually the act of a couple, but of an individual. Eighty percent of divorces in this country are unilateral, rather than truly mutual, decisions.[17] The divorce revolution has not, as is usually claimed, produced a straightforward increase in personal freedom. Rather the divorce revolution can be more accurately described as a shift of power, favoring the interests of one party over others: the interests of the spouse who wishes to leave over those of the spouse who is being abandoned and over those of the children whose consent is not sought.

Marriage, like a corporation or private property, is an institution that must be supported by law and culture if it is to exist at all. In the state of nature (as increasingly in the United States), marriage and cohabitation become indistinguishable. Marriage is a sexual option carved out of nature by law, faith, custom, and society. In other words, to have the choice as individuals to marry we must first choose as a society to create marriage.

For too long the collapse of marriage has been treated as a *natural* disaster, like typhoons, earthquakes, and tidal waves, causing pain and suffering that cannot be prevented, only ameliorated. Fifty years ago most marriages, by some good fortune, survived. Now most new marriages, by some ill-fortune, fail. The best we can do in the face of this mystery, we are told, is to be like the Red Cross after a storm: go through the wreckage, pick up the survivors, and carry on.

There is comfort in treating the collapse of marriage this way: If divorce and illegitimacy are inevitable, then no one must take responsibility for the devastation. If there is no solution, there is no problem.

This despair and inertia, however, are actively cultivated by those who do not want to see marriage revived; the postmarital culture is not without its fierce defenders. Marriage could not have collapsed without a strong push from those who found its abolition liberating. "Gradually," historian Glenda Riley notes in her 1991 book *Divorce: An American Tradition*, "proponents of divorce began to maintain that divorce was a citizen's right in democratic America; a civil liberty rather than a social ill."[18] Ditto unwed motherhood.

These divorce advocates are not necessarily mistaken about their own interests. The sexual revolution, like all revolutions, has its winners and its losers, although they are not neatly divided along sexual or ideological lines. For every woman who feels liberated by trading in her husband for a new life, there is a man who has been licensed to trade in his wife for a younger model. For every ambitious woman who has found release in the world of work, there is a woman who has lost the means to have and care for her own babies. Other, ambivalent young women, uneasily poised between the two worlds, are living with men they cannot get to the altar.

The divorce advocates and others who have benefited from the collapse of marriage remain strikingly unwilling to acknowledge the real costs of their desires. Former radicals, they have become true reactionaries, fierce defenders of the status quo. Faced with mounting evidence of the harm to children, society, and abandoned spouses, they look away, rationalize, or seek refuge in the belief that the changes they so devoutly sought and fought for were actually inevitable, the result of historical forces for which they need not assume personal responsibility.

Human nature is no different today than it was thirty years ago, and yet thirty years ago, most people who got married, stayed married. Today, most fail, and an increasing number never even try. When the majority of marriages fail and when millions of perfectly nice girls eschew marriage altogether, the failure is not merely private and personal (bad luck, bad judgment, bad morals) but public and institutional.

The voices of despair argue that times have changed, that under-lying forces ripping our marriages apart are too powerful to resist. A quick scan of international data, however, suggests that marriage and modernity are not nearly so incompatible as the divorce advocates would have us believe. Germany, for example, has an illegitimacy rate of 15 percent, half that of America's. In Italy the rate is 7 percent. In today's Japan, just 1 percent of babies are born outside of marriage, the same proportion as in 1970,[19] and the divorce rate is so low almost all minor children live with both their married parents.[20]

While America may never return to the low divorce and illegiti-macy rates of the past century, there is every reason to believe that we can, if we choose to meet these two simple goals: (1) stabilize mar-riage, so that the majority of lovers who marry succeed in their goal of making a permanent union of heart and hand, of spirit and flesh, and (2) reconnect marriage with childbearing so that each year more and more of American babies begin or continue their lives under the protection of a couple publicly joined by marriage vows.

Absent such an effort there is no sign that the decline of marriage is anywhere near over. Recent data strongly suggest that the real (as opposed to the crude) divorce rate has yet to level off: For those mar-rying in the late 1970s, the proportion divorced within five years was 22 percent; for those marrying in the early eighties, the proportion divorced within five years nudged up to 23 percent.[21] Since 1980, the illegitimacy rate jumped 66 percent and is still climbing, most rapidly among whites.[22]

If we fail to act, both the divorce and illegitimacy rates will most likely continue to climb, because the postmarital culture reinforces itself in an accelerating spiral of decline: Children of divorce are themselves particularly vulnerable to family disruption; and children raised in single-parent households, especially girls, are more likely to divorce or have children outside marriage.[23]

The alternatives to hope, faith, commitment, and progress are despair, doubt, anxiety, and decline. It is time for Americans to get out of the business of merely managing the decline of the family and begin the far more challenging but exhilarating task of recreating marriage. In that way, and only in that way, love will not only endure, but also triumph.

2

THE GOOD DIVORCE

WHEN DONNA WAS SIX, her parents embarked on a good divorce. It was just like the divorces so carefully described in children's literature, just the way the therapist prescribed, as in the *Dinosaur's Divorce*.[1]

Each parent was careful not to bad-mouth the other, and Donna's father continued to take an active interest in her life. After an initial three-year bout with depression, Donna's mother bounced back and remarried happily, as did her father. Today, everyone from both sides gets together for holidays and family occasions. Her dad and his family even attended her mother's second wedding, and vice versa.

At thirty-one, Donna is no divorce statistic. She is an indisputable success story: she is happily married with two children, and she recently graduated from medical school.

Nonetheless, Donna sought help from a therapist because she couldn't understand why for the past ten years, despite all the gifts and achievements that mark her life, she has been wracked by the fear that her husband, Anton, will walk out on her. "It was probably as 'good' a divorce as you can get," says Donna on her parents' split. But still, the unanswered—and unanswerable—question haunts her: "If my father could do this to my mother, could Anton do it to me?"[2]

In America, we measure problems in order to solve them. Social science emerged in the nineteenth century out of the faith that, with knowledge, we could triumph over even the most perennial human problems: hunger, poverty, crime, drunkenness, and vice. In many instances social science has proved a useful tool for understanding. But there is a danger in this approach: The measures may become our masters.

So we talk and think about family breakdown in terms of what it costs the taxpayers, instead of what it costs our children. We discuss the costs to children only in terms of the categories of social science, we adopt the language of pathology, and we discount nine-tenths of the injuries we do the children, because "no permanent damage" results thereby, at least damage as we know how to count it. "Most children [of divorce] will not suffer long-term serious harm," reassures Andrew Cherlin, a sociologist at Johns Hopkins University in Baltimore. "Most can adjust," concurs divorce researcher Mavis Hetherington, a professor of psychology at the University of Virginia, arguing that 75 percent of children in remarried families show no long-term problems.[3]

To sociologists, policy analysts, and other experts, the family is a kind of factory, and law-abiding, taxpaying adults are its chief output. Conceptualizing the family as a factory, researchers interested in divorce naturally focus on how it may or may not interfere with the production process: Are children of divorce well fed, well clothed, well educated? Are they given satisfactorily structured routines, appropriate responsibilities, effective discipline?

These are not unimportant questions and, as we shall see, the best answer social science can give is that the collapse of marriage significantly heightens the risk that our children will end up poor, hungry, ill, ignorant, violent, or dead. Nonetheless, imagining the family in this peculiar way limits our ability to see.

This *task-oriented* conception of parenting ignores, among other things, the essential, erotic dimension of family life. Somehow in the past few centuries eros has come to be synonymous with lust and so, in our day, it seems perverse to apply the word to family relationships. But in its original sense eros is the love that desires—that desires, above all, union with the beloved. This incorporation of another being into the boundaries of the self is at the heart of every good—and every dysfunctional—family. The closest modern equivalent we have is the psychological concept of "attachment," which suggests, if faintly, the similar urgent fusion of need, desire, and love. Eros describes not only the relation between husband and wife, but even more dramatically between parent and small child.

It is eros that drives the sacrifices, celebrations, jealousies, anxieties, and triumphs of family. It is eros that explains the huge efforts children make to please even the most unloving parents. And it is eros that describes why any rational adult would ever make the enormous donation of the self required to raise children, or for that matter, to stay married.

Sociologists, by contrast, keep their eyes firmly averted from this basic human reality, preferring to see family relations as a set of job titles. Anxious to reassure divorced parents strapped for time, energy, and money, divorce advocates enthusiastically join in endorsing the idea of *quality time*, which is the idea that a few minutes of undiluted attention each day can keep the child psychiatrist away.

Thus, Dr. Gardner, a professor at Columbia University Medical School and a psychoanalyst, assures parents that setting aside a few minutes a day to be alone with their children will prevent "pathological reactions." "The time need not be more than ten or fifteen minutes."[4] If ten minutes a day will do it, there is no real reason why divorced (or unmarried) parents could not fairly easily make up for the loss of an intact family.

Because of this task-oriented view of the family, for generations most divorce research focused on its effects on minor children. After the product of a factory has been distributed, the factory can have no more effect on it, right? After the car has been launched on the road, the auto manufacturer in Detroit can't very well influence any longer how well it drives, no?

But families are not very much like factories, and children are remarkably unlike industrial outputs. Only very recently have social scientists begun to investigate how divorce affects adult children. They have found, to their surprise, that the effects are profound.[5] It is not just young children or older teens who are emotionally devastated when their parents divorce. Even adults who have long since fled the nest experience their parents' divorce as a profound loss, an erotic catastrophe, a collapse of love's story that leads the story of their own lives toward grief.

What is the nature of this loss? One study of 115 adults whose parents divorced found that these adults "overwhelmingly described losses of important structural and functional components of their family ties" as a result of their parents' divorce, including "loss of family unity and traditions," "difficulty in arranging and restructuring family gatherings," and "problems with seeing both parents." Adult children "mourned the loss of their own children's relationship with grandparents" and reported "not feeling an integral part of a parent's remarried family."

Researchers found that "the specific family activities that were most affected by parental divorce were Christmas, Thanksgiving, birthdays… vacations, recreational activities and everyday family contact." The authors, to their surprise, did not find much support for the conventional wisdom that "late-life divorce has… a minimal impact on adult children because, typically, they have begun the process of establishing their independence."[6]

The fact that the breakup of the parents' marriage can profoundly affect adults long after they have left the parental home should flash a warning that there is something shallow and incomplete in the way in which we think and talk and make policy about the family.

Like Donna, Eric is no statistical casualty: he's no juvenile delinquent; he is not clinically depressed; he seldom misbehaved in class; he was never held back in school. His grades and his SAT scores were fine, thank you, as is his health, mental and physical. A senior at Yale, he is in no danger of slipping into the underclass.

By all usual social science measures, one would have to say that

Eric's dad didn't injure his son in any way by choosing to divorce. Any social scientist would point to his parents' divorce as a triumph.

But not Eric.

Eric is actually a two-time runner in the divorce derby. His "first father" moved away when Eric was just a toddler. His mother soon remarried a man whom Eric for most of his life called *Dad*.

Those early years were troubled ones. From first to sixth grade, "I was completely miserable for a really long time." The world, he thought, was "a pretty bleak place." Money was tight, emotions were tense, and, to top it off, Eric considered his new dad "a barbarian."

"He smelled different, ate different, and had a cruder manner than my mother. I was in full aesthetic revolt." Over the years his distaste dwindled, but "I always existed in a state where there was a separation between my father and mother."

He and his mom were separate from his dad. His mom and dad, as a couple, were separate from him.

Nonetheless, by junior high, life for Eric started to seem worth living. He was doing better in school, even in athletics.

"It seemed great," he says. "I came to believe all the world's problems could be solved if you played by the rules. My parents, by being cosmopolitan, hardworking people, myself by being a hardworking student, had succeeded. Life, therefore, could be perfected."

Then his grandmother, who lived with them, died, and his mother went into a lengthy decline, physically and emotionally. She was immobilized by back pains and bronchitis, and seemed very sad about her life.

As she withdrew into her sadness, Eric at last moved closer to his dad. Sitting in the den one day when he was sixteen or seventeen, the truth about his father suddenly hit him: "I really love this person."

One long-festering emotional wound had finally healed, one hole in the family heart had closed up. At long last, after a difficult struggle, Eric once again felt whole and happy. But not for long.

One day, in the fall of his senior year in high school, Eric came home and found his mom was alone and had obviously been crying.

"What's wrong?" he asked her over and over again. Finally she told him: "Your father told me he's been seeing another woman."

Eric stayed calm, rational, numb.

"Well, okay," he told her. Falling back on religious training, he added, "The thing to do is forgive."

"He doesn't want to be forgiven," his mom said. "He just wants to leave."

Eric's world fractured again. In a flash, the man who had been his dad for almost his whole life became his stepdad again. And soon, his ex-stepdad.

One of the little-remarked side effects of the divorce culture is that it makes your spouse—and sometimes your dad—less definitely member of your own family. The marriage bond is in one sense the closest human tie. Husbands and wives are bound up with each other's lives, become "one flesh" more intimately than even mothers and children—for mothers know and the children eventually discover that most of life will necessarily be spent elsewhere and with someone else.

Yet in another sense, the marriage tie is the family's weak link: a radical attempt to make "one flesh" out of what are intractably, unbearably two different and unrelated people. Marriage is the daring attempt to transform a biological stranger into your closest family member.

The paradox of marriage, and the source of constant cultural tension, is that "one flesh" is both a deep reality and a social fiction. Or, to put it more accurately, it is a cultural aspiration, a lie that individuals and society conspire to make true. Precisely because husbands and wives are not actually members of the same biological family, marriage is everywhere surrounded by ritual, constraint, and support. Tremendous social energy goes into making the aspirations of the marrying couple a reality.

When a culture replaces the marriage aspiration with the divorce ethic, the result is a dramatic change in the relation between husband and wife and, often, as in Eric's experience, between parents and children as well. When marriage is no longer a tie that binds, the older, prerational, and stubborn bonds of blood reemerge as dominant.

"I knew I had to make a decision," says Eric, "and I knew there could be no doubt who you go with: You go with your mother."

His mom was sick, depressed, often immobilized with back spasms. And the man Eric had just come to love was going to dump his mom and her problems for a new love: a family friend who was in many ways his mother's polar opposite—"ebullient, cheerful, smiley, thin, healthy."

Still calm, still rational, Eric went to his room and called "the wisest person I knew in the whole world." Eric told him the story in careful, clipped, mechanical sentences. Then he said what deep inside he really meant: "I failed," and burst into tears.

This happened five years ago. The distraught high school senior is now a polished college graduate. But when he reaches this point, he falls silent, struggling for control, unable to speak for several minutes.

This feeling of guilt is almost a sociological cliché, and he knows it. Children, we are told, often wrongly feel responsible for their parents' divorce. But Eric forthrightly rejects this interpretation of his own interior experience. He knows he was not in any sense the *cause* of his parents' divorce.

Still—"I'd always resented the 'You are not responsible' line," he tells me, struggling to express his own experience, outside the current psychological fashion. "I didn't feel causal responsibility. I felt an Oedipal complicity in evil. Oedipus didn't intend evil, but because evil is in the world, evil touches us. What I felt was not 'I'm to blame' but 'This is as much a besmirchment of my life as theirs.' I was involved in the evil around me."

Evil is a harsh word. But what other words can a son apply to the sudden abandonment by his father of an ailing mother? How else could a child experience his own demotion from a son to a stepson to an ex-stepson?

Though a social scientist might say Eric wasn't injured by the divorce, in his own mind his father's decision to leave his mother remains the central fact of his life: "Everything I've done since then is an attempt to atone or address this problem."

One thing still bothers him. Why was he, a seventeen-year-old kid, the only one who called evil by its name? "Why is it that something that by any reasonable light is destructive and wrong called up no communal response?" he asks, still puzzled.

It's not that Eric didn't go looking for one.

He went to his father and asked: How could you do this to my mother?

"He had no trouble justifying his own actions. He kept smiling at me and talking fulfillment language. He was unhappy. There was no point in continuing the relationship. He needed more sexual activity."

He went to his minister, seeking justice. "This is a religion of forgiveness," his pastor told him. "Yes, but my father is not penitent," Eric replied. His father justifies his actions. He thinks they are right.

Eric's family's friends mostly evaporated. The business community, "the only real community my father and mother had," didn't really care about right or wrong. After all, you can't do business only with people of whom you approve.

Eric was a teenager alone in a world where something terribly wrong was being done to someone he loved, by someone he loved— and no one else seemed to care. In fact, no one else seemed to notice.

His ex-stepdad is now happily remarried. His mother is not. Her business isn't going well. It takes energy to start over at fifty, and right now she doesn't have it.

"She is as unhappy and miserable as she can be," Eric says flatly.

For the spouses this is a typical divorce story. One—sometimes it's the man, sometimes it's the women, but almost always it's the one who wanted the divorce—emerges happy and victorious. The other—the one who was left, who needed to be taken care of—is not.

From a very young age Eric, like millions of other children of divorce, has been exposed to cruel failures of love.

As a result of his experience, unlike some children of divorce, he has thrown himself consciously and deliberately into faith, commitment, philosophy, and love. He has courted his future wife with care.

"Love can't be an emotion, because you can't depend on emotions," he tells me. "Love is an act of the will." Tragedy saved him, he believes, from shallow hedonism, and he is grateful.

Still, when asked if he worries about his future marriage, he says, instantly, "Totally. I worry that I'm as sinful as my father. I worry that I will forget the lesson of that; that my life will be overcome by desire at some point."

Behind that is another worry, one less easy for a man to confess than fear of his own sinfulness. It is Donna's worry, the fear of abandonment: "I'm hypersensitive to breakup talk," he admits. "I just get thrown back to the divorce. I can't talk about unhappiness as if it were related to love. It drives me crazy. It's so difficult for me to have any good relationship-management conversation."

Eric's story is by no means an unusual one. The damage he experienced cannot be captured in any social science measure. It is not primarily economic or psychological, but moral and emotional: He has been taught from an early age, not once but twice, by those he loved that love is not reliable.

However much he consciously rejects this view of love in theory, it haunts him in reality. He believes in love, but not instinctively, not as a normal reality, but through a tremendously difficult act of will. And in the background, the ghosts whisper: What if I'm wrong? What if I turn out as bad as my father?

And worse: What if she leaves me?

His story underscores one of the great missing links in the current divorce debate: The ways we commonly measure what children lose as a consequence of divorce do not capture the whole nature or extent of the loss they experience. A child whose family is broken apart does not become an adult unaffected by the experience. The divorce survivors carry within themselves the knowledge that what is most fundamental is also most fragile: A family is not a rock in a sea of stress, but a potential trap. In the water lurks the most primal terror—the terror of abandonment. The problem every child of divorce must face is how to depend on what one knows from experience is ultimately unreliable.

If the primary lesson a child learns from his parents' divorce is that love is not reliable, its corollary is that the family is not a person's most important commitment. What you want, the divorce culture teaches, is more important than what is good for the people you are supposed to love and even the people for whom you are responsible. When parents demonstrate to their children that the family is not, after all, the most important thing, that individual desires are more important than the solemn commitments that form families, the family loses its power to hold the loyalty of all its members.

Melissa is another of the divorce survivors—smart, pretty, and a prelaw student, she dreams of becoming a successful prosecutor. Melissa and her siblings were always welcome at her father's house after her parents' divorce, and he took his financial commitment to them seriously. After a difficult initial adjustment and some continuing anxiety about her mother (who is not doing well, financially or emotionally, ten years later), Melissa feels she is fine. It's her brother she is worried about.

As the oldest son, a teenager when their father moved out, he was supposed to become the responsible one, the new man of the family. The opposite happened. He withdrew from the family, borrowed the car without permission, stayed out late, and generally let the family know that he couldn't be counted on. Now in his mid-twenties, he has dropped out of college, works nights at a marginal job, and still lives with his mother. His attitude, Melissa told me, seemed to be, "If my dad can do whatever he wants, so can I." This is one of the ways divorce undermines the ability of families to transmit the virtues and loyalties necessary to sustain family life in the next generation.

In the public policy model, the family is a collection of *roles*, tasks performed, goods supplied. But many of these functions can be—and have been—taken over by nonfamily members or the market:

restaurants make food; laundries wash clothes; day-care centers supervise children; therapists, counselors, and friends provide emotional support. Parents are simply a set of individuals who merely take care of their children while they are too young to help themselves. Children may benefit from the material and emotional support of both a mother and a father, but there is no particular reason why, in theory, that mother and father have to be *married* to each other. In theory, parents could cooperatively raise their children in separate households.

At its extreme, this conception of the family leads to the conclusion that the family itself is dispensable: All its tasks could all be delegated. Thus one academic can blithely write, the family "is a package of roles related to the function of caring for and rearing children... The family is not the only social and legal structure that might evolve or be designed to execute this function.... Imagine by way of contrast a society in which the child rearing function is executed in an institution fully as public as courts, legislatures, and prisons. In this society.... the legal and social responsibility for the care and rearing of all children, the 'parental' role, is assigned to professional caretakers who represent, and are in the service of, the community at large."[7]

Another, even more influential, model of the family is the therapeutic model. Unlike sociologists' task-oriented conception, the therapeutic model emphasizes the emotional quality of relationships. But therapists share sociologists' conceptualization of the family as a set of individuals who relate to each other. Because the therapeutic model focuses narrowly on the well-being of the particular individual client, therapists find it easy to view divorce in a positive light— as the means for an individual to end a bad relationship and get the life he or she wants. What is missing from this picture of related individuals performing tasks and offering services, physical or emotional, is the family itself, an ordering of persons that is more than merely the sum of the individuals in it. Even the spouse who wants to leave may not see what is being lost.

The first and the most enduring loss—the one that takes place in every divorce—is the one that is almost never mentioned, the loss that affects children, parents, and spouses equally: the loss of the family story.

A young woman, call her Marie, sits in the living room with her father who, after thirty-five years of marriage, recently separated from her mother. They are looking through the family photographs, the old ones from the early sixties. There the whole family is, in grainy brown, at the Grand Canyon. Reminiscing, they go back further, to the fifties, back before Marie was born, to a photo of her mother taken soon after she and Marie's father met. Happily, the father tells her the story (she's heard it before): A group of young naval officers, out for a drive looking for girls, decide on a whim to stop at a nursing school. His face lights up as he remembers himself, a young man with big dreams, uncertain of fulfillment—a naval aviator flying into the unknown future, about to take the first great leap in his life story, about to win the girl. Together they would build a life, conquer the world.

Suddenly his voice drops. His eyes look away. He roughly tosses the picture of the young aviator with his arm around a pretty nursing student who would become his wife—her mother—to Marie. "You want this?" he says gruffly, with something like disgust, implying he has no further use for it.

The present had altered the past, disfiguring it painfully. The tale he had told himself about his life for the past thirty-five years was threatening to become a mere fairy tale, a lie.

Marriage is a powerful narrative of erotic triumph: of faith over doubt, of love over fear. The marriage plot affirms the potency of love, for from one's love springs a whole new creation, a new universe, a new family. In making a marriage, we make love real; out of our love we make something important indisputably *happen*. Because we dare to say "I do," the world is changed forever.

Or maybe not.

For the spouse who leaves, there is a new narrative to replace this lost love story. For the divorce winners, the marriage plot is superseded by the divorce quest: The lone individual who against great odds triumphs over adversity to achieve his (or her) passion. The great man who does not allow himself to be bound by society's petty conventions (such as the marriage contract) but who relentlessly pursues authentic experience wherever it takes him. The ugly duckling flowering into a swan. The peasant who becomes a prince.

But for the person who is being discarded (and very few divorces are truly mutual decisions), divorce is no quest. The spouse who left is not an actor in a new narrative because, for the spouse who is left, divorce is not an act at all—it is something that happens to him, something over which he has no control. Divorce transforms him into an object that is acted upon, a disagreeable bit player in someone else's story: a spear carrier or at best a villain.

It is an unbearable position. This is why so many people who passionately opposed their spouse's decision to divorce will, five years later, tell you, "It was the best thing that ever happened to me." The alternative is to remain in a failed story line, to declare oneself a permanent loser. And, in America, nobody loves a loser.

"Everything is easier for all of us," Laura says bravely. "Life is improving steadily, and all it takes is time, if we had only realized that at the start." But Laura's daughter has just had a second abortion, and Laura's second marriage is on the brink of failure.[8]

Despite their protestations many people cannot bear to part with the story of their life. They remain true to it, against their wishes, refusing to deny in their secret hearts the goodness of what they had, to accept the loss they have experienced. The divorce haunts them.

Older divorced women are particularly hard hit. In one study, ten years after the divorce, 80 percent of older women were financially insecure; almost half had experienced a decline in their standards of living. Half of all women who did not remarry reported a deteriorating sense of physical well-being: more colds, headaches, backaches, constipation, migraines, colitis, high blood pressure, and jaw pain— a catalog of ailments that married or remarried women do not report in nearly the same degree.

Of those who chose to leave the marriage, many are reasonably happy. They take not only pleasure but pride in placing their own needs first. For those women who did not choose the divorce, the losses entailed in the breakup of the marriage are devastating and hard to describe:

> Even though they are not isolated socially, they are intensely lonely. In comparing their lives today with their married years, they express a terrible feeling of loss. These women loved and cherished the roles of wife, mother, homemaker, and nurturer. They laid out the holiday decorations, cooked the traditional feasts, and passed the carving knife to the man of the house. Since the divorce, they still put out the decorations and cook the feasts for the children. But it is not the same.[9]

Gone along with the marriage is the story of the home and the woman who makes the home possible as the incarnation of love. However great their sacrifices for love, these women are no longer heroines, not even tragic heroines. The story does not simply end badly, it disappears. Love conquers nothing.

These women have their counterparts in those divorced fathers who disconsolately play Disneyland Dad when the treasured role as family man dissolves along with the family. Dispensing pleasures to their children to make up for the loss of the family structure, they also reel under the blow of being told that what they have dedicated their lives to doesn't count. What is the point of being a family man when the family has been first jettisoned and then reconstructed without you, by the woman you loved?

One inevitable consequence of a culture in which the divorce ethic replaces the marriage aspiration is that family boundaries become fluid, uncertain. People are sometimes members of your family and later not. You have your family, your mother has hers, your brother may have a third. Marriage, the incarnation of Eros, creates one out of many. Divorce shatters this family unity.

This churning cast of characters creates for children not, as optimists predicted, a larger circle of love, but a narrower and less reliable one. Two researchers have discovered, for example, that children from disrupted families are more isolated than children from stable marriages, that they depend more on teachers, counselors, and babysitters for support while at the same time perceiving these "outsiders" as sources of family conflict. Children from disrupted families are also more dissatisfied with the support they receive from friends.[10] Children who grow up in single-parent homes are less likely to marry, more likely to divorce, and more likely to have children outside of wedlock.[11] Lawrence A. Kurdek followed newlywed couples for five years and discovered that one of the best predictors that a marriage will fail was a history of divorce on the part of one or both spouses, especially if the wife brought children from a previous marriage into the new union.[12]

Thus over time, divorce begets more divorce, illegitimacy, and a striking reluctance to marry.

It is not that children of divorce are opposed to marriage. They are often remarkably conservative in their views of romance, expressing strong desires for love, commitment, and marriage, and an equally strong aversion to divorce. But to their own dismay, they often find that when faith in love wanes, fear is stronger than desire.

Rosita, with bright eyes and long curly black hair, is vivacious, charming, beautiful, and surprised to be told so (in her own mind, her mother is the beautiful one). She loves her work with troubled youths and has risen to a responsible administrative position in a private social service agency. But as she talks to me it becomes apparent her otherwise happy and successful life is shadowed by one strong and increasing anxiety. Recently she broke off an engagement, and now, in her late twenties, Rosita tells me she is afraid there is something wrong with her, that she can't, as the pop psychologists say, commit.

Rosita is a child of divorce, but not a good divorce. Her story is harrowing. After her parents divorced, her mother remarried a man who Rosita liked and who protected her from her mother's violent temper. But then they divorced, and Rosita experienced a second abandonment: Her stepfather made arrangements to see his own son—but not her. She started making trouble in school and was abandoned again: Her mom said she couldn't handle Rosita and dropped her off with an aunt and uncle in Puerto Rico. "She just left me and didn't come back." The final betrayal came when she visited her mother in New York and confessed that her uncle was sexually abusing her: Mom didn't believe her.

Being a social worker, Rosita tells me in best therapeutic language, "My development is arrested at age eight"—her age when her parents divorced.

This is one way of imagining what happened to Rosita, to see the psyche as an object, an organ that can sustain the damage and so become deformed. So Rosita with her professional knowledge of child development imagines herself a case of "arrested develop-ment"—as frailer, less mature, sicker than the average person, though on the contrary the history of her life betrays great inner strength and repeated triumphs over adversity.

There is another way of looking at it. Rosita's difficulty in trusting love is not the result of mental illness, but a perfectly rational mental clarity.

Maybe, I suggest to her, her problem is not *psychological*, not a deformation inside her, but something real that took place outside of her. At least three of the people who were supposed to take care of her and love her betrayed her. When Rosita tries to love, she takes with her that knowledge, the objective external reality that the people one loves cannot be trusted. For her, to love and to trust love is, as for Eric and so many children of divorce, a heroic venture.

The belief that the destruction of a family is a tragedy—if some-times an unavoidable one—has been replaced by a new, happier Walt Disney version in which when the family breaks apart the individu-als who once constituted that family discover alternate ways to meet their needs and achieve individual happiness. In Disney movies no one is shot through the heart.

This brave new vision of the family in which no hurt is ever per-manent is ideally suited to social science methodology, because unlike eros, its two-dimensional tasks can be observed, measured, and quantified. But why has this stunted view of the family, so improbable to the human heart, gained such wide currency? Maybe because in the divorce culture we have no other choice. To accommodate a 60 percent divorce rate, we must radically change our notion of marriage, transform our most solemn commitments into disposable preferences. We must view family loyalties, our ties to wife and children, as temporary and contingent, and, most fatal of all, we must reimagine love as transient.

Most children of divorce will not grow up to be "damaged" by the divorce, as we now commonly measure damage: Most will not be criminals, juvenile delinquents, psychotics, or high school dropouts. Many, thanks to their own courage and the devoted efforts of their parents, will grow up to be happy, successful, educated, and admirable human beings—the more admirable for having triumphed over adversity. That should not surprise us. Human beings can, as individuals, triumph over far greater adversity than the collapse of marriage. Even most concentration camp survivors grew up to be law-abiding, taxpaying citizens.

If the family were a factory created by the state to produce future taxpayers, divorce would pose few insurmountable difficulties. But even here, as we shall see, a culture of divorce may prove more problematic than the optimists have decreed. Because even though most children may survive divorce, the costs to a society of losing even an extra 10 percent or 20 percent of its sons and daughters to poverty, crime, drug use, illiteracy, illness, and death may be too high to bear—especially if divorce sets into motion a cycle of divorce and illegitimacy in which each generation's losses are magnified in the next.

But if the family is not a factory in which we are quasi employees, but instead an erotic narrative, then the question becomes not what does the law require, but what does love demand?

The costs of ignoring these questions, of casually permitting the divorce ethic to replace the marriage aspiration, are far greater than we have heretofore been led to believe.

3

THE VICTIMS
of CHOICE

IF THE GREAT THEME OF AMERICAN life has been progress, the unfolding melancholy melody of the postmarital culture is *downward mobility*. The postmarital culture is associated with persistent decline: declining health, declining fortune, declining physical safety, declining psychological security, declining education, and declining job attainment. The differences between children of broken families and children of intact families are not always huge, but the direction of the change is generally clear, consistent, and *negative*. In almost every measure of human progress, the collapse of marriage drags down the fortunes of men, women, and especially children.

Middle-class security is the most obvious casualty of marriage's collapse. The "feminization of poverty" is no longer a new story, but it bears repeating. Single moms are five times more likely to be poor than are their married sisters.[1] They are also nine times more likely than are married families to live in "deep poverty," with incomes of less than half the official poverty level.[2] More than two-thirds of ten-year-olds who live in single-parent families will have experienced poverty, compared to just one-fifth of children whose parents remain married, and the poverty is far more likely to be enduring. Overall, more than half of all poor families are headed by a single mother, more than double the proportion in 1960; and today children are almost twice as likely as the elderly to live in poverty.[3] David Eggebeen and Daniel Lichter calculated that increasing family breakdown accounted for almost half the increase in child poverty in the eighties.[4]

The costs of unwed motherhood are particularly staggering. In 1990, the median family income for unwed mothers was $8,337, almost half that of divorced women with children, and less than one-fourth the income of married mothers.[5] The child born outside of marriage is thirty times more likely to live in persistent poverty than is the child whose parents got married and stayed married.[6] Sixty percent of children whose mothers never married will be poor for most of their childhoods, compared to just 2 percent of children whose parents got married and stayed married.

Poverty is not the whole story. Most children will not become officially poor as a result of the collapse of marriage—merely *poorer*. Social critics from Barbara Ehrenreich (*Fear of Falling*) to Kevin Phillips (*Boiling Point*) write of growing middle-class insecurity, of a real and enduring anxiety that—for the first time in American history—the dream is failing: This generation may not be better off than the last. They point to a variety of factors, including a changing service economy, the decline of unions, Japanese and other international competition, and bad public policy. But all these threats, real and imagined, pale before the simple obvious fact: The greatest threat to the upward mobility of the poor and to the stability of the middle class comes not from the productivity of the Japanese but from the fragility of marriage.

Children of divorced affluent parents may well enjoy a higher standard of living than many children in working-class marriages. But within each class, the collapse of marriage relentlessly pushes children down the socioeconomic ladder. When a marriage ends, families are thrust into a world of relative instability, often moving to lower quality housing in less attractive neighborhoods.[7] The average child from a nonpoor family will suffer a 50 percent drop in income after divorce.[8] Only 10 percent of kids living with single moms enjoy a family income of more than $40,000 (the average for married couples), while the majority stagger along with a family income of less than $15,000 a year.[9]

Along with their children, women are particularly hard hit by marital instability. Greater participation in the labor force has not provided any protection from profound economic distress. Indeed, as Elaine Kamarck and William Galston recently pointed out, "The truth is just the reverse: Economically, the two-parent family is more rather than less necessary because more and more families need two incomes to sustain even a modest middle-class existence."[10] Today, younger divorced women have far more work experience than do women in the past, but this does not seem to protect them from the severe economic blows of divorce. One researcher compared the experience of women divorcing in the late sixties and seventies with more recent divorcees. To her surprise she found "little indication of change in the economic costs of marital disruption." Women divorcing in the eighties who did not remarry endured about a 45 percent drop in family income as a result.[11] Experience confirms what common sense suggests: Overburdened single mothers simply cannot compete in the labor market as effectively as married parents or childless singles.

Even for men, marriage is strongly associated with upward mobility. Social scientists argue whether this is because upwardly mobile men are more likely to marry or because married men with families to support work harder and longer, and in the end make more money. The answer is probably both. Women strongly prefer to marry stably employed men. At the same time, husbands tend to increase their work hours after the birth of children, while married mothers reduce their work hours.[12] A man's financial position is undoubtedly less threatened by the collapse of marriage than a woman's, but only comparatively so. Single men do not make as much money as married men and, after divorce, the suddenly single man loses much of the competitive advantage he gained from the discipline and rewards of family life.[13]

Poverty is one of the most easily measured effects of unmarriage as well as one of the most predictable. But it is not necessarily the most destructive to mother, child, or the nation. The evidence is now overwhelming that the collapse of marriage is creating a whole generation of children less happy, less physically and mentally healthy, less equipped to deal with life or to produce at work, and more dangerous to themselves and others. This evidence comes not from isolated studies but from hundreds of studies subsequently surveyed, critiqued, compared, and summarized by other scholars. No significant survey of the scientific literature contradicts these main conclusions:

- Reviewing thirty-two studies on the long-term effects of divorce, Dr. Edward Beal and Gloria Hochman concluded, "Adults of divorced parents have more problems and lower levels of well-being than adults whose parents stay married. They are depressed more frequently, feel less satisfied with life, get less education, and have less prestigious jobs. Even their physical health is poorer."[14]
- P. R. Amato and B. Keith, conducting a meta-analysis of revelant research, confirmed that even after controlling for income children of divorce do less well than children in intact families in many areas, including education achievement, conduct, psychological adjustment, self-esteem, and social relations. As adults, children of divorce will experience lower socioeconomic attainment and greater marital instability than children from intact families. "Data from over 81,000 people in 37 studies," they conclude, "suggests that parental divorce (or permanent separation) has broad negative consequences for quality of life in adulthood."[15]
- Sociologists Sara McLanahan and Gary Sandefur found that, even after carefully controlling for family background, growing up in a single-parent home is a distinct disadvantage: Teens who have lived in single-parent families are twice as likely to drop out of high school, twice as likely to become teen parents, and one-and-one-half times as likely to be "idle"—out of school and at home—as young adults.[16]

Summing up in the *Journal of Marriage and the Family*, Verna M. Keith and Barbara Finlay concluded that "parental divorce does have a negative impact on children and on adult status and behavior." They found that "educational attainment was lower for young adults who had experienced parental divorce earlier in life," and that adults whose parents divorced had "diminished psychological well-being." Their own study confirmed that children of divorce have lower educational attainment and that daughters have a higher risk of being divorced.[17]

Elaine Kamarck and William Glaston, two prominent scholars who joined the Clinton administration, surveyed the scientific literature and came to similar conclusions: "The economic consequences of a parent's absence (almost always the father's) are often accompanied by psychological consequences, which include higher than average levels of youth suicide, low intellectual and educational performance, and higher than average rates of mental illness, violence, and drug use... daughters of teenager mothers are more likely to become teenage mothers themselves, and are at higher risk of long-term welfare dependency."[18]

Children raised outside of the protection of marriage are more likely to become discipline problems, both at home and in school. Children in mother-only households were found to be at greater risk of developing "conduct disorder," regardless of household income.[19] And children from disrupted families were judged to be more aggressive, by their own, their mothers', and their teachers' accounts. These behavior problems were not short-lived responses to the divorce. Five years after the initial survey, the problems remained. A number of researchers also found that children of divorce, especially boys, were more aggressive than children whose parents stayed married.[20]

In some cases, minor and temporary behavior problems become permanent and dangerous. One of the strongest links to emerge in recent years is between the collapse of marriage and crime, a link we will explore in greater detail later in this book. One study of suicide and homicide rates in the United States using data from 1945 to 1984 found that of all social indicators, "only divorce rates were consistently associated with suicide and with homicide rates."[21] Another study found that, even after controlling for variables like poverty, "the greater the rate of divorce, the greater the homicide rate."[22]

Of all the risks of the collapse of marriage, perhaps the most horrifying and the least remarked is child abuse. Ironically, violence and abuse are routinely used to indict marriage and justify the divorce revolution. Sociologist Stephanie Coontz recently worried that "scare tactics" may cause couples to "stick it out for the kids" and thereby risk domestic violence.[23] Just recently, under the influence of this myth, a group of women legislators in Washington state introduced a bill to attach warnings about domestic violence to marriage licenses.[24]

Though married parents sometimes abuse their kids and each other, the reality is that the person most likely to abuse a child physically is a single mother. The person most likely to abuse a child sexually is the mother's boyfriend or second husband. In a University of Iowa study of 2,300 cases of sexual abuse, researchers discovered that nonbiological "father caretakers" were almost four times as likely as biological fathers to sexually abuse children in their care.[25] Another study by Martin Daly and Margo Wilson found that a preschooler who is not living with both biological parents is forty times more likely to be sexually abused.[26] Diana Russell's study of 930 San Francisco women reported that one out of six women raised by a stepfather was sexually abused by him, compared to one out of forty-three women living with their biological father.[27]

The mother's boyfriend appears to be an even greater potential risk to kids. One study found that, although they contribute less than 2 percent of nonparental child care, mothers' boyfriends commit almost half of all reported abuse by nonparents. As researcher Leslie Margolin concluded, mothers' boyfriends "committed 27 times more child abuse than their hours in child care would lead us to predict... a young child left alone with a mother's boyfriend experiences elevated risk of physical abuse."[28]

Sometimes a woman marries a violent and abusive man. But when a woman is not married, a variety of men drift through her and her children's lives and the chances that at least one of them will abuse her children increase dramatically. Furthermore, when marriage breaks down, the sexual economy of the household may become disturbed. Father figures enter the lives of teenage girls desperately seeking male attention, father figures who did not know their stepchildren as babies, father figures for whom the incest taboo is more theory than instinct.

Most stepfathers and boyfriends do not, of course, abuse the children in their care. Nonetheless, divorce, though usually portrayed as a protection against domestic violence, is far more frequently a contributing cause. The more unstable marriage becomes, the more children are put at risk of abuse.

Despite the growing body of evidence against divorce, however, it is not hard to find experts who demur. As the costs of the abolition of marriage become more and more apparent, strategies for denying the *obvious* become increasingly ingenious.

4

IN DENIAL

WHAT HAPPENS WHEN DESIRE AND REALITY CLASH? That's the question an increasing portion of America's cultural elite faced as they succeeded in putting the great sixties dream of maximizing sexual options into practice. Even children, they had argued, would benefit from the happy dust that would settle over the adult population as the taboos against divorce and illegitimacy crashed.

This initial optimism was battered by bitter personal experience and the findings of an ever more sophisticated array of social science research. And yet, faced with the necessity of abandoning the dream, or at least admitting its huge costs, America's cultural elite for the most part balked. As the evidence against the divorce culture mounted, the arguments of its defenders became ever more intricate, Byzantine, and irrelevant.

One fine example of this dedicated unwillingness to admit the lessons of experience was offered up last year in *Rules of Engagement*, a book by *New Yorker* writer Lis Harris that profiles four American marriages. In her introductory essay Ms. Harris offers up some of the most common and least persuasive arguments ingenious minds have invented to defend the status quo. For example, one argument is that marriage isn't really in trouble, because people still get married, or as Ms. Harris puts it, "Less than ten percent of the population lives to age sixty-five without marrying" a figure "pretty much the same as in the eighteenth and nineteenth centuries."[1] Well, yes, but up to 65 percent of new marriages fail and one-third of all babies are now born out of wedlock. Or, another argument is that the rise in divorce is inevitable, so we might as well lie back and enjoy it. Ms. Harris cites the first U.S. Commissioner of Labor, who remarked as early as 1888 that "Law does not create divorce."[2] Actually (as we shall see), several recent studies suggest that changes in divorce law may account for as much as 25 percent of the surge in divorce since the sixties.

Finally, wielding an argument only a social scientist could love, Ms. Harris reassures us that divorce is not really a problem, because the divorce courts are really only stepping in for the Grim Reaper. The divorce rate, she argues, has "merely taken up the slack left by the radical shift in the mortality rate. In 1850 only 2 percent of the American population lived past age 65; today 75 percent does."[3] But if divorce were merely replacing death in some natural process of marital dissolution, divorce courts would be filled with raging octogenarians. In reality most divorces occur among younger couples married for relatively short periods. Despite the ravages of disease and childbirth, the average colonial marriage lasted twice as long as the average marriage today.

Puritan marriage occupies a curiously disproportionate place in the imagination of intellectuals like Ms. Harris, who devotes many pages to arguing that marriage is in great shape today, compared to the "Puritan husband and wife [who] were all but smothered by the *communitas.*" This is an intellectual strategy no sane person would apply to any other social problem. Imagine a *New Yorker* writer arguing that poverty is no problem today because our poor are rolling in dough compared to our Puritan ancestors, or that AIDS isn't a real pubic health crisis because in the Puritan's day syphilis, tuberculosis, and cholera killed so many more.

Not every apologist for the divorce culture goes to the same lengths as Ms. Harris to argue that despite the disasters accompanying the collapse of marriage this is still the best of all possible worlds. Yet even many far more moderate and respected voices succumb to the temptation to minimize the damage.

Many distinguished scholars, such as Frank F. Furstenberg, Jr., and Andrew Cherlin, now acknowledge that divorce has some negative effects. But they argue that these are mild. After all, they point out, many children of divorce are doing well. A phrase one hears frequently in these discussions is "serious permanent harm," which most children, by the standards most experts accept, do not sustain. Most children whose parents divorce will not become delinquents, drop out of school, or lapse into permanent depression.

These experts underestimate the effects of divorce and illegitimacy for two reasons. The first is methodological. As social scientists they are committed to a process of analytically separating causal forces that in the real world are inextricably intertwined.

Many researchers, for example, spend considerable energy and ingenuity in teasing out what percentage of the damage divorce causes is due to lower income and what is due to "the divorce itself." Yet studies that control for income can actually understate the true consequences of divorce. In the real world, less money is one of the most consistent by-products of the collapse of marriage; it is precisely divorce or the failure to marry that drives most of these women and children into poverty.

This simple intellectual tactic—first deconstruct marriage into its component parts, then claim it is the parts, not the whole, of marriage that are essential for children—is used over and over again by experts as an attempt to minimize the importance of marriage for children. Take, for another example, the case of infant mortality. By the late eighties, American infants were dying off at a rate almost one-fifth higher than in Norway, 50 percent higher than in the Netherlands, and fully twice as high as in Japan.[4] These numbers have been widely remarked, and during the recent health care debates they were often cited as an argument for bringing European-style National health care to America. The evidence, however, as Nicholas Eberstadt of the Harvard Center for Population and Development Studies first pointed out, strongly suggests American babies are suffering less from our private medical system than from our decision to privatize marriage and withdraw from it public, legal, and cultural support.

If anything, American babies are receiving unusually advanced and aggressive medical treatment compared to their European counterparts;

one reason that, compared to other Western countries, "American babies at any given birth weight appear to have unusually good chances of surviving the perinatal period, regardless of race."[5] Moreover, poverty appears to contribute only very slightly to the risk that a child will be born with low birth weight, a predictor of infant mortality. Among whites, babies born to families with incomes below and above 150 percent of the poverty line are equally likely to have a low birth weight; about 5.6 percent do. Among blacks, poorer families are only slightly more likely to have a low–birth-weight baby: 12.9 percent versus 11.4 percent.[6]

So, what accounts for our high infant mortality? Marriage, says Eberstadt, is a far more powerful predictor of infant mortality than money: If the mother is unmarried, the risk of death to her infant more than doubles. So powerful is the relationship between marriage and infant survival that marital status proved a more important predictor of infant mortality than did age or education of the mother, or even whether the baby was "wanted." Despite the well-established link between education and infant health, *a baby born to a college educated unwed mother is far more likely to die than a baby born to married high school dropouts.*

Yet just as the link between marital status and infant survival emerged, experts came forth to disparage it, using once again the strategy of deconstruct and conquer. It is not marriage itself that is important, they argued, but the access to economic resources, better health plans, and the social and psychological support that marriage typically provides. The Centers for Disease Control, for example, argued that "the marital status of the mother confers neither risk nor protection to the infant; rather, the principal benefits of marriage to infant survival are economic and social support."[7] It is not marriage per se, you see, but all the benefits marriage provides, indeed consists of, that protect children.

Undoubtedly, one reason marriage is better for babies is "greater access to resources": two heads, two hearts, and two pocketbooks are better than one. The partnership of marriage allows parents to divide the chores—physical care, breadwinning, and maintaining morale—to the benefit of all concerned, especially baby. The knowledge that marriage provides such crucial supports for children was once considered a strong reason to discourage men and women from choosing to raise babies outside of wedlock. Now, oddly, it serves as a rationale for attempting arduously to create through public policy some inevitably inadequate substitute for the real thing, from day care, to the WIC program, to programs to make "deadbeat dads" come across with the monthly check.

Manipulating government programs and extracting child support may keep more kids above an arbitrary poverty line; no social program can give divorced or never married families the economies of marriage. Nor can the law compel the kind of enormous sacrifices, from working overtime, to taking a second job, to mortgaging the house to pay for college, that married fathers routinely make for their children, but which divorced fathers seldom do. The collapse of marriage leaves everyone poorer. For children, the decline is partly fueled by the immutable law that two households cannot live as cheaply as one. But it is driven also by the inexorable reality that over time mothers and fathers who are not married develop conflicting economic interests and competing family obligations. Once the bond between husband and wife is broken, the tie between parent and child becomes increasingly defined by legal commitments rather than erotic ones. Outside of marriage, many men flee their legal obligation and fail to visit their children or pay child support. These are the "deadbeat dads" that are so widely condemned. But millions more do something almost worse: they meet their legal obligations to their children, scrupulously, meticulously, down to the letter of the law.

Jarrett, a twenty-two-year-old son of a distinguished archeology professor, works in a book store to earn money for another quarter in college. At the rate he's going, he'll be twenty-five before he graduates—*if* he graduates. What about his father? "You're a college professor," he says he'd like to tell him "…You got a good education, but what about me? You care more about your stepchildren than you care about me. You were so anxious to get rid of me that you prorated my last child support check to end on the tenth of the month that I turned eighteen."[8] He'd like to tell him that. But he doesn't dare—he might lose his father altogether.

All too often, college-educated fathers like Jarrett's come to feel that meeting their legal obligations for child support is enough—what is not legally required cannot reasonably be expected of them. In Judith Wallerstein's study only one-third of affluent divorced fathers chose to help pay for college. Ten years after their parents divorce, 60 percent of young adults were on a downward educational course compared with their fathers.[9]

Wallerstein's sample is not representative: more than three-quarters of both mothers and fathers in her study had at least some college; one-quarter of the men held advanced degrees in medicine, law, or business administration. It is the sample's very unrepresentativeness in this regard that makes the results so shocking. White, educated, upper-middle-class children—the very class for whom divorce is thought to be least a problem, because the kids are least likely to end up on welfare or in jail—may be among those hardest hit by the collapse of marriage.[10] McLanahan and Sandefur's careful analysis of four large, nationally representative samples confirmed what Wallerstein's data suggest: Middle-class families suffer an even larger-than-average drop in living standards after divorce, falling by some 50 percent.

The divorce culture exerts a relentless downward pressure on the ability of families to transmit not only money but values, aspirations, and opportunities to the next generation. One study that attempted to assess the effects of divorce on social mobility concluded that family disruption "substantially increases men's odds of ending up in the lowest occupational stratum." Divorce has produced a new "inability of families to pass on advantages to their children."[11] Daughters who divorce require far more financial aid from their aging parents than their married sisters.[12] In turn, they are able to give less social and financial support to their own adult kids.[13] Divorce drains the collected capital of the generations, taking resources from both kids and grandparents to meet the urgent needs of the current generation of adults.

As misleading as the strategy of deconstruct and conquer may be, the experts who downplay the consequences of marriage's collapse make a second, even more serious error. They treat failed marriages as isolated events affecting almost exclusively those directly involved. Looked at this way the moderate or temporary harms sustained by most children from most divorces can seem minor. If we restrict ourselves to the question, will any particular child survive a particular divorce—will he or she grow up to be a mentally competent, law abiding taxpayer? then the answer in most cases is probably yes. Although almost all children find their parents' divorce painful and traumatic, and the vast majority will experience a significant drop in their standard of living, most do not become juvenile delinquents or high school dropouts.

To judge the true effects of widespread marital collapse, however, we must ask another question, what happens when a whole society—or a large subsection thereof—adopts a risky pattern of child rearing?

Marriage is not a just consumption item. It is a social institution, like government or a corporation. Social institutions exist to allow individuals to join their energies, moneys, and ambitions to create certain goods they could not easily produce on their own, such as law and order or the Empire State Building. They engage men and women not just as consumers but as producers. Our most grievous and destructive erotic error has been to forget this in the case of marriage, to demote marriage strictly to a consumer good, constructed solely for the gratification of two individuals for as long as both feel gratified. The great differences between animals and man, the source of much of his dignity, is that he not only eats, but *makes.* And of all human institutions, marriage is one of the most productive, because it takes two biological strangers and makes them next of kin, jointly bound to the care of children. But since marriage is not just a private pleasure, its collapse creates burdens borne not just by the men and women who choose to leave, or even by their own spouses or children, but by other people's children, whole neighborhoods, and the nation as well.

Take, for example, the behavior problems in school that divorced and fatherless children display significantly more often than children from intact families. One boy (and it is disproportionately boys who disrupt classrooms) who acts up can disrupt the learning of every child in the class. Studies of effective schools have concluded that one of the most important factors affecting a student's academic achievement is the level of disorder in school.[14] All the time a teacher must spend just maintaining order is time lost to learning. In our schools, as in our streets, the collapse of marriage is nurturing a generation of children unresponsive to adult authority, prone to misbehavior, with emotional needs and psychological traumas that make it far more difficult not only for them to learn, but also for teachers to teach.

Perhaps no more vivid example can be offered of the social as opposed to the individual effects of divorce and unmarriage than the resurgent crime wave. By 1990 there was every reason to believe America could expect some respite from our three-decade-old crime wave. By the eighties criminals began to receive harsher sentences. More important, the demographics of the country shifted in ways that seemed to predict a substantial relief from crime. Crime, especially violent crime, is over-whelmingly committed by young, unmarried males. Although single men constitute only about 13 percent of the population over 14, they commit nearly 90 percent of major and violent crimes.[15] The more young, unmarried men in the population, the more potential criminals. Thanks to the baby bust in the early eighties and continuing into the nineties, the proportion of young adolescent males declined, which is why criminologists and demographers expected the crime rate to drop.

Overall crime rates did ease somewhat, but not nearly as much as expected. Violent crime rates were horrifyingly stubborn. In America's big cities, with populations of 250,000 or more, from 1985 to 1991 the homicide rate actually rose 40 percent. In America's small towns, with populations between 25,000 and 50,000, the increase in the murder rate was identical over the same period.[16] In five states and the District of Columbia, the leading cause of workplace deaths is now murder.[17]

Although by 1995 criminologists were congratulating police forces for a modest overall drop in the crime rate, they were also warning, in the words of Princeton's John Dilulio, "this is the lull before the storm." Forty million kids age ten and under are about to become teenagers, many of them "fatherless, godless, and jobless."

The modest lull was caused in part by a decline in violent crime among adults over age eighteen. But the crime rate among younger males, raised in the postmarital era, skyrocketed. Over the past thirty years the juvenile crime rate has more than doubled; the juvenile homicide rate has almost tripled.[18] Between 1985 and 1991 alone the homicide rate among boys aged 13 to 19 rose from 13 murders per 100,000 to 33 per 100,000, a 154 percent increase. [19]

Crime and murder rates have jumped for both black and white young men, but the biggest jump has occurred among young black men—the same group that experienced the greatest degree of father absence and least likelihood of marriage. From 1983 to 1993 the proportion of young black men ages 18 to 24 who murder more than doubled, rising from about 1 murderer for every 1,000 young black men to a point where today, about 1 out of every 500 young black men murders someone. (The comparable rate for young white males is about one out of every 5,000.)[20] In one national survey, 40 percent of teens said they knew someone who had been shot in the past five years.[21]

The evidence that young men and boys raised without fathers at home are significantly more likely to become criminals is now overwhelming. Violent crime continues unabated in large part because the proportion of young men raised without fathers continues to rise. Within a few years the boys of the baby boomlet, an astonishing and growing proportion of whom are growing up without fathers, will reach their crime-prone years. Violence among young teens is already rising. As these boys move into the prime murder years—18 to 24 years old—the killing fields will multiply.[22]

Many of these murders are less about drugs or money than they are about "turf," that emblem of masculinity—evidence that for these boys the gang has replaced family, community, and nation. In the absence of a strong, positive role for men in the family, boys seek male identification elsewhere, and the great historic rival of the family and community is the gang. The emotional power of gang membership is its ability to provide a role, an established and valued part in a meaningful story. In particular, a gang provides a specific role for the boy's maleness—a role that is conspicuously absent in the larger society as he knows it. As one *New York Times* reporter noted, "Talking with gang members... makes it clear that the gangs offer what many teenagers have missed in their own childhoods: family, rules to live by, power, respect. Boys who will kill without remorse use the word love to describe their bonds with their street friends."[23]

The link between marital collapse and crime is certainly a *social* phenomenon in the most obvious sense of that word: The children who are killed in the drive-by shootings or gang wars are killed by the children of other parents who divorced or never married. But violent crime is a social consequence of marital collapse in another deeper and perhaps more frightening sense as well. The link between fatherlessness and crime is not only to individual fatherless boys but to neighborhoods in which marriage is no longer a norm. Of all the studies on the relationship between fatherlessness and crime, it is those measuring the effects of a pattern of unmarriage throughout a community that are the most persuasive and disturbing. When one couple divorces, the chance their son will become a juvenile delinquent may be quite low. But when a whole community adopts the pattern, everyone's sons and daughters are at risk.

Josefina Figueira-McDonough investigated a link between juvenile delinquency and high school dropout rates in Maricopa County, Arizona, an area with a large, disadvantaged Hispanic population. What she uncovered went against all her training. "Contrary to most past theory and research," she found "dropout rates have no impact on delinquency," even though dropout rates among Latinos are extremely high. What did predict delinquency rates? The greater the proportion of single-mother families *in a neighborhood,* the higher the delinquency rate.[24]

Two sociologists, Robert J. Sampson and W. Byron Groves, who analyzed data from hundreds of British communities came up with similar results, uncovering statistical links between the proportion of single parenthoods *in a neighborhood* and virtually every type of major crime, from assault to car theft.[25] And when Douglas A. Smith and G. Roger Jarjoura set out to uncover the "causes" of crime, they analyzed data on 11,000 people in three different urban neighborhoods. What they found was the powerful and disturbing effects of the collapse of marriage. While both poor neighborhoods and black neighborhoods suffered more violence than average, the single best predictor of the degree of violence in a given community was once again the proportion of single-parent families. So powerful was the connection between disrupted families and crime that, once family status was controlled for, neither race nor income had any effect on the crime rate.[26] The good news is that neither poor people nor African Americans have any special taste for rape, assault, and murder. The bad news is that fatherless boys—and boys living amid fatherless boys—do.

"It takes a whole village to raise a child," says the African proverb. This is true. It often takes more than one married couple to create a safe environment for children. More than one married couple—but hardly less. Because when marriage fails as the normal, usual, and generally secure institution for raising children, communities fail also. Other social relations begin to be marked by the same uncertainty and anxiety. A community begins to be dominated by fear precisely at the moment it begins to lose faith in love.

When a neighborhood—or a country—jettisons basic moral rules, individual allegiance to the rules becomes more difficult, costly, and perilous. In such a society (or antisociety), the costs of marriage—its restrictions and responsibilities—must still be borne by individuals. Meanwhile the benefits of marriage, which come in part from living in a community where marriage is recognized as the norm, are sharply reduced for all, including the married. The payoffs for responsible behavior, which traditionally include being welcomed to live among the similarly responsible, begin to disappear. Marriage cannot be sustained in a community in which it is considered a lifestyle option.

Optimists point out, correctly, that most children of divorce or children born out of wedlock will not become murderers. Even in America's inner cities, most people are law-abiding. But a society that, in each generation, progressively loses an extra 10 percent or 20 percent of its children to drugs, crime, suicide, ignorance, or mere idleness and despair is a society defined not, as America has always been, by upward progress but by slow decline. If we fail to restore marriage, our children will find it small comfort to live in an America in which each generation is only "moderately" worse off than the last.

For too long we have pretended that the collapse of marriage is a purely private affair with only private consequences. People choose to divorce for their own reasons, and it hurts nobody but themselves. Women decide they don't need marriage to become mothers, and as long as they stay off welfare it's nobody's business if they do. Preoccupied with individual desire, they pretend their desires have no costs, that human interests never conflict.

Why not trade in your spouse who has become intellectually or sexually unstimulating, if it's nobody's business but yours? Why not unload that troublesome male ego and pursue your personal growth unfettered, if it doesn't cost anything? Why shouldn't governments and society allow the economic and legal protections afforded marriage to erode, if marriage doesn't matter or matters only to the two people involved? Why make the sacrifices of remaining in what feels like a mediocre marriage, if, as parents are everywhere told by the therapeutic community, the sacrifice doesn't do our children or anyone else any good?

But these things do matter because marriage is a public good, not just a private one, and the pain and suffering scattered by its dissolution are not confined to the two spouses or even to their own children but devastate the entire community, which ultimately cannot survive marriage's abolition.

Seventeen-year-old Michelle Jensen was not herself a child of divorce. She lived in Davenport, Iowa, with her parents. Her father Mark is an electrician. Her mother works behind the counter at a local gift shop. A good student, Michelle volunteered at the Zion Lutheran Church nursery school on Sundays. Summers, she worked at a camp for disabled children.

Her parents' marriage, if not glorious, was secure. But even in the pleasant blue-collar neighborhood where she lived, gangs like the Vice Lords were beginning to make their presence felt. Like many girls, Michelle found herself attracted to the swashbuckling young males who "looked so cool with their tattoos and red gang bandanas." She dated a gang member and counted the other Vice Lords as friends.

One warm summer night in August 1993, Michelle told her parents she was going to babysit, then drove out instead to a party at the house of a friend named Tony Hoeck. Drinking gin and malt liquor, several of Michelle's friends decided to rob a convenience store. They needed a get-away car and wanted Michelle's. When she refused to turn over her keys, Tony ordered a boy named Chris Felgenhauer to knock her out. But the ensuing struggle made so much noise that Mrs. Hoeck woke up and told Anthony to get Michelle out of the house because she was drunk.

The boys told Michelle they would just take her home because she was too drunk to drive. Once on the road, one of the teens stopped to relieve himself. Michelle got out of the car and began to walk away. One of the boys, Justin, took out his sawed-off shotgun and ordered her to stop. He counted five. She walked on. So he shot her in the head, the shot ripping away part of her skull.

The gang decided against robbing the store that night, because it was too crowded. Instead they stopped off at Hardee's for some burgers before heading back to the murder scene to prove to other gang members they really had killed someone.

When one of the teenagers, Jason, was asked by the police if he found it hard to eat after seeing Michelle shot, he replied, "No, not really, I was hungry. I wasn't even thinking about it."

For those who prefer to treat the collapse of marriage as a personal choice, or as somebody else's problem—a black problem, a ghetto problem—Michelle's is a chilling story. All six of the teenagers who murdered Michelle were white. Five of the six came from what used to be called "broken homes."[27]

5

FATHER HUNGER

THIS IS THE THEORY: Every day in every way fathers are getting better and better.

"Until recently," as two eminent family scholars optimistically maintain, "a father could feel he was fulfilling his parental obligations merely by supporting his family.... Today, however, the role of father is beginning to demand much more active involvement in the life of the family, especially with regard to child rearing."[1]

"An increasing number of men are now taking the primary responsibility for child rearing or are sharing equally," agreed a psychologist in a popular advice book.[2]

That's the theory. Jason is the reality.

Jason is a well-loved, nine-year-old, tousled blond boy who laughs easily and chatters with adults. He lives with his mother, Lori. His dad lives fifteen minutes away.

"He's okay," says Jason about his father, swatting away a tear. "I don't know when he's telling the truth or when he's actually going to show up."

Lori, a loving affectionate mother, is worried. Jason appears to be a normal, well-adjusted kid. But once in a while he tells his mother he wants to kill himself. "Issues of potential loss affect him deeply," she says. "I've been dating a guy for one week and [Jason] already wants me to marry him and make him his daddy."[3]

I know what she's talking about: father hunger.

It's an ache in the heart, a gnawing anxiety in the gut. It's a longing for a man, not a woman, who will care for you, protect you, show you how to survive in the world. For a boy, especially, it's the raw, persistent, desperate hunger for dependable male love and for an image of maleness that is not at odds with love. Signs of it are everywhere, if you know what to look for.

I first saw it in my own six-year-old son's eyes as he watched, riveted to the screen, the phenomenally successful "Teenage Mutant Ninja Turtles."

Homeless and born of radioactive goo, the valiant turtles, nurtured by their surrogate father, a giant ninja-master rat, must save a city and a boy from the ravages of the predatory male, Shredder.

The dramatic tension is created by the boy's need to choose between moral poles: Will he accept the authority of the good dad or the lures of the evil one? The home or the gang? The father or the fascist?

"I am your father," Shredder hypnotically booms at the gang of teen boys he has assembled.

"You call this a family?" one of the heroes replies scornfully.

In the end, "all fathers love their children," the rat guru reassures the troubled boy, who then rejects the gang and reunites with his own father.

Father hunger has produced a sudden explosion of unlikely television families in which a perplexing multiplicity of loving fathers care for motherless children, including "Full House," in which three adorably blond little girls are raised by three loving and affectionate men—their dad, their dead mother's brother, and his best friend—and "My Two Dads," in which two men are so determined to be great dads that, despite their uncertainty as to which of them is actually the father, they agree to raise a little girl together.

It has emerged even more clearly as the major theme in motion pictures aimed at boys: in sports films such as the wildly popular *Mighty Ducks*, in which the boy finds in his coach a kind of surrogate father and tries to get him interested in his single mother, and even more obviously in films such as 1994's *Getting Even with Dad,* in which a clever but sad young boy blackmails his divorced father into spending time with him and in the end makes his dad fall in love with him again. The summer 1994 hit *Angels in the Outfield* began with a boy wistfully asking his drop-in dad, "When are we going to be a family again?" "I'd say when the Angels win the pennant," his father replies scornfully, before zipping off on his motorcycle.

Thus the collapse of marriage has created a modern fairy tale in which the wickedly absent father is replaced by a warmly loving father figure or, even better, is transformed by a child's love into the devoted dad of every kid's dreams.

Celluloid fathers like these are raised up by entrepreneurs who are quick to spot unfulfilled appetites. And for all the losses the end of marriage entails for children, one of the most painful and enduring—and the most common—is the loss of the father.

The first way fathers are lost is physically. Therapists may reassure children that "though Mommy and Daddy don't love each other anymore, they will always love you," but children of divorce know better. For most, domicile is destiny: Only one-third of all children living apart from their fathers get to see their dads as often as once a week.[4]

For the first year or so, fathers make a special effort to see their children. As life goes on, as they or their children move inconvenient distances away, or as they acquire additional emotional obligations to new wives or girlfriends or stepchildren or new babies, or as the crisis subsides and the children seem to be getting on fine, or as men grow weary of facing the continual hostility of ex-wives, or for a hundred other reasons or no reason, fathers' contact with their children dwindles rapidly. Ten years down the road, two-thirds of all children of divorce have virtually no contact with their fathers.[5] As four distinguished researchers concluded, "Marital dissolution typically involves either a complete cessation of contact between the nonresidential parent and child or a relationship that is tantamount to a ritual form of parenthood."[6]

Children whose parents fail to marry in the first place have even less dependable connections to their fathers. On average, the child born outside of marriage spends just six months living with his father.[7] As time passes, the same pattern of the disappearing dad emerges, but more strongly. Three-fifths of unwed fathers whose children are age two or younger see their kids regularly. But by the time the kids reach the age of seven and a half, less than a quarter of unwed fathers still see their children frequently.[8] Altogether, as University of Pennsylvania researchers concluded after one large-scale survey of children, "Fathers, in particular, were more likely not to have had any contact at all than to have seen their children even once in the past twelve months."[9]

Put the divorce and illegitimacy statistics together and you come up with this disturbing trend: *A baby born today stands a roughly fifty–fifty chance of keeping his father.* Previous generations lost fathers to the grave, but this is the first generation of Americans for whom paternal abandonment has become the norm. This is the first generation of American kids who must face not the sad loss of fathers to death, but the far more brutal knowledge that, to their fathers, many other things are more important than they are.

Father hunger is the bane of single mothers everywhere, who often find to their surprise that not all love is personal, merited, or based on intimate acquaintanceship. Penelope Rowlands, a never-married San Francisco magazine writer with a five-year-old son, was shocked by it: "My son began asking for his father before he was two. I'll never forget it. He said, 'Why no daddy?'"[10]

Bonnie is forty-five, with light brown wavy hair and large eyes with big circles under them. She is a teacher of deaf children and the never-married mother of eight-year-old Michael. She and baby Michael lived in Germany for seven months. Then, feeling she needed a family, she came back to the United States and lived with her mother. "At first I went to every family gathering. I put a lot of emphasis on getting him together with his cousins and aunts and uncles. But still, even with all these people around him, I realized it's not the same. Something was missing. There's this hole."

This hole is in Michael's heart. He has seen his dad on only a few visits, here and in Germany. His father pays no support, but he tells Bonnie he will send money for airplane tickets "any time." In the past Bonnie has taken Michael to Germany to visit his dad. Because she has very little money, they both have to stay in his dad's apartment. When they do so, Michael tries to make his mom and dad hold hands.

This year, Michael is mad at Bonnie because she refuses to take him to Germany. "It's too painful," Bonnie says.

What's too painful? Seeing how much her son loves his father, even though his father does nothing for him, even though he was carelessly cruel in his disregard for her.

Though children seldom see their fathers when marriage dissolves, they do not forget them, even when their mothers wish they would. In the postmarital culture a startling gap arises between mothers' perceptions and children's perceptions of who counts as a family member. In one large-scale study fully half of the children who did not live with their father nonetheless named him as a member of their family, while only one in twenty of their mothers did so.[11]

"Most children do not give up on their fathers, even if they are ne'er-do-wells who have abandoned them without a backward glance," notes Judith Wallerstein. "Children turn around and construct a credible image of the father they never knew from any scraps of information that they can collect and tend to idealize him in the process."[12]

Therapists tell mothers like Bonnie that they shouldn't interfere with this idealization process. In the light of reason and the best interests of the child, they are right. But whose blood is that cold? Certainly not Bonnie's. Michael is not just her child, but her whole family, her great love, and her ruling passion. She is not a particularly angry person, and she has tried very hard not to let her feelings interfere with Michael's well-being. But still, the man Michael loves and longs for is the man who desperately pressured her to have an abortion, who never gave her a dime or a helping hand as she struggled—

a stranger in a foreign land with almost no money to take care of a baby, and who has never helped her since. He is the man who didn't want her and, worse, didn't want the greatest treasure she could offer—Michael. And her son loves him.

In a good-enough marriage, the mother helps the child idealize the father. She, like the child, has every interest in exaggerating his good points and minimizing his flaws. When family members go their separate ways and withdraw from the family as a unit, either through divorce or failure to marry, this union of interests collapses both emotionally and economically. This is one manifestation of eros (the longing for union with another self); A husband experiences his child's and his own economic interests as one. He works for his family. A father who is no longer part of his son's household, however, experiences his son's support as a kind of tax on his own new household and often on his ability to attract a new wife and support a new family. He particularly dislikes that his child support money will unavoidably help his ex-wife or ex-girlfriend as well as his kids. Full of ambivalence, the good man pays anyway and the bad man absconds. Either way, he and his children learn that, when marriage ends, the financial and erotic interests of family members fundamentally diverge.

Fathers have their own complaints: about the awkwardness and artificiality of the postdivorce relationship with their children, about the demotion from head of the household to "Visiting Daddy."

"Few people realize how difficult it is to transplant the relationship from the rich soil of family life to the impoverished ground of the visiting relationship."[13] From the fathers' standpoint, many are just doing the best they can in a difficult situation. Maybe they did not want the divorce anyway (the majority of divorces are at least formally initiated by women);[14] maybe they desperately wanted to be real fathers in real families and instead are thrust into this fractured half-a-dad position, each visit a reminder of what they have lost. Maybe the kids are hostile too or acting weird because of the divorce or because of their mother's hostility—who knows? The dad usually doesn't. The financial squeeze is tight, and, of course, he resents helping support a woman who wants his money but doesn't want him. If having a father was so important for the kids, why couldn't she stick around and stay married, like she promised?

Under these circumstances, the man who stays in touch and pays his child support regularly is likely to feel quite good about his performance as a father. His children are likely to feel differently.

The divorced fathers in Wallerstein's study were an unusually committed group, compared to national averages. Very few had completely abandoned their children. (Ten years after the divorce, only 10 percent of the children in Wallerstein's sample saw their fathers only once a year or less.) This greater paternal involvement is consistent with studies that show educated men are most likely to keep in contact with their kids after divorce.[15] Wallerstein's children were drawn from middle-class families in which the fathers were mostly college-educated professionals.

These fathers—generally remarried, holding down demanding professions, and living busy, complicated lives—made special efforts to keep in touch with their kids. For the most part, they paid their court-ordered child support. From their point of view, they have done well in a difficult situation, certainly much better than the average man.

The children felt and experienced the same situation entirely differently. "Most fathers in our study thought they had done reasonably well in fulfilling their obligations whereas three out of four of the children felt rejected by their fathers." The father says, "My door is always open. My son is welcome to come visit me anytime, and I'll give him anything he needs." The son says, "I'm not welcome in his house. I feel awkward and uncomfortable there. All I do is watch television while he talks to his friends."[16]

What mattered to children, in Wallerstein's experience, was not the amount of time, but the quality of the relation. Boys who saw their father as moral and competent and who felt valued by him did very well. When a father was seen as bad, weak, or unconcerned, the boys were likely to suffer "low self-esteem, poor grades, weak aspirations."[17]

Unfortunately, a mother who has been abandoned by or who has left her children's father is generally not in a very good position to help the children see their father as good, strong, and concerned. If the father has abandoned his family, it is hard for the mother to see him as loving. And if she has left, how can she justify that decision to herself if he is so good?

In divorce, both the children and the father feel the loss of the mother's love for the father. To a considerable and unrecognized extent, the father's role is sustained through and by women. When women (many for very understandable reasons) refuse to take on this burden, the child suffers the loss as well.

These underlying erotic truths help explain one of the great puzzles in the sociological literature: the great difference between orphans and "divorce" orphans.

Children have very different psychological reactions to parental death and parental divorce. Children who are orphaned react by internalizing. They frequently withdraw for a time, in grief, to mourn. By contrast, children of divorce, especially boys, are far more likely to externalize, to act out and become behavior problems. Similarly, girls who lose a father to death often become shy and reserved with members of the opposite sex, while girls in divorced families often respond by launching into precocious, sexualized relations with males. Children of divorce are also far more likely to end up divorced as adults, compared to children who lose a parent to death.

Of the two ways to lose a father, death is better. As Robert Emery, surveying the evidence, concludes, "Compared to children from homes disrupted by death, children from divorced homes have more psychological problems."[18]

This finding is in some ways surprising. Given the way sociologists conceptualize the family—as a set of tasks and roles—there ought to be little difference as a result of how the father is lost. Both represent cases of "paternal absence"; in both cases, mothers must take up the slack left by the loss of their partner, a daunting task that may lead to role overload. Some have gone so far as to argue that something called "family breakup" is really not much more common today than it was a hundred years ago, when divorce rates were low and illegitimacy almost nonexistent, but many more children were orphaned.

This apparently sensible analogy turns out to be nonsense, for it pretends that the loss of a full-time wage earner and occasional diaper changer is more important than the loss of love.

Children may often *experience* a parent's death as a form of abandonment, but at some deep level they know, or come to understand, that this is not true. Death, unlike divorce, is not a failure of love. Moreover, in death, unlike divorce, the mother who remains still loves and admires the father. She may even idealize him far more in death than in life. Death may deprive children of their father's flesh-and-blood presence, but the *story* of their father—of the man who made them, loved them, protected them—remains intact.

The same disturbing truth emerges from another set of social science research. In the aftermath of the divorce revolution, experts put much emphasis on the need for both parents to keep close ties to their kids after a divorce. Surprisingly, the evidence is mounting that even frequent visiting is no balm for father hunger. Even when fathers stick around after divorce, children may feel abandoned. Overall, children of divorce who see their fathers do no better than children of divorce who do not see their fathers.

In the NSC study, for example, the amount of contact children had with absent fathers made little difference in their well-being. As Furstenberg and Cherlin note, "Teenagers who saw their fathers regularly were just as likely as those with infrequent contact to have problems in school or engage in delinquent acts and precocious sexual behavior."[19]

Here is the puzzle the current research poses: Although inside of marriage the presence of an active father makes a great difference in children's well-being, the presence of that same father, outside of marriage, seems not to have the same benefits for children.

The father's role is particularly fragile and vulnerable to disruption outside of marriage. Not surprisingly, noncustodial mothers are more likely than noncustodial fathers to keep in regular touch with their kids. Far more surprisingly, children who do not live with their mothers are almost as likely as children who do not to report they have a good relationship with their mothers. But when the father moves out of the home, the paternal relationship deteriorates rapidly: 69 percent of children who live with their fathers report a good relationship, but only 36 percent of children with an absent father say they have a good relationship with him.[20]

More than half of the children whose fathers don't live with them say they don't get all the affection they need from their fathers. Again, those who saw their absent fathers frequently did not evaluate their relationships more favorably than those who saw them infrequently: Overall, only half of absent fathers were viewed as "family" by their children, compared to all fathers living with their children and even 70 percent of stepfathers living with the children.

Psychologists and other child-care experts have begun to emphasize the importance of fathering. What they have not done is insist on a much more politically risky point: The only reliable way to be an effective father is inside an intact marriage to the mother of your children. Instead they promoted a fantasy of finding new ways to involve fathers in children's lives outside of marriage. Joint custody, for instance, swept the land, new rhetorical attacks on deadbeat dads were launched, and parenting groups for unwed fathers began to spring up.

Such programs raised the possibility that we could deflect the damage of divorce or unmarriage before it happened by transforming divorced husbands and never-married men into dependable fathers. Divorce (and failure to marry) could be remade into a kinder, gentler institution.

As part of this new spirit of optimism, the Clinton administration proposed a new federal program: job training, parent education, and counseling programs for unwed fathers.[21]

"People are only starting to recognize the importance of including teen fathers," says Beth Grube, dean of social work at Fordham

University's Tarrytown campus, which is starting a new program for young unwed fathers. "It's not only good for the father, but for the mother and child."[22] But the peculiar problems unwed fathers face are not easy to overcome. Consider the case of Hassam Lemons. Hassam was a seventeen-year-old unmarried father of a baby girl when he entered a program run by the National Institute for Responsible Fatherhood, a Chicago-based group that motivates young unwed fathers to take responsibility for their kids. When he and his girlfriend split up, Hassam dropped out of his daughter's life.

"The people from the institute kept saying, 'Where's your child? That's really taking it out on her.'" So Hassam made contact again, and, now that he has found work as a handyman, he says he'll pay child support. There is one complication, however. He recently fathered another child, and now he says he needs to spend more time (and presumably money) with his new girlfriend and their new baby.

Hassam means well. But outside of marriage, he finds it almost impossible to be a committed father. Marriage unifies the erotic interests of the family. In marriage, a man and a woman give themselves to each other in a sexual union that includes a promise to care for each other and for any children who result. Released from marriage, the erotic interests of individuals necessarily fragment as the family diversifies.

What does it mean to be a good father? At a basic level, a father shows his children and their mother that he loves them by putting their needs first. His sexuality is (in theory) at his wife's disposal, not other women's—and therefore cannot threaten the well-being of his children. His income is their income. His emotional energy and financial energy are also theirs.

But what if there are two mothers and two children to care for? His commitment to both cannot be supreme. Even for men who wish to be responsible fathers, for all practical purposes one set of children must be subordinated to another. When, as is often the case in families fractured by divorce or failure to marry, the father is a man of very limited resources, struggling to get by in a world where the wages of less-educated men are falling, the difficulties of being a good dad to two or more sets of children intensify. But for all fathers, time, energy, and money are limited commodities.

Several studies confirm that, for the father, "remarriage frequently introduced new parental obligations… weakening his ties with his biological offspring. In effect, sociological parenthood took precedence over biological parenthood."[23]

Nor are the erotic dilemmas all of the fathers' own making. Ricky Hall, for example, is twenty-five years old and currently enrolled in Beat the Streets, a Cleveland job-training program for unwed fathers. Ricky promises he'll pay child support as soon as he finds a job and says wants to visit his kids right now. But his former girlfriend has acquired a new boyfriend—who, Ricky fears, is the jealous type. "I could go and start trouble, but I choose not to," he says.[24]

The mother's erotic interests also diversify outside of marriage— where marriage unites her desire for partner and children, unmarriage divides it. Her new romantic partner may or may not be interested in her children, he may be more or less resentful of the energy and attention they divert from him, and he may or may not be tolerant of her ex-lover, i.e., her children's father. Outside of marriage, a mother's love for her children and for her lover are frequently at odds.

In difficult circumstances, some men choose to abandon their children. Others are simply forced to *prioritize*. The children demoted to second best know it and suffer for it.

David's mother and father divorced several years ago. She moved back to New York to be closer to family. Every summer, David visits his dad and returns heartbroken. "David's so hungry for his father, but his dad never spends time with him," his mom complains. "He always has to tag along with his father's new wife's daughters."

But as David's dad points out, what else can you expect? "These kids are my family," he points out to David, not unreasonably, from an adult point of view. Nevertheless, David will never feel like his father's first priority. For the few weeks David gets to see his dad, David will always have to split his father's care and attention not with his brothers and sisters (as most children do), but with a couple of strangers. To David, it doesn't seem fair. To David's father, it seems the best he can possibly be expected to do.

If liberal visitation rights cannot make a divorced dad into a real dad, joint custody—for which the experts held out such high hopes—has been deeply disappointing. According to Furstenberg and Cherlin's review of the literature, "Joint *legal* custody seems to be hardly distinguishable in practice from maternal sole custody."[25] The evidence on the effects of joint physical custody is less established (as the number of such families is quite small), but at least two studies also suggest that children in joint physical custody "were no better adjusted than children from the mother–physical custody families."[26] Children in these families may see their fathers more but, like other children of divorce, they do not necessarily do any better as a result.

One reason may be that when divorced fathers see their kids more often, mothers and fathers have more reason and opportunity to quarrel. Major conflict between parents is one of the worst emotional stresses a child can face.[27] What is important is not merely the physical presence of the father, but the moral unity of the parents that marriage represents. When eros fractures, the child experiences intense loyalty conflicts, beholden to two parents who no longer love, or are loyal to, each other.

Not surprisingly, young teens whose parents were divorced were almost four times as likely to say they experienced "family-related moral dilemmas" as were children of intact families. Moreover, children of divorce face moral conflicts very different from children in intact families: "The early adolescents of divorce were concerned with deciding which parent to live with and not hurting their feelings, whereas the early adolescents from intact families were concerned with fighting with siblings." (And yet children of divorce were four times more likely than children in intact families to say they had problems with peers and friends.)[28]

Marriage is the vehicle by which, throughout history, society has tried to create firm, reliable ties between men and their children—to institutionalize the impulse of paternity. In marriage, men make a commitment to care for the children their sexual acts may produce. In marriage, men have a reasonable certainty that the children produced are in fact their own.

The current fumbling attempts to arduously reproduce these ties outside of marriage are without precedent and are unlikely to succeed. Because marriage and parenting are not, as the experts have imagined, job labels that can be transferred from one employee to the next as personnel shift but, instead, are imperatives of eros.

Eros is love—but not selfless, disinterested love. Eros is love that is full of need, full of desire, love sustained or enriched by the most powerful human drive: the desire not to be alone in an impersonal imperturbable universe we cannot affect because it does not care. Eros is love that seeks above all union between self and other.

It is the name we commonly apply to love between men and women, but it is also the only word that adequately describes the love that children feel for their parents. Though eros is full of need and desire, it transcends mere affection, pleasure, or even self-interest, as the narrow rationalists understand it. We can hear Eros' divine imperative, painfully and perversely twisted, even in the voices of children abused by their parents—children such as Melissa, a ten-year-old girl now living in a residential treatment center for children too disturbed for ordinary foster care. Her parents' rights were severed because, although they had plenty of food for themselves, they neglected to feed Melissa. "My parents used to lock me in a closet," she tells an interviewer matter-of-factly. "I miss them."[29]

And in the heart of parents' love for their children is also this same eros. Good-enough parents identify with their children, make sacrifices for their well-being, and rejoice in their achievements because they see their children as part of themselves—and also because they see themselves as part of their children. Psychologists, witnesses to disturbances of eros gone awry, tend to discourage this close identification between parent and child, to see it as suspect, problematic. But whatever neurotic problems may be caused by "smothering" are nothing compared to the profound psychoses produced when no parent forms this wild, erotic attachment to a child—when the child is left to grow up alone in a universe that does not care.

Perfect eros is rare between men and women, parent and child. A love that is both profoundly attached, deeply desiring, and perfectly disinterested must be rare. What is surprising is how closely, in how many cases, so many parents actually approach the ideal. In marriage, mothers and fathers routinely make sacrifices—of time, money, energy, freedom—for their children, far beyond what the law can require.

For fathers, in particular, marriage plays a crucial role in attaching them to their children. Marriage creates a unity of interest between them and their children, and a distinctly male role in the family. When marriage dissolves, or is ignored, this crucial tie between men and children apparently is not just weakened, it is transformed in ways that are hostile to the interests of children and to their profound desire for union with both their parents.

It is not biology, but law, custom, and mores that make fathers out of men, and family an institution out of eros. The fact that the tie between father and child is less "natural," that is, more fragile, more a product of culture, than the tie between mother and child, does not mean that it is less important. Culture is man's natural state, humanity's inescapable destiny.

The greater fragility of fatherhood does, however, mean that attaching men to their children—creating a tie so firm a child's heart can rely on it—is a social problem, in the way that creating attachment between women and their children is not.

How do we give children the fathers they need and long for? Marriage is the ancient answer to that ancient problem, and none of the modern solutions that attempt to re-create the father outside of marriage appear likely to assuage our children's hunger.

Nor, as we shall see, will just any sort of marriage do.

6

THE LUMPY FAMILY

To know where marriage is headed, you have to look at where it has disappeared. Take the strange case of Woody, Mia, and Soon-Yi.

An improbable sex scandal erupted between America's premier comic and his ethereal unbride. Woody felt betrayed. He had played by the rules, followed love fearlessly, without regard to convention. "The heart," he said, "wants what it wants."

So why was everyone so mad at him?

In the courtroom, Woody made his plea for custody. Everything he said was true. He and Soon-Yi were consenting adults. Surely in this day and age we do not crucify anyone, much less movie stars, for having extramarital affairs. And he and Mia weren't even married. All he wanted was what was best for his children.

"Was it in the children's best interest to sleep with their sister?" Mia's lawyers shot back.

An unanswerable objection. But to see it, you have to stand in a certain place. Say about two-and-a-half feet tall.

For Woody, as for so many today, relationships are bilateral and contained: He and Mia were once lovers, now they are not; he and Soon-Yi became lovers; Soon-Yi and Mia are adopted mother and child. He and Satchel are father and son; Satchel and Soon-Yi are brother and sister. Woody knows Soon-Yi is not his daughter, not even his stepdaughter. That she is his son's sister simply never enters his mind. That is a relation between Soon-Yi and Satchel—what could it possibly have to do with Woody?

There are no unchosen bonds. Obligations today arise only out of the choices we make. Woody chose to adopt Dylan and not Soon-Yi, who had a father.

This understanding of personal relations as defined by bilateral choice is at the heart of the new postmarital culture.

Woody and Mia's family may be unusual, but some of its key assumptions are shared by a huge proportion of American households. When families are created through divorce and remarriage, sociologists hail them as a new type of family form: the blended family. Blended families are very common.

One-third of all marriages today are remarriages for at least one of the spouses.[1] About one out of five married couple families contains stepchildren. About one out of three Americans now has some immediate stepfamily ties: either a stepparent, or a stepchild, or a stepsibling. If the current rates of divorce and remarriage hold steady, demographers estimate, about one-fourth of all children will spend some time living with a stepparent.[2] Nearly half of all Americans will be in a step relationship of some kind.[3]

Great hopes have been pinned on the blended family. Increasingly battered by the dramatic changes brought on by the collapse of marriage, Americans now seek refuge and reassurance in the institution of remarriage.

"Neither the rising age of those who marry nor the frequency of divorce necessarily means that marriage is becoming a less prominent institution than it was in earlier days," says sociologist Stephanie Coontz. "Ninety percent of men and women eventually marry, more than 70 percent of divorced men and women remarry, and fewer people remain single for their entire lives today than at the turn of the century."[4] This optimism is not confined to the Left. "Nine out of 10 divorced Americans get remarried," neoconservative columnist

Ben Wattenberg asserts even more optimistically. "That's not exactly the portrait of a nation that's given up on marriage."[5]

Many children are going through divorces, experts told us, but not to worry. Because of remarriage, few will end up in single-parent families. Americans are not turning away from marriage, but simply substituting good marriages for bad. Through remarriage everyone wins: Men and women get happy marriages, and children get happy families.

For adults, there is some truth in the idea. A certain portion of divorced Americans do indeed hit Cupid's jackpot: They rise from the purgatory of divorce into the paradise of a more satisfying marriage.

But do their children also rise? A growing wealth of data is emerging to show that one of the key assumptions of the divorce culture— what is good for adults of a family must be good for their children as well—turns out to be a myth. They call it the *blended family*, but if truth-in-advertising laws applied to sociologists, they would relabel it the *lumpy family*.

Expert optimism was battered by two discoveries: First, remarriages turned out to be even more unstable than first marriages.[6] Second, and even more devastating in psychological terms, children in stepfamilies do no better on average than children in single-parent homes.[7] While remarriage does raise household income—remarried families are almost as well off in terms of income as intact families[8]— the money may not be as available to children. Stepparents and non-custodial parents are far less willing to lay out cash for college than parents in intact marriages.[9]

Children living with single parents or in stepfamilies are both more likely to drop out of high school than children of marriage. In one national study, 85 percent of teens from intact families graduated from high school, compared to just 67 percent of children from single-parent families. Again, remarriage proved to be no cure for what ails marriage: Although the income in stepfamilies was almost as high as that of intact families, teens whose parents remarried were actually slightly less likely to graduate from high school than teens from single-parent families.[10] Teens in stepfamilies were almost as likely as teens in mother-only families to have required psychological help within the past year. Both groups were about three times as likely as children in intact families to need such help.[11]

Another study found that "disturbed adolescent functioning" is just as common among teens in stepfamilies as in single-parent families, and much more common in both than among teens in intact families. Remarriage, the author concluded, "does nothing for the psychological health of adolescents in the medium term."[12] After surveying the recent literature, Furstenberg and Cherlin came to the same sad conclusion: "It appears that children in stepfamilies have the same frequency of problems as do children in single-parent families."[13]

The most damning indictment of the divorce culture comes not from short-term studies of children, but from long-term research on adults. Two researchers recently investigated the effects of family structure on achievement among Americans adults ages twenty-five to sixty-four. They found that both children living in mother-only and in mother/stepfather homes had lower socioeconomic attainment and completed less education; those who lived in such families "for longer periods achieved fewer years of education than those who lived in these family types for fewer years." Overall, they concluded, "Living in a mother/stepfather family has as much negative effect as living in a mother-only family."[14]

It turns out that it is not *the two-parent* family *but any* intact family that holds substantial advantages for children.

What accounts for this profound gap between theory and reality, between marriage and remarriage, between the blended and lumpy family? As recently as the late seventies, sociologists Frank F. Furstenberg, Jr., and Andrew J. Cherlin reminded us, "Researchers behaved as though remarriage merely restored the simple nuclear family that divorce had broken apart."[15] This simple faith grew, once again, out of the way sociologists conceptualized family and parenting as essentially a set of tasks to be performed. In this functionalist view it is understandable, perhaps, that single parents may not perform (on average) as well as married-couple families because they have literally twice as much to do. Sociologists refer to this excessive burden single mothers face as *role overload*. But when the single parent remarried, they believed (a priori and without much evidence) that the tasks of parenting could again be split between two parents, relieving the mother and restoring to the children the advantages of the intact family.

Failing to understand the erotic relations that are at the heart of family life, they failed to predict what, sadly and surprisingly, later research strongly suggested: Remarriage is not only not necessarily a cure; it is often one of the risks children of divorce face. "Through divorce and remarriage, individuals are related to more and more people, to each of whom they owe less and less,"[16] note Furstenberg and Cherlin. "As blended families become the norm, the responsibilities of family members become more complex, more ambiguous and more open to dispute," say researchers Ahlburg and DeVita.[17]

While true, these critiques capture only part of the weakness of remarriage as an institution. In the lumpy family, the very question of who is a family member becomes ambiguous and open to dispute. In the lumpy family, household members are related to some people, but not to others. Family obligations and family loyalties fragment, as children as well as new spouses face a question seldom posed in the intact household, who counts as family?

The NSC asked a large sample of Americans this question: "When you think of your family, who specifically do you include?" The results showed what any reader of fairy tales might predict—stepfamily relations are not like intact family ones. Stepchildren living in the home were fifteen times more likely than biological children not to be named as part of the family. And children were three times as likely to exclude a stepparent living in their households as a biological one.[18]

As two sociologists recently put it, in surveys "stepchildren consistently expressed more negative description of relations with their stepparents than did children in nuclear household with their parents. And stepparents who were raising both biological and stepchildren reported that stepparenting was more problematic and less rewarding."[19] In the National Survey of Children, close to half of parents with both children and stepchildren agreed that their stepchildren did not think of them as real parents, it was more difficult to be a stepparent than a natural parent, it was more difficult to discipline their stepchildren, it was more difficult for them to love their stepchildren than their biological children, and their children would have been better off if they had grown up with two biological parents.[20] *Only half of adults with stepchildren identified them as members of "their close family."*[21]

Acquiring a stepfather provides children of divorce an opportunity for another warm and loving relationship with an adult male. It provides a divorced parent with the opportunity for a more satisfying relationship with a spouse. But remarriage also provides an opportunity for renewed marital conflict, jealousy, and a new round of fights between natural parents, and competition for the time and energy of the mother. Remarriages are a fertile arena for conflicts between stepparent and a child whose young life has already been marked by many such conflicts. "If I love my stepfather, will I betray my father? If my mother loves my stepfather, will she forget about me? Just because I like my stepdad, does that mean I have to put up with his kids barging around here like they own the place?" And underlying that, the more heartbreaking question, who comes first?

When David's mother, Ann, moved in with Barry, David remembers how everything changed. "He wouldn't allow my sister and me to be with my mother in her room. He'd lock the door and keep us out. Before, we'd hang out in her room and watch movies. When he came that just stopped."

"When [kids] were living with Mom, it was 'You're my best buddy,'" says Elizabeth McGonagle, a social worker in Ballston Spa, New York, and founder of Banana Splits, a support group for children of divorce. "Then along comes Prince Charming and the child all of sudden has to go to bed on time."

Ann experienced the same kind of loyalty conflict later on, when she moved in with a new man, her fiancé, Lee. "He didn't feel that he came first," she noted. "My children come first. That caused a lot of conflict for us as a couple and a family—jealousy, anger, blame."[22]

Sibling rivalry in stepfamilies can be exacerbated by the child's sense that the new marriage is not as legitimate as the one that produced him: First, she leaves my dad, now she spends all her time with this squalling baby. Or, I love my little sister, but I don't see what she sees in that jerk, her father.

The possibilities for loyalty conflicts are manifold because the erotic interests of the families have diverged. Recognition of this reality is what has made the stepfamily so suspect (from the child's point of view), the object of fear and fairy tales that center on the child's recognition that his interests and his stepparents' interests are not the same: The wicked stepmother may want to kill me off to keep her husband's goodies for her own children.

It is not, of course, that erotic conflicts never emerge in intact marriages. Husbands may feel shunted aside when wives devote all their energies to a new baby; wives may feel unappreciated when husbands are more physically demonstrative with their kids than with them; very occasionally, children may feel their parents are so in love with each other that there is no need or room for them.

Spouses may violate the terms of the marriage, without dissolving it, in ways that create similar erotic conflicts. A disruption of the family's unity occurs when parents defect temporarily to engage in extramarital affairs. Frank Pittman, a psychiatrist who teaches at Emory University, observes, "The impact of parental affairs on the lives of children is very much the stuff of tragedy," producing symptoms of insecurity such as "clinging, bed-wetting, thumb-sucking, fire setting, temper tantrums, or night terrors." For adolescents, "Shoplifting, running away from home, and setting fires to the house, are frequent ways of acting out.... Suicide attempts among children and adolescents are a frequent response" to a parent's infidelity. Pittman says these are dramatic attempts by the child to get an answer to the question, Who is more important—your child or your affair? "The child may be shocked, and truly suicidal, upon learning the answer to that question."[23]

Creating a unity of love within a family is no easy task. But marriage is designed institutionally to minimize conflicts, while unmarriage multiplies them.

Even a warm and affectionate relationship with a stepfather, while a great gift, does not seem entirely to compensate a child for the loss of a full-time father. "Among children with stepfathers, those very or quite close to the stepfather have more positive school outcomes and are much more satisfied with their families," writes James L. Peterson. However, children living with both biological parents are still more likely to be very satisfied with their families and more likely to be doing well in school, even compared with those children in stepfamilies who are very or quite close to their stepfather."[24]

The best news for kids about remarriage? In the NSC, about half of the stepchildren whose parent and stepparent were still married said they felt close to their stepparent and wanted to be like the stepparent when they grew up. The worst news? Many stepchildren will have to go through the breakup of their new family. Of all the risks to which remarriage exposes children, one of the most common and least remarked is *redivorce*.

Half of all children will witness the breakup of a parent's marriage. Of these, close to half will *also* see the breakup of a parent's second marriage.[25] Ten percent of children of divorce will go on to witness three or more family breakups.[26]

And while children in remarried families do no better, on average, than children living with single mothers, children in redivorced families do far worse. "The worst outcome," James Peterson continued, "in terms of needing psychological help, was for children living with a parent who had been divorced or separated after a second subsequent marriage."[27]

Alan Booth and Paul R. Amato recently published the results of a longitudinal study tracking more than twelve hundred Americans. They found that those who experienced multiple divorces reported the highest level of anxiety and depression as adults, as well as more troubled marriages and higher divorce rates. One study found that children in repeat divorces were given lower grades by teachers and lower approval ratings from their peers.[28]

Many more children will endure breakups of other kinds that are not reported in Census Bureau statistics. Divorced parents not only frequently remarry, they may quite naturally be involved in serious relationships that do not lead to marriage. Children of divorce share their mother not just with a stepparent, but with live-in boyfriends or other serious lovers. If the child doesn't like his mother's boyfriend, he must still deal with his own hostility and the disruptions in family life that ensue. And if he becomes fond of his mother's new friend, different emotional issues, in their own way just as difficult, are raised.

Consider the case of Carly, whose parents embarked on a difficult divorce when she was three. Carly has many strengths. She is a lively, outgoing, intelligent, and articulate child, with two parents who are devoted to her, but not to each other. This has been very confusing and saddening for Carly, who witnessed angry exchanges, insults, and verbal abuse between her two beloved parents during the divorce and its aftermath.

How does the adult postdivorce world look through the eyes of the child? There are some good things about it.

The ugly fights that broke out in the middle of the divorce diminished after Mommy moved out with the kids but, three years later, Daddy in particular is still extremely angry. Once in a while his control breaks, and he calls Mommy obscene names.

In the past three years, Mommy has had two special friends who spent a lot of time with Mommy, Carly, and her brother, Matthew—taking them to movies and out for Chinese food, even sometimes helping with homework. Carly likes Mommy's current special friend, but she misses Vinny, who no longer drops by. Recently Matthew asked to speak to Vinny, but Mommy said that she didn't think Vinny wanted to hear from her. So Carly decided to help her brother out. She went to the phone and called up Vinny. Maybe her Mommy was right. Maybe she said the wrong thing. "Mommy and us are seeing somebody named Emil now," she told Vinny. "He buys us pizza, and Mommy stays in his room."

Meanwhile, her father is also on his second serious girlfriend. The first one was nice. She had a boy named Ben. After her father broke up with his girlfriend, she and Matthew still saw Ben sometimes, because their mothers would get them together, so that's not so bad. Especially since Daddy soon got another girlfriend—a super one from Carly's viewpoint. Kathy is very nice and lives with Daddy, so she's always there when Carly goes to stay with Daddy on weekends.

Today, though, Carly is sobbing. Kathy is leaving. She has to go back to graduate school. Kathy used to "protect" her, she says, from "the boys." They would go into her bedroom and shut the door. "When the boys knocked on the door, she said, 'Go 'way, we're doing girl things.'" Now, when she visits her father, there is a great big hole where Kathy used to be.

From an adult perspective, there is nothing particularly unusual about Carly's parents' postdivorce romantic life. Frivolous relations, if they had any, were kept out of the children's sight. Serious loves, potential mates, they understandably wanted to integrate into their family lives. But from a child's point of view, a year is a very long time. In Carly's case a year meant about 20 percent of her young life—a long time to spend falling in love with someone who drops you completely and mysteriously for reasons you can't fathom.

Adults in postdivorce romances seldom accurately assess the effects these relationships may have on their children, and, even if they did, their options are limited. To keep your love life completely separate from your children is not only logistically difficult but emotionally awkward—it means keeping your partner and potential mate completely shut out of the other most important part of your life. The original marriage may be dead, but eros is not, and parents' drive to unify their love lives remains powerful, especially for women. There is a falseness and an artificiality in keeping the great loves of one's life entirely separate. It is directly at odds with the essential impulse of romantic love. Moreover, when considering remarriage, parents quite naturally and reasonably want to see how their children and their partner get along.

The result for children is the repeated experience from an early age of love failing—both between adults and between adults and children. In sharp contrast to children in intact families, children of divorce or nonmarriage repeatedly undergo the experience of seeing family-like members enter and drop out of the picture. The initial experience of love's failure and the abandonment most children experience in the immediate aftermath of divorce is confirmed again and again in the years ahead. These children learn that giving your heart involves not just the chance, but the likelihood, of great pain. No wonder these children of divorce are, as researchers find, especially hungry for love, fiercely conservative in their views of marriage and family life, firmly committed in theory to lifelong marriage, so much more anxious to attain it—and yet so much more likely to fail to get what they long for.

What is marriage? Before, we knew without words what marriage was. Now we don't know at all. A piece of the heart? A business arrangement? An exchange of vows? A contract? A sacrament? A state of the heart? An unstated ideal? Who counts as family? This was Woody Allen's dilemma, and it is shared in an increasing number of ways by an increasing number of men, women, and children.

In unmarriage, the relations between people are fluid, self-defined, intense perhaps but inherently (that is, by definition) unstable. In unmarriage the relationship is not defined by status, but by emotions. Your lover is the person you love or at least with whom you make love. Your child, on the other hand, is something else: a person you ought to love. You may fail in love, and many parents do. But your child is not any less your child because you have failed. Having a child creates a bond, a duty. Having a lover, by contrast, creates expectations.

"The person who is having sex is the person who is having the relationship," Soon-Yi told her mother. It was the cruel truth. In our culture, the connection between people is created and sustained by physical intercourse; it ends with orgasm and begins anew with the prospect of the next orgasm.

None of the relationships in an unmarriage impinges on any of the others. How can they, when the purpose of any relationship is to enrich the life of the individual who chooses it? As sociologist Andrew Cherlin puts it, men and women "are more likely today than in the past to evaluate their marriage primarily according to how well it satisfies their individual emotional needs. If their evaluation on these terms is unfavorable, they are likely to turn to divorce."[29]

No relation between two people can put a demand or a duty on a third party, nor can demand or duty even be put on one of the first two parties at a third point in time. Each relationship remains an affair of two individuals that, in the modern, postmarital mind, leaves all the other relations unaffected.

The family is not a system to which all members belong; the family in at least some members' minds (like Woody's) virtually disappears. In this way, the interests of the family are put asunder; individuals in the household have family ties to some members, but not to others.

Because the goal of the new love contract is the happiness of each individual partner, it is inherently temporary—it lasts as long as both people perceive themselves better off together than apart. Because it is conceived as an affair between adults, the new marriage contract inherently subordinates the welfare of children to the welfare of adults.

But that is not exactly right: It is not that the new partners care less about their children. Like Woody, they simply cannot conceive that the marriage relation is the children's business.

Surely children need a mother and a father, but how can it matter whether the mother and the father are married to one another? In fact, won't the children be better off if the adult partners are individually happier?

How things look depends on where you stand.

In the late sixties, when Mia fell in love with André Previn, things looked different. On the magazine cover, pregnant with twins by another woman's husband, she gazed at us with dewy eyes raised above conventional sexual morals, a new madonna, a modern fertility goddess. The heart (those eyes, that radiant face, told us) *wants what it wants.*

So in the years to come, she continued to build her rambling, unconventional family in unconventional ways; as many women do today, she placed more faith in her personal powers than in the social institutions, such as marriage, that were so visibly crumbling around her.

And when her personal powers failed, with a child and a lover—most terribly both at once—on what ground could she stand? If marriage is fraught with danger, unmarriage (like remarriage) has proved to be no safer haven.

Since the late sixties, when Mia photographically flaunted her fertility, experts have launched a determined assault on what they saw as outmoded attitudes toward marriage and divorce. In great measure, they have succeeded.

In place of the old narrative, which portrayed family loyalty as a solemn good, even worth enduring some personal unhappiness, we have built a powerful new story around the institution of divorce, portraying it as the archetypical American story of renewal, rebirth, the individual's triumph over circumstances, a personal declaration of independence.

For many this story is true: Getting a divorce is an exhilarating choice. Being divorced, however, or having one's parents divorce, is something else altogether.

But how things look depends on where you stand.

And for the past thirty years American law and American society have stood with the victors of the sexual revolution (with which the divorce revolution is inextricably bound). We have worshipped at the feet of these golden gods and goddesses, even to the point of sacrificing our children to them.

Erotic conflicts are hardly new. What is new is our relentless optimistic tendency to believe that such conflicts do not exist—to imagine that it is happiness, not love, that unifies. What makes one parent happy, must make all happy—children and jettisoned spouse alike. We stand with the victors in the race for happiness, enjoying their victory and savoring their happiness. Because they are happy, we insist that what they have done must be good—that everyone else must be happy too.

Nowhere is this strange new blind faith more evident than in our recent attempts to remake unwed motherhood.

7

MURPHY'S SISTERS

MURPHY BROWN WAS NOT THE ONLY ONE. Mary Jo, a divorced mother on the hit TV show "Designing Women," chose to be artificially inseminated by the sperm of a Mormon bongo player. One of the "Trials of Rosie O'Neill" was to discuss artificial insemination with her psychiatrist. Teddy, the bad sister in "Sisters," was upset to discover she was pregnant; Rebecca of "Cheers" was upset to find out she was not. Hannah on "Anything but Love" discovered that tests can lie. Ava of "Evening Shade" prayed about her home pregnancy test: "Please, God, please don't let it be blue."[1]

By October of 1991—the first four weeks of the TV new year—at least seven sitcom women were either pregnant or considering it: Only Ava, who didn't want a child, was married.

Nine months later, Murphy Brown gave birth on national television not only to a baby boy but to a fierce debate on the subject of unwed motherhood. Then-Vice President Dan Quayle's speech denouncing Murphy Brown set off a furor of television round tables, op eds, and letters to the editor. "I wish there were a word stinging enough to express the man's bumbling villainy," sputtered one angry young female New York columnist.[2] Murphy's choice, as one *New York Times* reporter approvingly put it, sent a strong message to the American public: "Women who want children do not need or necessarily want a spouse underfoot."[3] A growing number of women—and not just inner-city welfare mothers—would seem to agree.

In January of 1993, Irene Sang, a single thirty-three-year-old Pasadena optometrist and civic leader, became one of Murphy Brown's spiritual kin: She got pregnant with donor sperm and was planning to raise a child while "raising nary an eyebrow," as news reports put it. "I'm very responsible," the Rotary Club member told the *Los Angeles Times*. "People had to take a second look and say, 'Wait a minute. If Irene has done this, there must be some legitimacy to it, rather than illegitimacy.'"[4]

"Pregnant Teen-Agers Are Outcasts No Longer," trumpets a *New York Times* headline. Instead, "Today, pregnant teenagers are even beginning to be viewed by some of their peers as role models." In Eau Claire, Wisconsin, April Schuldt, five months pregnant, is elected homecoming queen. In Hempstead, Texas, almost one-third of the cheerleading squad gets knocked up over the summer. High school officials, under threat of a lawsuit by the National Organization for Women, reverse their decision to bar pregnant cheerleaders. At Manhattan's Chelsea High School, both the president and secretary–treasurer of the student council become pregnant and are encouraged to remain in their highly visible leadership positions.[5]

The eighties saw an explosion in unwed motherhood that shows no signs of subsiding. In 1982, 15 percent of all never-married women between the ages of eighteen and forty-four had had a child. By 1992, the number had leaped to 24 percent.[6] Illegitimacy is no longer only a problem of black families, or poor families, or irresponsible teenage girls. By the late eighties, black teenage mothers, for example, were responsible for less than one-seventh of all illegitimate babies born in the United States.[7]

The fastest rate of growth in unwed motherhood is among white women past their teen years. During the eighties the teenage birthrate actually leveled off. Despite a bump in teenage births in the early nineties, the new trend toward unwed motherhood, as two researchers noted, "is driven primarily by women age 20 and older."[8]

More than two-thirds of out-of-wedlock births are to women in this age group. In 1970 about one-fourth of unwed births were to moms over age twenty-four. By 1988 one-third of unmarried births were to women at least twenty-five years old—old enough to know better.[9]

Though the majority of unwed mothers still come from poor backgrounds, the ranks of educated or professional unwed moms are rising sharply. Call them Murphy's sisters. Consider two different measures of middle-class status: education and occupation. Between 1982 and 1992 the proportion of single women with some college education who bore out-of-wedlock children more than doubled, from 5.5 to 11.3 percent. Similarly, as recently as 1982, just 3 percent of never-married professional women had had a child, but by 1992 more than 8 percent had.[10] College-educated women today are more likely to become unwed mothers than women as a whole were in 1960.[11] They are even more likely to approve of other women doing so.

The increasing number of births to unwed adult women reflects two intertwining trends: decreasing marriage rates, which means women are single (and therefore at risk of unwed pregnancies) for longer periods of time and a sudden loosening in the cultural link between marriage and child rearing. More and more women view having an illegitimate child not as an unfortunate accident, but as a legitimate choice.

And the trend is still growing, because the jump in numbers of out-of-wedlock births has been accompanied by an even larger collapse in norms. In 1974, at the height of the sexual revolution, just 31 percent of women agreed that "there is no reason why single women shouldn't have children and raise them if they want to"; by 1985, 49 percent of American women agreed.[12] And today the proportion of younger women considering unwed motherhood is even larger. According to a 1994 *New York Times* poll, 55 percent of teenage girls now would consider having a baby outside of marriage.[13] Today only about one-third of whites and one-quarter of blacks and Hispanics say they "strongly disapprove" of having a baby outside of marriage. Disapproval is even weaker among two groups with special influence on the culture of married childbearing: young women and the well educated.[14]

In just ten short years, unmarried childbearing has evolved from a fringe lifestyle to a mainstream choice. Ann Harrison, thirty-four, a program director for a Christian radio station, is the living embodiment of this change. Seven years ago, she says, she got "carried away" one night with her boyfriend and ended up pregnant. Today, she is actively considering having a second illegitimate child by choice. Sure, she says, "A father and a mother are ideal for a child. So life is less than ideal. News bulletin." She might consider starting a relationship but "very few people catch my eye. I'm really kind of tired and busy."[15]

In 1982 (the year I became an unwed mother) just 16 percent of white unwed mothers over the age of twenty-four said their pregnancies were deliberate. Five years later, the majority (55 percent) of those unwed moms deliberately chose to get pregnant.[16]

Why are so many smart, educated, professional women even considering unwed motherhood? Consider the case of Barb, who at thirty and as a Ph.D. candidate, certainly qualifies as one of Murphy's sisters.

Like many smart young women I know, Barb wants a baby.

She would be an ideal mother, or so she thinks, and so do I. At thirty she is energetic, intelligent, educated, warm, funny, and affectionate, although perhaps a bit of a space cadet. At thirty, she hasn't yet found Mr. Right. So, like many other single women I talk to, she is thinking of going it alone. Already at thirty, if she ventured to procreate, she would, in the terminology of the medical profession, be an *elderly primagravida*. She is a Census Bureau statistic waiting to happen.

Barb sounds the familiar lament, the mad mating call of the modern young woman: "Where are the men? I believe in love and relationships. I'd much prefer to raise a child with a partner. But where do I go to get one?"

I sympathize. Something has gone strangely awry in the socialization of young men. Just since 1980, the proportion of men ages thirty-five to thirty-nine who have never married has risen until today almost one out of five men of that advanced age is still a bachelor.[17]

But in Barb's case, the perfidy of men is clearly not the whole story. She is gorgeous, smart, sexy, charming. But whom does she date? Other women's husbands, unemployed artists, new-age monks who take (and break) vows of celibacy. To Barb, herself a child of divorce, interesting men, sexy men, *masculine* men, are those who pose, well, difficulties.

The culture of courtship that shaped her, that shapes all of us, has given her the tools to maneuver skillfully in the gap between sex and love, to become an artisan of the orgasm, a condom connoisseur, but it has left her pathetically deficient in the art of making a happy family. For this sexual task, she is as useless and helpless as her unmate, the pristine bachelor with his carefully stocked kitchen and his carefully garaged car. In love, she and her bachelor unmates are as pathetic and dangerous as Tyrannosaurus Rex: roaring sexual giants ineffectually reaching out with puny, underdeveloped hands.

For a whole generation of American women now approaching middle age, dating is preparatory not to marriage, but to mating. To date is to put oneself in the sexual market for years. (As for the marriage market—where does that exist?) At over twenty-six for men and over twenty-four for women, the median age at first marriage has risen to its highest level in one hundred years. The proportion of women in their early thirties who have never married has almost tripled, from 6 percent in 1970 to 16 percent in 1990.

What impression of male–female relationships does fifteen to twenty years of dating and mating and serial monogamy give to women? The dominant motif of romantic love as these women have experienced it is of repeated failure; enduring love appears increasingly improbable. After you have fallen in and out of love a dozen times or more, how do you believe in love? And how do you dare to hope that love will lead to a happy marriage?

Again and again this theme of repeated failure, and abandonment, emerged from the lives of the educated unwed moms I interviewed. Many, clearly drawn toward children, had a history of repeat abortions with men they loved.

Jeanine is one of these highly educated unwed moms, with a master's degree in history and a successful career as a nurse. Jeanine first thought of becoming a single mother when a boyfriend cruelly threw her out on the street, back in 1981. She went into a deep depression and moved in with her father for a while. In her late twenties, after a series of disappointing relations with men, Jeanine began to despair about marriage. Her tumultuous love life was punctuated by a ten-year off-and-on relationship with a man who "just couldn't commit." When she became pregnant by him, he told her "not now," which in her mind meant "probably later." When she got pregnant a second time, she flew out to California to talk things over with her dream lover. "If you don't have this baby," he told her, "there's nothing I wouldn't do for you." She relates the line with hard-earned disgust in her voice. She heard the same tantalizing vagueness, the "not now" that carried grand intimations of future satisfaction. But this time, she would not be fooled. "I told him I had already had one abortion for him. I had done that for love of him. That was enough."

The underlying cultural logic linking illegitimacy and divorce becomes suddenly visible in the lives of middle-class, educated women like Jeanine who have had or are considering an out-of-wedlock pregnancy. In the underclass, these links may be obscured by the harshness of the social environment, the disorder, decay, poverty, crime, and especially the male unemployment that make marriage seem objectively difficult for many poor women to obtain. When all the men you know are either drug dealers or unemployed, unwed motherhood can seem a pretty reasonable choice.

But women like Barb, Jeanine, and the rest of Murphy's sisters do not face such bleak alternatives. Their problem seems not to be finding men willing to marry them, but finding marriageable men sexually attractive. Underlying their erotic attraction to the elusive, undependable man is a profound ambivalence toward marriage, an ambivalence rooted in the collapse of marriage around them, which many have experienced firsthand in their own parents' failed marriages and divorces.

When marriage becomes sufficiently unstable, to many young women a husband becomes not a source of security but a potential hazard. When your husband is no longer firmly a member of your family, the impulse for a family—for enduring, dependable love—can take the shape of the desire for children rather than marriage. "A lot of women have to grapple. Would they like a child who's biologically connected to them or a man who's not so connected and who might divorce them?" points out Dr. Barbara Bartlik, president of the Women's Medical Association. "A child's more of a sure thing. It's a closer bond. You'll never be separated."[18]

Many young American women develop an almost superstitious fear of marriage, as if marriage, rather than being the perquisite for divorce, was somehow its cause. Farrah Fawcett, one of the earliest of the current crop of Murphy Browns—the celebrity moms who celebrate unwed motherhood—had lived with Ryan O'Neal for more than ten years when she made this comment: "Growing up I saw married people being unfaithful. I thought, what's the point? Marriage is a contract. It kills romance. We don't need a contract."[19]

Conversely, a good marriage has become such an elevated, demanding ideal—entailing among other things continuous adventure, romance, and self-fulfillment—that it seems, for an increasing number of women, an impossible dream. In justifying their own decision, single women who choose to get pregnant do not hesitate to say that a good marriage is preferable. But, they imply, a really good marriage is so unlikely that, for practical purposes, unwed motherhood is a perfectly reasonable second choice. "Single parenthood is not a bad second to a superb marriage, and a poor marriage is a poor third," says Emily, an unwed mother and a freelance writer with a southern drawl and solid, middle-class Episcopalian roots.[20]

"I would say that, in the ideal world, two parents who love each other and are doing a great job together would be better than a single parent," agrees Joyce, another unwed mother who is a sociology professor at a midwestern university. "But I still hold that a good, really involved single parent who wanted to have the child is better than most of the homes I have seen."[21]

Pundits and policymakers may treat illegitimacy and divorce as separate phenomena—to say as Dan Quayle did in his Murphy Brown reprise speech in 1994, "I'm not talking about a situation in which there is a divorce"—but today's generation of younger women knows better. They are living out the cultural logic we have created for them. With a 50 percent to 60 percent divorce rate, even if one makes it to the altar before the maternity ward, there is no longer any security for oneself or one's children in marriage. Moreover, if (as we have been telling women for the past twenty years) there is nothing wrong with forming a single-parent family through divorce, how can creating a single-parent family without putting kids through the added trauma of divorce be wrong?

One important reason that large numbers of elite American women are engaging in fantasies of unwed motherhood is that American culture over the past thirty years has largely failed to articulate the role that fathers play in children's lives—indeed it has been actively hostile to the idea that women and children need men at all. Marriage could not have been so removed from its privileged place, reduced to a lifestyle option, had fathers not been turned into the latest disposable item in the nursery.

In sociological literature this was often accomplished by simply airbrushing fathers out of families. Fathers were not so much derogated in the sociological rhetoric as simply ignored. The shift in focus that left fathers out of the picture was accomplished primarily through a shift in language. "Broken families" and "fatherless families" fell out of the rhetoric of research and were replaced by new linguistic entities: "single-parent families" and "two-parent families." Notice that even the supposedly traditional "two-parent family" is a strange, sexless thing. Two parents may be better than one, the name implies, but nothing in the name suggests that either parent must be a man.

And the single-parent family? It lacks nothing. By its very name it becomes complete unto itself. Social scientists began to argue that "single-parent family systems are not inherently disorganized nor necessarily detrimental to individual members. Rather, they simply differ in structure and internal organization.... The major problem faced by single-parent families is not the lack of a male's presence, but the lack of a male income."[22]

"Can we stop defining [the female-headed family] as a scourge and view it for what it is," asked columnist Judy Mann, echoing the professional rhetoric, "a demographic group that has particular needs, much the same as the elderly or two-parent families with children?"[23]

If single-parent families are just another "demographic group," as Judy Mann urges us to believe in the prestigious pages of the *Washington Post*, then men are dispensable after all. Women don't need them, and children don't need them either. In elite opinion, fathers have come to be seen increasingly as a kind of luxury for children, nice but not necessary.

Some young women considering unwed motherhood (especially those whose parents are still married) do acknowledge the importance of fathers, but they do not see any link between getting a father for their children and getting married. In white, educated middle-class America, just as in the black family a generation ago, the rise in divorce is swiftly being followed by a collapse in norms connecting marriage and childbearing. "I imagine finding a man who wants children but doesn't want to get married," one attractive, well-educated, twenty-something professional woman told me. Women can imagine anything they like, but the reality is that men who are not married do not become dependable fathers. As we have seen, even divorced fathers—men who had established relationships with their children inside marriage—typically do not maintain strong emotional relationships with their children, nor do they see them more than a few times a year.

The female fantasy of the unwed father who stays around is nevertheless surprisingly persistent. Women contemplating unwed motherhood, who fear and distrust social institutions, especially marriage, turn to a do-it-yourself approach to family relations. They persistently believe against all evidence that through the power of their personality they can surmount the familial destruction they witness around them. They don't need laws, pieces of papers, or institutions such as marriage to create successful families. By dint of careful selection and much thought, they can find a good, dependable man without having to marry him. If that plan fails, they can raise children without fathers, often relying on their parents' rather than their own marriage to provide support for their children.

These fantasies are enhanced or encouraged by a barrage of quasi-official propaganda that misleads many women into swallowing the myth that the mother–father household is unnecessary because, allegedly, so many families do all right without it. "Less than 10 percent of American households are traditional father–breadwinner, mother–homemaker families," elite female leaders like Rep. Pat Schroeder repeatedly claim, leading many single women to believe that the male role is now virtually redundant. Most mothers work, we are told, and their children need only the "quality time" that can be given at the end of a long workday. Under these circumstances, mothers in single-parent families may appear to have few disadvantages compared to mothers in married households. But the vast majority of *married* mothers either don't work or work part-time.

Even among two-career couples, marriage offers parents more time and energy for children than either spouse could provide alone. Yet even two-career couples complain bitterly about the lack of time for family needs. In one 1989 poll of employed mothers, 83 percent (and 72 percent of employed fathers) said they were torn between their jobs and the desire to spend more time with their families.[24]

Single mothers complain the most bitterly. One researcher investigating the "time crunch" in family life found that, in one focus group, "single mothers were the dominant voices… the most vehement and outspoken critics of single-parent status." One single mom, who works more than twelve hours a day, eats only one meal a week with her son, a fact that fills her with grief and anxiety. "It's hard for a single parent, very hard." Another single mom who works eighty-four hours a week said plaintively, "I would like to spend more time

with my son, hugging him…. I see that there is a lot of hate and confusion and upset in him, and that's just one thing I would like to do
is hold my child."[25] When *Glamour* magazine—most of whose readers have some education—asked its readers to describe "the highs
and lows" of being unwed moms by choice, fully half expressed serious regrets about their decision.[26]

Girls contemplating unwed motherhood point to the real-life
Murphy Browns, celebrities who have out-of-wedlock births without
losing social status. Donald Trump's current, Marla Maples, who was
a married man's mistress and then the mother of a divorced man's
illegitimate child, was treated on the occasion of her child's birth as a
kind of American Princess Di. Real live princesses, like Stephanie of
Monaco, do no differently. I see her, the picture of grace and maternal devotion, her baby in her lover's arms, on the page of this morning's newspaper with the caption, "Princess Stephanie of Monaco and
her companion Daniel Cucruet cuddle their newborn daughter
Pauline, born May 4…. Little Pauline is their second child."[27]

Increasingly, elite voices are trying to draw a distinction between a
Marla Maples Trump and an April Schuldt (the Eau Claire,
Wisconsin, homecoming queen). In crude terms the distinction
amounts to this: Donald Trump's illegitimate children don't cost the
taxpayers money.

For perhaps the first time in American life, the arbiters of culture
are trying to establish a new, explicitly double standard of sexual
morality, the dream of aristocrats everywhere. Right and wrong are
one thing for the rich and another for the poor, the rich claiming
unwed motherhood as a kind of class privilege. Poor black women,
who believe they have cannot find a reliable, employed husband,
must abstain from having children. But rich, educated white women
can do as they like since, presumably, the taxpayers won't be asked to
pay for it. And in our current impoverished dialogue, the costs
directly borne by taxpayers are the only ones that count.

Liberal columnist Richard Cohen put the new class privilege in the

Washington Post thus: "A middle-class woman of some means… is perfectly capable of raising a child by herself…. The children of affluent single mothers are not likely to concern us. They are not likely to become wards of the state, and they are not any more likely to become criminals than other children are."[28]

Nor is this view confined to liberals. After the Murphy Brown fracas, conservative economist Herbert Stein pondered in a *Washington Post* column whether Quayle "might be saying that it is wrong for a wealthy, educated, intelligent woman… to have a child without a husband." If that were the case, he noted disapprovingly, "Quayle casts the first stone at this woman."[29]

More loudly than the aristocrats of old European courts dared proclaim, today's elite are trumpeting that exemption from sexual morality is a class privilege. Money buys the right to love when and as one wills.

But this line between rich and poor will not hold. No self-respecting American will put up with it or allow her life to be shaped by so dubious a moral ideal. If unwed, pregnant Marla Maples Trump can be a media princess, why shouldn't April Schuldt be a homecoming queen? (At least April's boyfriend wasn't married.) Is a billionaire's sperm sacred? "If you can treat some unwed mothers with respect, then why not do the same for others?" asks April, not unreasonably.[30] And there are other reasons.

Richard Cohen's claim is flatly wrong. Fathers are as important in the lives of middle- or upper-class children, especially boys, as they are in those of the poor.

The same theme of downward mobility, evident in patterns of divorce, is displayed even more starkly among unwed mothers, even educated ones. The relative drop in the economic and emotional well-being of educated unwed moms may well be even larger, because children of college-educated *married* mothers enjoy tremendous advantages.

Yet as many as 90 percent of children of unwed mothers end up on welfare.[31] Many of the rest will hover uneasily just above the line.

Almost every college-educated unwed mom I interviewed relied on welfare for a time, except for two whose fathers both happened to be multimillionaires. In fact, a baby born to a college-educated single mother is more likely to die than is a baby born to a married high school dropout.[32]

Unwed mothers, doing double or triple duty with little or no relief, are simply less likely to be consistently effective parents than married mothers, and their children show the effects. Once again education or class status doesn't erase the advantages of marriage. Even after controlling for income, children of unwed mothers are two and a half times more likely to develop conduct disorders than do other children.[33] A 1988 University of Illinois study of twenty-five hundred young men and women concluded that, even after adjusting for family income, the absence of a father significantly reduced the educational attainment of boys.[34] An earlier University of Rhode Island study found that boys without fathers at home scored lower on achievement tests even after controlling for IQ and socioeconomic status.[35]

The great law of unmarriage is and remains *downward mobility*. Education does not spare kids the heartache of rejection by their fathers nor does it transform women into Supermoms, capable of rearing, educating, and supporting children without any support.

Murphy Brown's dilemma is this: she wants emotional ties without being tied down; she wants the gratifications of motherhood without the obligations of family; she longs for love and is afraid of it, afraid that marriage—enduring love between man and woman—is out of her reach.

In this case, the personal is also the political. The brouhaha over a fictional character revealed deep cleavages in America's political culture. For the Right, these cleavages were made embarrassingly clear when presidential spokesman Marlin Fitzwater, after backing Dan Quayle's attack on Murphy Brown, was reminded that Murphy Brown had considered and rejected getting an abortion. Abruptly reversing himself, Fitzwater declared, "The 'Murphy Brown' show [exhibits] prolife values which we think are good." How to discourage single motherhood without pressuring women into abortions is a problem—partly real, partly rhetorical—the American Right has yet to resolve.

Even worse is the conundrum of how to discourage unwed motherhood without punishing unfortunate women. To advocate making worse the lives of people whose lives are already very difficult is both bad morals and bad politics. By the morning after his Murphy Brown speech, Dan Quayle was "clarifying" his remarks to explain that he had the greatest respect for single moms. When sex was acknowledged to be the privilege of the married, then "stigmatizing" unwed mothers made moral sense. In today's sexual environment, punishing unwed mothers may amount to punishing women because they are unlucky.

The results of male flight from the family are becoming disastrously obvious. But, trapped by the rhetoric of choice, America's elite—most especially its female elite—has found no way to say, simultaneously and convincingly, that being a single mom should be a woman's choice *and* that men should be responsible for helping raise and support the children women *choose* to have. If it is a woman's choice whether to have a child, why should men have to bear the burden of that choice?

Focusing exclusively on welfare mothers, as the Right increasingly wishes to do, misses the real story: the upheaval in all children's and women's lives when the link first between sex and marriage, and then marriage and parenthood, is broken.

To solve Murphy Brown's dilemma we must stop pretending that all choices are equally good. We must remind women that babies do not exist for the gratification they give mothers (or fathers)—they are human beings whose needs should be paramount. America's more privileged daughters must surrender the class prerogative of denying their children fathers simply because they believe they can keep their kids off welfare. The old American imperative—each generation better off than the last—cannot survive the new morality.

Life is imperfect. The problem of coping with out-of-wedlock births, like the problem of marital breakdown, is an old one. But the problem reaches epidemic proportions when, as now, we try to pretend that it does not exist. A pregnant unmarried woman who believes (as I do) that abortion is wrong faces difficult and imperfect choices—hasty marriage, unwed motherhood, or adoption. The difficulty of the choice cannot be erased by pretending that raising a child outside of marriage is just another lifestyle choice, for the one who chooses may not be the one who pays the price. It is our children—and our children's children—who suffer for adults' increasing unwillingness to accept the necessity of marriage.

To restore the marriage norm, however, will require resurrecting, for a generation of women steeped in despair over love disguised as optimism about choices, faith in the possibility of love.

8

THE BAD MARRIAGE

AMERICAN FAMILY LIFE is haunted by two elusive specters, one a dream, the other a nightmare: the ideal divorce and the bad marriage.

The bad marriage is the last, best hope of the divorce advocates, the bogeyman compared to which even divorce, illegitimacy, sudden poverty, downward mobility, educational decline, psychological suffering—in short, even the postmarital family—looks good. In the founding myths of the postmarital culture, the bad marriage is defined in contrast to that which has liberated us from it: the ideal divorce. The irony, as David Blankenhorn, author of *Fatherless America*, has remarked, is that the ideal divorce—with its sharing, caring, respectful, cooperative co-parenting—looks a lot like a great marriage, minus sex. The bad marriage is the demon compared to which anything looks good. According to the myth, the ideal divorce is what we get when the demon is exorcised.

Anne Lamott became a national spokeswoman for single motherhood with her bestseller, *Operating Instruction: A Journal of My Son's First Year*. When her toddler son, Sam, sadly told everyone in his nursery school that he didn't have a daddy, "I wanted to fall through the floor writhing in pain." But she comforted herself with this thought: "There are a lot worse things than not to have a dad. I think it is worse to have a bad dad. I think it is worse to be raised in a bad marriage than it is to be raised by a reasonably happy and healthy single mother."[1]

She has a lot of company. "In many instances, a single parent is more desirable than two parents," agrees one college sex education textbook. "When the home has been plagued by battles and bitter feelings, children often fare better when the war is finally ended."[2]

"The belief that married couple families are superior is probably the most pervasive prejudice about family life in the Western World," maintains Judith Stacey, a sociologist at the University of California at Davis. "Research indicates that high-conflict marriages harm children more than do low-conflict divorces.... In short, the research scale tips toward those who stress the quality of family relationships over their form."[3]

One of the driving ideas of the postmarital culture is that the happiness of adults is so crucial to their success as parents that divorce will make them even better parents. As Professor Norval D. Glenn puts it, as Americans became convinced that adults "could not be good parents unless they were well-adjusted and self-actualized," the old belief "that unhappily married parents should stay together for the sake of their children was widely replaced by a belief that they should divorce for the sake of the children."[4]

The power of this idea can hardly be overestimated, for it eliminated most of the uncertainty and potentially tragic conflict in troubled marriages. Under expert tutelage many parents came to believe staying in a struggling marriage made them bad role models for their children. "What pushed me over the edge [to divorce] was that I was training my children to think this is what a relationship is about—total emptiness," as one mother put it.[5] Thus, continuing a troubled marriage came to be seen by many not as an act of courage, strength, or fidelity, but as a kind of perverse masochism, or at best a failure of nerve. The moment this crucial idea was adopted, the divorce ethic culture triumphed over the remnants of the marriage ideal.

The conventional wisdom is now that divorce is better for kids than staying in a troubled marriage. But is that true? Our current faith in divorce's beneficent effects did not come out of nowhere. A great deal of evidence confirms that serious family conflict is very damaging to kids. Within intact families, the research suggests, psychologically speaking, "the negative effects of persistent marital conflict" can be "as great as that of enduring several" divorces and remarriages.[6] But the same research suggests several important caveats: First, before divorce can even begin to look like a better option for kids, the marital conflict that leads to it must be both intense and *sustained*. For example, one study compared the level of marital conflict with children's emotional health at two five-year intervals. Children whose parents were divorced, separated, or remarried were twice as likely to need psychological help as children whose parents stayed in a marriage with minor or moderate conflicts. Even children whose married parents had "high-conflict marriages" at the start of the survey did better than children whose parents broke up. The only group of children who did worse than the divorced group were children whose parents reported high conflict at both time periods in the survey.[7]

In other words, this and other research suggests, divorce or separation may benefit children whose parents are locked in a marriage that is and remains hateful for a long period of time.

There is, so far as I have been able to uncover, little reliable data on what proportion of divorces is precipitated by the intense sustained marital conflict that is so damaging to kids and what proportion of divorces occurs in what (from the child's point of view) might be called "good-enough marriages." Most divorces, researchers have found, are marked by intense ambivalence, even on the part of the spouse who chooses to divorce. As sociologist Joseph Hopper puts it, "At the same time that they listed complaints, however, divorcing people easily reported good things about their marriage. They liked having someone at home, someone to talk with about their day. They described camping trips, holidays and birthdays, the dream of having one's own family and home. They loved their children. They described feelings of security, safety, and comfort."[8] Despite the divorce culture, many battered women (married or not) continue brutal relationships, while many marriages that end in divorce don't appear to have unrelenting angry hells.

But what about those sustained high-conflict marriages? Do the data suggest divorce is the best option in those cases? The answer is yes, but with one important proviso: *only if the divorce leads to less conflict.* One University of Georgia study, for instance, compared the school performance of children in four categories: low-conflict intact families, low-conflict divorced families, high-conflict intact families, and high-conflict divorced families. As expected, children in low-conflict intact families did significantly better than any other group. Next came children in low-conflict divorced families. They performed slightly better than children in high-conflict intact families.

The children who did the worst of all—and considerably worse than children whose parents remained in bitter, angry marriages— were children from high-conflict divorced families. "Divorce may be a plausible option if it leads to less parental fighting, but it is a horrendous option if it does not," the researchers concluded. "High conflict in conjunction with divorce was significantly more detrimental to the functioning of adolescents."[9]

Here is a question few have bothered to ask: Does divorce lead to less conflict? One reason very few inquiring minds wanted to know the answer is that the assumption that divorce ends marital conflict is built into the very language of social science. "Marital conflict" is a label that implies its own solution: To put an end to marital conflict, you only have to put an end to the marriage. But of course what really bothers children is not that two spouses are fighting, but that their parents are fighting. Yet divorce advocates frequently compare angry marriages to low-conflict divorces on the magical assumption that a piece of paper called a *divorce* will put an end to parental fighting. In other words, they compare an exaggerated vision of bad marriage with the phantom virtues of the ideal divorce.

But as most people now know from experience, divorce—far from ending parental conflict—often raises the ante. It provokes angry exchanges, bitter feelings, and even uncharacteristic acts of violence between parents.[10] We who live in the divorce culture know this. It is an unavoidable aspect of our cultural terrain. We have all watched formerly civil and even affectionate couples in the divorce process degenerate to name calling, raised voices, random acts of unkindness, or, worse, bloody physical battles.

Constance Ahrons' 1994 book *The Good Divorce* is a decidedly optimistic study of middle-class divorced couples. Yet she found that just 12 percent of divorced couples enjoyed low-conflict " good divorces." And these couples had not left high-conflict marriages. Instead almost all of them had enjoyed close, friendly relations prior to divorce. Most had called their spouse their "best friend." Good divorces typically do not heal angry, conflict-filled marriages, but terminate friendly ones. And even good divorces were unstable: Five years later, a third of these friendly divorces had degenerated into open conflict, often when one or both ex-partners remarried.[11]

Ahrons' study confirms what common sense suggests: Divorce is typically marked by much conflict, and the acrimony endures for many years. She constructs a typology of parents' postdivorce relations. It is not a pretty picture. In 50 percent of middle-class divorces, she found, parents engage in bitter, open conflict, becoming what she calls "angry associates" or, even worse, "fiery foes."

"Every time I need to change any plan, try to discuss anything, all I hear is her constant barrage of 'What a lousy father'... usually she carries it one step too far and then I explode," said one such father.

"I try to control my temper but he just pushes my buttons, and we end up screaming and I just hang up," said a mother. "It wrecks my day and I know it upsets the boys."

Five years later, Ahrons found only a minority of angry divorcing couples had managed to improve relations with their exes. After five years, two-thirds of the angry divorces remained mired in hostility. Even one-quarter to one-third of the good divorces had degenerated into open angry conflict.[12] Studies like these do not indicate that divorce is doing much to end parental conflict.

Too often, in divorce, conflict escalates into physical violence. In Judith Wallerstein's study of middle-class divorced parents, more than half the children witnessed physical violence between their parents, whereas before the divorce more than three-quarters had never seen violence in the home. Another study of marital rape confirms that violent attacks frequently begin during the process of divorce.[13]

The bitterness often continues for years. Ten years after divorce, Wallerstein found, fully half the women in her study and one-third of the men are still very angry at their exes. "True, some couples were no longer standing in the same kitchen screaming at one another; they were screaming on the telephone instead. Or they fought face to face while dropping off or picking up the children" Wallerstein continued.[14] Nor does the end of marriage spell the end of romantic turmoil for the custodial parent. The love lives of divorced mothers are not necessarily stress- or conflict-free merely because they are not married to their new love partners. As one researcher pointed out, many single mothers were caught not only in "ongoing chronic conflict with ex-spouses" but also in "repeated conflict and separations from boyfriends."[15]

Even when divorce makes adults happier, it does not necessarily make them better parents. A fair reading of studies like these suggests that, as psychologist Frank Pittman put it, brutal marriages may be bad for kids, but boring marriages are fine. Marriage, even a less-than-satisfying union, provides certain intrinsic supports for parenting, and these structural supports can be more important than the attitudes or aptitudes of the particular individuals. When marriage dissolves, the spouse who is left with the children usually faces a harder task than when the marriage was intact—and must meet it with *less* emotional, financial, and logistical support. Meanwhile, the spouse who leaves often abandons any substantive role as a parent.

Dale Burrelle, for example, left his wife, Betty, when she started acting like a maniac. On one occasion she kicked a hole in the side door of the garage. She cried suddenly or just as suddenly burst out screaming. Her erratic emotions probably had something to do with her mother's recent sudden death in a car accident. But around this time, she took the kids to visit her sister and her husband "decided he really liked living alone, without all the commotion." So he left.

When her husband left her, Betty Burrelle was indeed a "psychiatric case," deeply distressed and depressed: first her mother died, and then her husband left her—with three kids under the age of eight and $450 a month in child support. While married, her husband had been a devoted father, spending evenings reading bedtime stories to his kids. Now he sent his child support regularly and called occasionally.

A year after the divorce Steve, the oldest, was crying himself to sleep every night. Fifteen years later, despite above-average intelligence, Steve graduated from high school with just a C average. He is still living at home, working part time at a bowling alley.

Tanya, his eighteen-year-old sister, has a good job, a high school diploma, and big plans for a future in art and design. But she marches into Dr. Wallerstein's office saying, "I want to see my records.... I want to know why I've been unable to be by myself, meaning without a guy, without sex, since junior high school."[16]

The Burrelle marriage, like many that now end in divorce, was not a brutal, violent one nor was it wracked by frequent conflict. Even their divorce was not one of the worst, not marked by frequent bitter infighting. But however depressed she may have been before her divorce, can anyone really doubt that for Betty Burrelle the divorce itself—her husband's sudden disappearance, her consequent financial distress, the loss of her home and family—made her recovery from her mother's death much more difficult and imposed new, enduring burdens on her and her children?

No sane person goes through life without experiencing grief, distress, depression, anxiety. One of the purposes of marriage is to offer adults emotional support in times of trouble and to give children an alternate source of stability when one parent is temporarily disabled by personal troubles.

A University of Washington study tried to measure these structural benefits of marriage by dividing 117 households with young children into three groups: "maritally distressed" couples, "maritally supported" couples, and unmarried mothers. As expected, mothers in "maritally distressed" households reported more disobedience problems than mothers who found their marriage satisfactory. A good, or at least good-enough, marriage makes a big difference in children's lives. But the unmarried mothers reported the most problems of all: Compared with both groups of married mothers, "single mothers reported more parenting stress and perceived their children as having significantly more behavior problems." Researchers observing the children agreed: The children of single mothers displayed more "deviance and noncompliance" than did the children of unhappily married mothers.[17]

Fathers are an important source of discipline in the household, not primarily because fathers are tougher or scarier than mothers, but because women who have the emotional, financial, and social support of marriage are themselves more effective disciplinarians. Not burdened with the tremendous stress single mothers endure, they are better able to apply the moderate, loving, consistent enforcement of order to which children respond. Even women who are unhappy with the degree of intimacy in their marriages, feel unappreciated, or who fight with their husbands often enjoy significant economic and psychological support—the feeling that someone will care for and her and her children.

The divorce story that dominates our culture goes something like this: Many married people are very unhappy. They fight a lot, which is very bad for the kids. Divorce gives adults a new shot at happiness. Children are saved from all that fighting, and through their parents' remarriage get a better role model of adult love. But for most kids the story is only a fairy tale. The good divorce is an ideal that, experience painfully teaches us, is no less difficult to achieve than the good-enough marriage—and the returns to men, women, children, and society are far less. The brutal fact is this: more divorce has not led to less conflict or even to happier marriages or to more children living with happily married parents.

Faced with the collapse of marriage, some experts maintain a fallback position: Though the institution of marriage may be sick, the individuals in marriages are healthier than ever. Now that unhappy marriages are easier to end, it stands to reason that those remaining are happier. Unfortunately, this comforting idea, generally presented as self-evident, isn't true.

Norval Glenn, a sociologist at the University of Texas at Austin, was one of the first to notice what the data are actually telling us. In the late seventies, buttressed by data showing that many divorced parents remarried happily, he and a colleague concluded, "divorce and remarriage seem to have been rather effective mechanisms for replacing poor marriages with good ones." In other words, more divorces mean more happy marriages.

Today Glenn notes that "it has become almost standard practice among marriage-and-the-family and family textbook writers" to argue "that the steep increase in divorce since around 1965 does not indicate that there has been a corresponding deterioration in marital success.... Rather, it is argued, persons may simply have become less willing to tolerate unsatisfactory marriages."[18]

The data suggest otherwise. Despite high divorce rates, the proportion of American adults who are unhappily married has not changed. But the number who are happily married has dropped sharply, from more than half of Americans in 1973 to less than two-fifths today. The proportion of people in intact first marriages who report their marriages are "very happy" actually dropped about 4 percent between the early seventies and the late eighties.[19] Meanwhile, again despite the epidemic of divorce, the proportion of kids living with unhappily married parents has not changed. But the proportion living in what all family experts agree is the ideal situation—a happily married family—has dropped sharply: Whereas in 1973 a majority of kids lived in happily married families, today less than 40 percent do.[20]

Call it an unexpected case of erotic stagflation: higher divorce rates *and* unhappier marriages, a combination as irrational and illogical (according to the conventional wisdom) as the fact that premarital cohabitation increases rather than decreases a couple's likelihood of divorce.

The decline in happiness has not affected all married folk equally. After the revolutionary changes in sex, marriage, and family life, what group has been the biggest loser in the happiness sweepstakes? Younger married women.

Current wisdom has it that marriage used to be an oppressive institution for women, but that it has lately improved. Again the data suggests otherwise: Despite the tremendous changes in modern marriage—the movement of women into the labor force, the decline of patriarchal authority, the emergence of egalitarian marriage styles— it is the youngest women who have been the biggest losers on the happiness scale. Overall, since 1970 the decline in the proportion of "very happy" wives is modest: about 4 percentage points. For younger married women, however, the drop has been more dramatic: Between the early seventies and the mid-eighties, the percentage of married women ages eighteen to thirty-one who were "very happy" dropped from 44 percent to less than 35 percent. Meanwhile, the happiness levels of never-married men in this age group *almost tripled*.[21] Glenn concludes, "It appears that recent changes in marital status and in the effect of marital status on happiness have led to a distinct decline in the happiness of women."[22]

Apparently a divorce culture affects far more than just people who divorce. When marriage as an institution visibly erodes, the consequences are felt by all of us—young and old, married and unmarried.

The divorce ethic does not tend to promote strong, independent women, but nervous, anxious ones. Catherine Johnson interviewed couples for a study of happy marriages. She was struck by the intensity of the fear of divorce evinced by younger wives, even those in happy marriages. Women like Elaine Stassen, who in her late twenties wanted to stay home to care for her infant son, but didn't dare. "I watch

'Donahue' and 'Oprah,' and I see it all the time: the men turn forty and leave for a younger woman." Elaine returned to grad school to calm her fears, but it didn't help much. The divorce culture has instilled in Elaine a sense that "things just aren't under your control." Her husband in this tranquil marriage has no such fears: "'Oprah' and 'Donahue' are directed at women," he says. "I never even think about it."[23]

Some divorce advocates try to celebrate this uncertainty, urging us all to strive for that highest spiritual level at which the enlightened ones realize, as guru John Bradshaw puts it, *"There is no human security. There is no one who will always take care of us."*[24]

For those of us who have failed to reach such an elevated stage of spiritual growth, this proposition is not only disheartening, but also one profoundly hostile to marriage. People marry because they want the security of dependable love. When marriage becomes a fifty–fifty proposition (or worse), the married are no longer receiving the great good that marriage is supposed to confer.

Meanwhile, the daily burdens of marriage must still be shouldered, which creates a creeping tendency toward what one married man of my acquaintance called "The Chump Factor"—the fear that he is allowing himself to be cheated or taken advantage of. He who is madly in love with his wife may never experience more than a passing temptation. But what if you find yourself slogging along in an average marriage, wondering whether a good-enough marriage *is* good enough? In a culture that is constantly lecturing that you owe it to yourself to be happy, ridiculing the notion that duty honorably performed is one of the pillars of the good life, and implying that by failing to divorce you may be psychologically damaging your kids, how can such a marriage seem good enough?

After all, as Glenn comments, "If a person constantly compares the existing marriage with real or imagined alternatives to it, the existing marriage will inevitably compare unfavorably in some respects. People are hardly aware of needs that are currently being well served, but they tend to be keenly aware of needs that are not being satisfied."[25]

Experts and laymen who use the bad marriage to justify divorce mistakenly treat the bad marriage as a fixed, easily discernible thing. In their black-and-white world, there are good marriages that survive and bad marriages that ought to end in divorce.

Divorcing couples frequently rewrite their own marital history to create such black-and-white clarity after the fact. They are busy creating a new storyline for their own lives; to justify the divorce, they persuade themselves that their marriages were very bad indeed. Incidents or character traits that are treated as annoying problems when a spouse is determined to stay married evolve into marital crimes when the same spouse is determined to leave.

One recent in-depth long-term study of fifty-six married couples found it was impossible to predict a divorce by merely looking at how a couple interacts: Placid, friendly marriages and volatile, dish-throwing marriages may be equally stable. What really foretells a marriage's future "is how a couple retells their past.... When a marriage is unraveling, the husband and wife begin to recast their earlier times in a negative light. Previous disappointments become dramatically enhanced."[26]

Similarly, sociologist Joseph Hopper, in an intriguing study called "The Rhetoric of Motive in Divorce," found that prior to divorce both the spouses who leave and the spouses who are left describe "similar experiences and feelings of being trapped; at the same time, they described good things they did not want to forgo."

After making the decision to divorce, however, the spouses who decided to leave began "negating the good things and emphasizing the bad.... They described marriage as a functional arrangement and they explained their divorces in terms of emotional and practical needs being unfulfilled.... Complaints about lack of communication turned into: 'I never got any support and intimacy from her, which is what I needed.'"

Meanwhile, the abandoned spouses lay claim to the good side of the marriage. "They began comparing their relationships with those of friends and relatives, emphasizing the ways in which their own were superior."

To the objective eye, nothing seems inevitable about these divorces: "It seemed that many outcomes were possible in nearly every marriage that I learned about. The partners might have stayed together, for example. Or the noninitiating partner might have been the one to call the marriage off."[27]

With few exceptions, the good and the bad marriages turn out to be not entirely different things, but two different stages of the same marriage, or the same marriage in two different people's minds. Looking at longtime happily married couples, one discovers that many, if not most, of these at one time looked like very bad marriages indeed. A good marriage is often not so much a matter of choosing carefully as of loving well—and stubbornly.

In Catherine Johnson's study of one hundred couples, all of whom had been married at least seven years, 60 percent were very happily married. (Only 2 percent seemed very unhappy; the rest were, in the author's words, "suffering from 'ordinary' woe," their marriages "marked by ongoing, if usually minor, friction.") Yet of the long-married very happy couples, a fourth had at one time sincerely considered divorce, often for very serious causes.[28]

Marjorie Williams, a twinkly great-grandmother in her eighties, is still happily married to Henry, the man she met and wed during the Great Depression. Today, she and her husband travel around the world and are on close terms with their two daughters as well as their grown grandchildren, all of whom are doing well personally and professionally. "Theirs," according to Johnson, "was a highly functional and highly successful family relationship."

You couldn't have predicted it from the way things started. During their early married life, Marjorie and Henry were poor. To make matters worse, Henry gambled away much of what little money he earned as a street vendor. Though she longed to stay home, Marjorie had to work to support their two daughters. When her husband came home with his depleted earnings, Marjorie was often very angry. But, says Henry, "She never stayed mad at me overnight. There was always a good-night kiss."

"How many of us," Johnson wonders, "taking care of two small girls aged one and two on an inadequate income, could muster a good-night kiss for a husband who had come home with half his paycheck squandered on card playing?"

Marjorie never ignored Henry's vices, but she always emphasized her husband's good traits. She saw him as a good man, "as honest as the day is long, an excellent father who was always generous with his girls." In time he stopped gambling. The Great Depression passed, and he went on to become the wonderful husband, father, and provider she now remembers (and lives with) in joy and love.[29]

The purpose of the marriage vow is to help human beings keep their commitments to love when their emotions, or simply their fatigue, threaten to wash those commitments away. When people take love seriously, they find capacities for love and for patience. And they give their beloved a chance to grow in love as well. When couples stay together because they believe in their vows, their duty, their commitment to each other (quite apart from their own happiness), in the end they often realize happiness as well.

In the postmarital culture, troubled couples are not only *not* encouraged to live up to their marriage vows, they are actively encouraged, after "working" on their marriage for an appropriate period of time, to divorce. The lack of faith that friends, family, and experts have in the value of the marriage undercuts their own commitment and their faith in that of their spouse.

In his late twenties, Mark Johnson returned to grad school where, surrounded by students and physically separated from his wife, he began (to put it mildly) to conduct himself as an unmarried man: He drank heavily on occasion, dabbled in cocaine, and propositioned more than one young coed. His wife, Marie, insofar as she was aware of the situation, responded to this treatment with understandable coldness and resentment. The marriage tie frayed, but did not snap. Still, a few months after the birth of his first son, Mark began to discuss the possibility of divorce. Everyone he talked to—grad students, professors, friends, all voices of respectability—

echoed the new popular wisdom: "You can't stay married just because you are supposed to."

One conversation stopped him. "I don't want to lose my grandson" was all his usually silent father said. Soon afterward, Mark made his decision. He returned to his wife because, as he put it, "It was the white, upper-middle-class, Christian Republican thing to do." It was a direct rebellion against the prevailing divorce ethos, which insists that marriages held together merely by moral commitment, by the belief that it is wrong to divorce, are dead, empty, lifeless things.

That his wife took him back was a tribute to her own firm commitment to marriage. Over the next few years, she endured many more failures of love at his hands. More babies came, and, despite his advanced degrees, he had difficulty finding and keeping a job.

Yet somehow, buttressed by their moral commitment to marriage as much as by their emotional love for one another, Mark and Marie made it through what appeared to be a very bad marriage to create together something entirely different.

It is a few years later, and I am at their home on a holiday. Mark is wrestling on the floor with his three young sons, who are obviously very much in love with their father. And they are not the only ones. As Marie passes back and forth through the kitchen, preparing the holiday meal for friends and family, one thing is very obvious: Mark cannot keep his hands off of his wife. This bad marriage is now alive with warmth, affection, and even sexual passion. It is a moving tribute to her strength of character, a triumph won, not without considerable pain and effort, of faith over fear, of love over suffering and doubt.

The bad marriage haunts us in part because we have reduced the marriage commitment to a single, grim, frightening phrase: Couples should "stay together for the sake of the children." The vision it conjures—of loveless, bitter, tight-lipped martyrs living in hell with their equally miserable kids—is impossible to uphold as a moral ideal.

To restore marriage we need a commitment both more grand and more gripping, more sacrificial and oh so much more satisfying—

not a saga of slow death, but a story worth living for, with leading roles not for victims but for tarnished heroes: all-too-human beings *loving each other well*, both for their own sake, and for the sake of the children of their love.

It is not a vision of heavenly paradise, but of earthly homes, neighborhoods, and communities. Hell is what happens when this vision breaks down.

9

AFTER MARRIAGE

AMERICA IS PRONE TO APOCALYPTIC VISIONS: Alar-poisoned apples, tainted water, soil erosion, asbestos fog, overbreeding women, immigrant hordes, a hovering mushroom cloud.

It is the underbelly of our relentless optimism, our utopian fevers: the melancholy counterpoint to the dominant theme of triumph and mastery that is the American story.

America is prone to apocalyptic visions. Here's mine:

It is a summery day in June on an urban playground. Teenagers shoot hoops, children play on swing sets, parents and old people sit quietly on the benches.

Raphael Rympel, a ninth grader who emigrated from Haiti with his family, is doing what he usually does: hanging out near the monkey bars. A man comes up to Raphael and starts to argue, then suddenly pulls a silver pistol from his waistband. He fires one shot, into the ground, to impress Raphael. The bullet ricochets, and an eight-year-old girl, Carmella, cries out in pain. The man starts to walks away but Raphael keeps yelling at him. Abruptly he turns and shoots twice. Raphael crumples to the ground, dead.[1]

This was just one afternoon in one neighborhood, Crown Heights, and by no means the worst one, in one American city in New York. But here is my nightmare: There is no escape from Crown Heights—because every neighborhood in America is just like it.

Far-fetched? Not for many African Americans, for whom the nightmare seems to have already arrived. In a 1994 poll, more than 75 percent of black adults said they feared that their own children or children they knew would become victims of violence. A majority believed that half or more of black children would become teenage parents, have their lives destroyed by drugs, or get into trouble with the law. More than three-fourths of black teens surveyed viewed violence in school as a serious personal problem.[2]

Their fears are grounded in grim realities: Each year, nearly half of all young African American men who die are murdered.[3] Homicide was the leading or second-leading cause of death among black children in 1988.[4] And most black children will experience bouts of poverty: The average black child will be poor for at least four out of the first ten years of life; one-third of black kids will be poor for seven out of ten years.[5] "We have a black-child crisis worse than any since slavery," declares Marian Wright Edelman, president of the Children's Defense Fund.[6]

The African American family experience in this country is usually treated in the public debate as the exception to the norm, a pathology induced by racism or welfare in a distinct community set apart from middle-class, mainstream mores. Even those on the Left who laud the extended black "matriarchal" family as a strength tend to isolate what has happened to the black family from the rest of the culture, to view it as a distinctive and uniquely African American phenomenon. Many on the Right, for their part, seek comfort in the idea that the social disorder caused by family breakdown is a strictly black problem. Carl F. Horowitz, for example, in a recent issue of *National Review*, offered many statistics documenting that the underclass remains disproportionately African American and Hispanic and concludes: "These enormous discrepancies in racial composition cannot help but cast severe doubt upon predictions that mainly white communities... will soon be in much the same straits as black ones today."[7]

But what if what has happened to the black American family is not so very different from what is happening to the American family as a whole? What if the experience of African Americans is not a racial anomaly or localized pathology, but a leading indicator?

If this is the case, the black experience of family breakdown is important, not only because it has cost the taxpayers money, and not just because it has injured so many black American children, but also because it constitutes a kind of petri dish in which the forces buffeting all American families can be seen and examined.

Is marriage infinitely adaptable to new social conditions, as trendy sociologists like to maintain, or can it be destroyed? What is the relation between divorce and illegitimacy? Under what conditions does marriage cease to be the norm and become the exception? And what will life be like for children, the women who care for them, and the men who don't, in the brave new world after marriage?

What has happened to marriage in the black community is both a tragedy and a warning: It can happen in other communities. It already has.

The collapse of African American marriage is a shockingly new phenomenon, occurring with breathtaking swiftness, and within living memory. As recently as 1940, blacks in every age and sex group were actually *more* likely to marry than whites.[8] Only 18 percent of black women who married in the 1940s eventually divorced, a rate only slightly higher than that for white women of that era. But, of the far smaller number of black women who married in the late sixties and early seventies, 60 percent have already divorced.[9]

As recently as 1960, fully three-quarters of all African American babies were born to married couples[10] and two-thirds of black children lived in two-parent homes (intact or stepmarriages). Today only a third of black children have two parents in the home.[11]

Black children are only half as likely as white children to be living in a two-parent household, and are eight times more likely than white children to live with an unwed mother. For black children under six, "the most common arrangement—applying to 42 percent of them—was to live with a never-married mother."[12] Even under slavery, a black child was more likely to grow up living with his mother and father than he is today.[13]

Many black Americans still make the long march to the altar, but among those who do marry, marriage has become an extremely fragile institution: Black marriages are almost twice as likely to end in divorce as white marriages.[14] Remarriage is also far less common: Only about one-third of divorced and separated black women remarry within ten years of their separation, compared to almost three-quarters of non-Hispanic whites.[15]

Among African Americans, marriage as we have known it—an enduring union for the mutual love and support and protection of husband and wife, parents and children—has all but disappeared. As Andrew Cherlin concludes after summarizing the data, "Marriage has become just a temporary stage of life for blacks, preceded by a lengthening period of singlehood and followed by a long period of living without a spouse... for blacks, even more so than for whites, a long, stable marriage is the exception rather than the rule."[16]

What happened? The two most popular explanations might, for the sake of convenience, be called the conservative and the liberal stories.

In the conservative account, associated with Charles Murray, the villain is welfare, which undercuts marriage by offering poor black women an alternate and more reliable source of income than poor black men. In the liberal story, the problem is a lack of jobs. William Julius Wilson contends that rural blacks moved to northern cities just as blue-collar manufacturing jobs dried up. Without decent jobs, black men became less willing and able to marry and maintain families. Divorce and illegitimacy rates soared.

Both stories, as far as they go, are probably true. Both, however, fail to go far enough.

One difficulty with Wilson's thesis is that sophisticated analyses suggest it can explain only a small percentage of the problem. Two independent studies using two different methods have reached the same conclusion differently: "Changes in the employment of young black men explain about 20 percent of the decline in marriage rates since 1960."[17] To explain 20 percent of so great a problem as the collapse of the black family is no small feat. Nevertheless, as sociologists Robert D. Mare and Christopher Winship conclude, "socioeconomic factors cannot account for the drastic decreases in marriage rates during the past thirty years. It is necessary therefore to seek alternative explanations."[18]

If, as the popular debate suggests, poverty or welfare policy were solely responsible for the state of black marriage, unmarriage would be a strictly underclass problem. But in fact—and almost unnoticed in the acrimonious argument over the underclass—marriage is also evaporating among working- and middle-class blacks.

Over the past twenty years, for example, the illegitimacy rate among black female high school dropouts has roughly doubled. Among black female college graduates, the illegitimacy rate has *tripled.*[19]

Moreover, the drop in marriage rates was almost as large among employed black men as among all blacks.[20] In theory, employed black men, insofar as they are comparatively rare, ought to be hot commodities, with high rates of marriage. From the women's point of view, that may be true. But it takes two to tango. With many to choose from, employed black men may feel less pressure or inclination to settle down with one woman.

Even given that welfare makes it possible, albeit barely, for women to support children out of wedlock, how is it that so many women decided doing so was their best option? How did marriage as a cultural or moral ideal fail so suddenly and completely?

In the sociological literature and public policy debates, divorce and illegitimacy are generally treated as discrete phenomena. People divorce for certain reasons, it is supposed, and have children outside of marriage for other reasons. But the African American experience strongly suggests that this sharp cleavage is artificial: Rising divorce and illegitimacy rates are intimately connected, directly and indirectly, in simple and in complicated ways.

The obvious link between divorce and illegitimacy is the decline of marriage as a family-forming institution.

Here is a stunning and little-noticed fact: Between 1960 and the mid-eighties—precisely the years when the *percentage* of black children born out of wedlock soared—the *birthrate per unmarried woman* (i.e., the rough likelihood that any given unmarried black woman would have a child) *declined* by more than 25 percent.[21] Because more and more black women remained single, the *number* of out-of-wedlock births that did rise, but only gently: from thirty-five illegitimate births per one thousand minority women of childbearing years in 1960, to about forty by the mid-eighties.[22]

So why did the black illegitimacy ratio skyrocket? Not so much because single black women were having more children, but because married black women stopped having babies.[23]

Had married black women continued to have children at the same rate as in 1960, the percentage of black children born out of wedlock would have risen only slightly—from 23 percent in 1960 to 29 percent by 1987.[24]

The flip side of the illegitimacy explosion is what might be called the *marital implosion*: African American women now average *less than one child while married*.[25]

This is an astonishing development. As recently as 1960 the average black woman had slightly more children in marriage than the average white woman. By 1970 the races had reversed position, with black women averaging slightly less than two children per marriage, while white women averaged 2.39. By 1980 the married black birth rate had slipped further, to average just more than one child per marriage. Today the black marriage averages less than nine-tenths of a child.[26] The birthrates of black married women have fallen so sharply that absent out-of-wedlock childbearing, the African American population would not only fail to reproduce itself, but would rapidly die off.[27]

Many scholars find these facts reassuring because they seem to reduce a supposed massive rise in illegitimacy to a statistical glitch. In absolute terms, the number of African American children being born out of wedlock is only slightly larger now than it was in 1960. So what's the big deal?

These experts fail to recognize that marriage and childbearing are being severed in two ways; black single women are having somewhat more babies and black married women are having far, far fewer. The net result is a very big deal: Illegitimacy is replacing marriage as a way to produce children among African Americans.

The first half of the equation, Why are so many young black women having babies out of wedlock? has received a great deal of attention. But the other side of the coin is equally, if not more, important: Why are black marriages increasingly nearly childless?

Since most research has focused not on marriage, but on its absence, the data are only sketchy and suggestive. A married couple, disinterested in or afraid to have children are not, in themselves, a "policy" problem: They do not ask for or require government programs to rescue them from the consequences of their decision, consequences such as more wealth, leisure, and peace and quiet. But individual decisions multiply into new social norms. When not some, but most, black married couples are reluctant to have children, then marriage is failing in its prime social function: to nurture and protect the next generation.

Part of the reason black women have so few children during marriage is that so many have had children before marriage. This is one simple and direct way in which illegitimacy affects marriage: Babies born out of wedlock drive out those born within. Women coming into a marriage with a child are likely to be older, associate childbearing with financial and personal hazard, and believe they have completed their family. Such women will be far less likely to think of marriage primarily or even substantially as a path to motherhood, and also less likely to teach their children, younger friends, and relatives—or their men—to think about it in that way.

Married women with illegitimate children are also less likely to have children while they are married because their marriages are more fragile: Divorce and fear of divorce, research suggests, are some of the prime reasons women forgo children.[28] As Kathleen Gerson, a professor of sociology at New York University, found in her suggestive study of sixty-three middle-class women, "The experience of instability in marriage or in a heterosexual relationship was one of the most powerful and disorienting events initiating a process of reassessment and change away from domesticity.... In most cases the decision to establish greater commitment to work involved not one, but two related choices: the choice to take work more seriously *and* the choice to forgo bearing a child."[29] When marriage becomes unreliable, childbearing seems much too risky.

Here is where the chain of causality becomes an ensnaring web. Fear of divorce makes women prepare for it, both by working more hours outside the home and by avoiding children. But marriages in which the wife works full time are more likely to end in divorce. Mare and Winship sum up the evidence: "The higher a woman's earning and the greater her permanent commitment to the work force relative to her husband's, the less likely she is to remain married."[30]

Understanding this dynamic allows us to recognize another disaster disguised as progress—the troubling reality behind the cheerful statistics Republicans like to present on the success of black married couples. Married blacks have made impressive statistical gains. Only 12 percent of black married-couple families are poor compared to 61 percent of female-headed families.[31] A recent analysis of 1990 census data discovered that in Queens black married-couple households earn slightly more money than their white counterparts.[32]

How did they do it? The American way—by working harder than their neighbors. "In black households, both husband and wife were more likely to have jobs than in white households, and they worked longer hours as well."[33] And it does not happen just in Queens. To achieve middle-class status, black women, in particular, must and do work more often and longer hours than their white counterparts.

The consequences for childbearing are great. Like whites, but far more rapidly, the black "family" is maintaining its middle-class status by shedding its children.[34] When women must work full time, each additional child becomes a tremendously costly proposition. Children cost money directly, but they cost even more in time, energy, and opportunity for the mother.

When divorce is sufficiently common, fears for their own future security drive wives to work full time, which both increases the divorce rate and makes rearing a child from marriage more costly.

For those with only a newfound, hard-won, and tenuous hold on the good life, the effects of marital fragility on childbearing may be even stronger than for the largely middle-class women Gerson surveyed. Children may become a threat to, rather than an incentive or reward for, marriage.

When divorce rates beget fear, marriages no longer beget children.

Under this combination of circumstances, the culture begins to bifur-cate. Marriage remains an excellent vehicle for status aspirations—for those who want to make it. But to forge ahead, those in the driver's seat are increasingly forced to chuck out all nonproductive passengers—they have become an economic threat to the well-being of married adults. Marriage increasingly becomes a way of improving the economic and perhaps emotional well-being of adults, but not a means for channeling the love, energy, and money of adults toward children.

In the next generation, daughters affected by the cycle of divorce—divorce begets illegitimacy, which begets more of both—are more likely to both divorce and become unwed mothers.[35] Daughters raised in single-parent households launch into sex earlier—because they are less supervised, they often crave male attention, and they have observed their own mothers' romantic lives. A mother with an active postmarital sex life may be less interested in or effective at postponing her teenage daughter's premarital sex life.

One study found that, compared to their older married counterparts, young unwed moms had far more negative attitudes about relations with men. Only 25 percent of the unwed teen moms had clearly positive views of men, compared to 71 percent of the older married moms. The unwed teen moms were also more likely to view marriage as a highly problem-atic relationship, which the researchers attributed to "a significantly higher incidence of divorce in their families of origin" than were the mar-ried mothers. Absent fathers, they believe, make these teen girls "partic-ularly vulnerable to involvement with men who would treat them badly."[36]

There seems to be a tipping point at which marriage becomes so fragile and divorce so common that an increasing number of women decide it may be safer to dispense with marriage altogether: Illegitimacy surges in the wake of a surge in divorce. Between 1940 and 1960, divorce, once relatively rare, became a common experience among African Americans. In the next twenty years, illegitimacy made the same great leap: In 1960, only 23 percent of black births were out of wedlock, but by 1980, 55 percent were.

The same pattern—a generation of divorce engendering a generation of illegitimacy—seems to be emerging among whites, albeit somewhat more slowly. Between 1960 and 1980, divorce, once experienced by only a small number of white Americans, became more common than not. And between 1980 and 1990, as the children of those broken marriages reached marriageable age, the white illegitimacy rate jumped from 11 percent to 18 percent. By the year 2000, if present trends continue, nearly 40 percent of all babies will be born outside of marriage.[37]

Just for the moment we may be able to maintain the illusion that divorce and illegitimacy are separate and wholly distinct phenomena. Like the front and back of the bus, illegitimacy for blacks and divorce for whites. For the moment, the illusion is made easier by the fact that unwed motherhood is still relatively rare among white, college-educated women. Yet for the people who make, or fall into, the relevant decisions, divorce and illegitimacy are both distinct entrées into a similar lifestyle: single parenthood. Which is why despite differences, divorce and illegitimacy are inevitably connected by a deep cultural logic, by prevailing cultural ideas about marriage: How favorably or unfavorably men and women view single parenthood depends on the stories of marriage and family that dominate the culture and the incentives toward marriage, both economic and moral, that are created and sustained by the community.

Are two parents necessary, or simply desirable? Do children need fathers, or can mothers do it all? How hard is it to be a single mother, anyway? How hard is it to get and stay married, and is the effort worth it?

The answers a community offers to questions like these will shape men and women's attitudes toward both divorce and unwed motherhood. A society that enthusiastically approves of divorce will make at least one partner happy and will have difficulty telling unmarried women that it is wrong to have a baby, if doing so will make them happy.

Unmarried women who consider having babies are often acutely aware of this connection, comparing themselves in this regard (and not unfavorably) to divorced women. "One of the things he is spared that children of divorce go through," says Emily, a freelance writer and unwed mother of Ethan, "is the fighting and using the child as a crowbar on each other."[38]

This is part of the divorce paradox: The less demanding and restrictive marriage is, the less useful and attractive it becomes. When marriage no longer offers security to women raising children (which it can do only by securing the partners reasonably firmly in their obligations to each other, whether the bonds are legal, religious, cultural, or erotic), more and more women opt for the even greater insecurity of unwed motherhood. Marriage becomes not the only acceptable (or even the best) means of creating a new family, but a partnership between adults for the purpose of raising the adults' quality of life. Children become a risky hindrance to this struggle to get ahead—and a tremendous point of vulnerability in the event of divorce. The child-prone go ahead and have babies without marriage. The status-oriented get married but increasingly fear having children.

The more unreliable marriage becomes, the more couples eschew it for more casual couplings. Men see little reason to marry. Because if marriage seems a high-risk partnership to women, to men (especially good men) it begins to look like a chump's game where, if you act in good faith, you tie your devotion, work, and wealth to a woman who will not necessarily respect the bond. Women, meanwhile, afraid to depend on men, sharply increase their work commitment and drastically cut back on children.

As divorce becomes more the rule than the exception, stigmas against it inevitably wither away. It is not possible to stigmatize a majority practice. Unwilling to pass judgment or risk breaches with their friends and siblings, people no longer say out loud that divorce is bad, even for the children. Instead, they congratulate one another on having the courage to create a new life for themselves and their children.

And as the stigma against divorce collapses, so, too, inevitably the stain against illegitimacy. If single-parent families are as good as two-parent families, even for the children, why wait for marriage? If it is okay to create a single family through divorce, why not do it without subjecting yourself and your kids to the trauma of divorce?

As young lovers become increasingly anxious about getting "had" in marriage, cohabitation not only increases but gains respectability, aided by the older, divorced generation's difficulties in defending an institution they abandoned. Couples living together begin by insisting on the same social advantages as married couples—being invited to the same dinner parties and allowed to sleep together under their parents' roof. Finally, they begin to ask for the same legal benefits. Cohabitation, the great historical rival of marriage, begins to win the competition. "Relationships" drive out marriage as bad money drives out good. A less reliable and therefore cheaper security submerges the unique rewards of being married.

In this way a culture of divorce begins to displace a culture of marriage, and marriage itself becomes unable to perform its great historic function: committing the love and money of adults to their children—and to the future.

Today, the white family stands poised, eerily, almost exactly where the black family was twenty-five years ago, before its rapid descent into a postmarital world.

- In 1960, 23 percent of black children were born to unwed mothers. Today the proportion is nearly the same for whites, and the rate is rising rapidly.[39]
- In 1969, 43 percent of babies born to black high school dropouts were illegitimate. Today almost 40 percent of babies born to white high school dropouts are illegitimate.
- In 1960, only 60 percent of black women ages twenty-five to twenty-nine were married. In 1990, only 62 percent of white women in this age group were married.[40] Today the average white woman will spend only 43 percent of her life married, very close to the 40 percent a black woman spent in marriage in 1950.[41]

"The changes in family structure that occurred among blacks are a leading indicator of what may happen among whites," writes Reynolds Farley. "Barriers to the educational and occupational advancement of black women declined recently, and they were strongly motivated to upgrade their position in the labor market because of the restricted economic gains of black men. Improvements in the earnings of black women, however, made marriage less necessary, made it less desirable to stay in an unpleasant marriage, and may have made it easier for husbands to dissolve marriages. If the earnings of white women rise, compared with those of white men, will we find that white families increasingly resemble current black families? Two decades from now will the majority of white children be born to unmarried women? Will 30 or 40 percent of white children live below the poverty line?"[42]

The collapse of marriage has created an emerging sexual economy in which there is an extraordinary discontinuity between the sexes: To succeed, a man had best marry and have children. To be financially secure, a woman had best remain single and childless.

Women, both black and white, are responding to this situation, quite rationally, by rapidly disinvesting in family life and refocusing on the world of work. This is no longer merely a matter of choice or preference (as it may have been in the sixties and seventies), but a response to scarcity—to the fear and anxiety with which today's young women approach sex, marriage, and children.

A 1994 *New York Times*/CBS News poll of American teenagers revealed that only 57 percent of teenage girls considered it very likely that they would have children, and only 26 percent deem marriage as essential to their own happiness (compared to 38 percent of teenage boys).[43] Meanwhile, fully 55 percent of America's teenage girls said they would consider having a baby outside of wedlock.[44]

We know that marriage can be made to disappear. It has already largely happened in the black community. It is happening in the American family at large. The question is, What will we do about it? As Paul E. Peterson wrote in *The Urban Underclass*, "The most powerful force contributing to the formation of the urban underclass, perversely enough, may be the changing values of mainstream American society, in which the virtues of family stability, mutual support, and religiously based commitment to the marriage vow no longer command the deference they once did."[45]

All children, but especially the children of the poor, are paying the price for the sexual liberation of the well-to-do. The sexual and social mores that weakened marriage in the black community were the mores relentlessly peddled by white elites. The cultural, economic, and legal factors that undermined the black family are having the same effect on the white family and the family throughout Western Europe and Canada. The interrelated factors of rising divorce, failure to marry, skyrocketing illegitimacy, lower in-wedlock births, and lower male wages first experienced by African Americans are fast becoming the crises of the Western world.

PART TWO

❧

THE
CULTURE
of
DIVORCE

10

DECONSTRUCTING MARRIAGE

In 1880 Pope Leo XIII declared, "To take away from man the natural and primitive right of marriage, to circumscribe in any way the principal ends of marriage laid down in the beginning by God Himself in the words *Increase and Multiply*, is beyond the power of any human law."

Lately, however, as two legal scholars noted, "It does not seem to be beyond the power of the American courts."[1]

Over the past thirty years, quietly, and largely unremarked outside a narrow group of specialists, American family law has been rewritten to dilute both the rights and the obligations of marriage, while at the same time placing other relationships, from adulterous liaisons to homosexual partnerships, on a legal par with marriage in some respects. To put it another way, by expanding the definition of *marriage* to the point of meaninglessness, courts are gradually redefining marriage out of existence.

The deconstruction of marriage is usually described (by courts as well as critics) as a way of increasing individual choice. This rhetoric ignores the reality that marriage consists of a special packet of reciprocal rights and responsibilities designed to both protect family members and make family life attractive, to unify the interests of family members in a mutually supportive way. As these responsibilities blur—as they must when marriage is made indistinguishable from relationships in which the parties have few, if any, responsibilities to each other—and the rights are parceled out to the unmarried, marriage itself begins to dissolve. The more other relationships begin to acquire the rights of marriage, and the more the law declines to enforce the special responsibilities of marriage, the more ghostly and insubstantial the marriage commitment becomes.

Marriage is a sexual option carved out of nature by custom, faith, society, and law. Marriage cannot be created by an individual, or even a couple, alone. In marrying, spouses acquire rights and assume obligations not only for themselves but on behalf of their yet-unborn children. At the heart of the idea of marriage is the *vow* by which two people pledge to transform the emotions of love into a durable, higher, and external reality, transcending the transience of human feeling. Like a soldier's oath it is meant to sustain heroic efforts when they seem merely exhausting or dispiriting or terrifying, but which if abandoned would mean a personal and moral loss incomparable to the momentary relief of quitting. But soldiers are not sustained merely by their oaths; similarly, where society, custom, and law cease to uphold and sustain the marriage vow, where the obligations of marriage are made purely optional, and where the rights of marriage are granted to those who do not accept its obligations, then marriage functionally ceases to exist.

The numerous innovations blurring the legal distinction between marriage and nonmarriage—knocking marriage off its pedestal—are scattered throughout family law. But they share a common theme: They conceptually discard the essence of marriage—the creation, from two individuals, of a new legal unit—and substitute a notion of two individuals temporarily paired in a series of nonbinding decisions. Legally and philosophically, the law has been deconstructing marriage into its component parts—a Chinese menu of love in which one takes one's pleasures from column A.

This is the distance traveled in just a few short years by the Supreme Court. In the famous 1965 case of *Griswold v. Connecticut,* the Court declared that, in marriage, "We deal with a right of privacy older than the Bill of Rights—older than our political parties, older than our school system. Marriage is a coming together for better or for worse, hopefully enduring, and intimate to the degree of being sacred." But by 1972, in *Eisenstadt v. Baird*, the Court had no problem dissolving the sacred union: "Yet the marital couple is not an independent entity with a mind and heart of its own, but an association of two individuals each with a separate intellectual and emotional make-up. If the right of privacy means anything, it is the right of the *individual*, married or single, to be free from unwanted governmental intrusion." For that and other reasons, the Court ruled, it was a violation of equal protection for the law to treat married and unmarried individuals differently.

In a review of the case, penned only a year later, constitutional scholar John Noonan pointed out how far the Court had gone toward disestablishing marriage: "The vital personal right [to marry]... is not the right to exchange magical words before an agent authorized by the state. It is the right to be immune to the legal disabilities of the unmarried and to acquire the legal benefits accorded to the married. Lawful marriage... is a constellation of these immunities and privileges. To say that legal immunities and legal benefits may not depend upon marriage is to deny the vital right."[2]

The Court's deconstruction of marriage came about in the context of an increasing and (some might think) obsessive concern for sex. Marriage came to be seen not primarily as a covenant or contract with a legally enforceable content, but as a particular variety of sexual practice in an era when sex itself was being conceptually privatized, redefined as a private indulgence of an individual, by an individual, for his (or her) own individual gratification. Soon, not only were the courts declining to use the law to enforce sexual morals, they had begun to use the Constitution to protect violators of the old sexual code, not from the police but from anyone—from outraged spouses to landlords—who might be disposed to impede the gratification of the sexually liberated or support the rights of spouses.

Both courts and legislatures, for example, have discarded legal devices designed to protect the marital relation from outside intruders, phasing out lawsuits for intentional damage to marital consortium, enticement, alienation of affection, and criminal conversation. In other words, cads could no longer be sued by husbands for seducing their wives. These actions in law were abandoned on the grounds that, if the spouse consented to extramarital sex, the adulterous third party ought not be held responsible for damaging the marriage. In business, enticing a party to a contract into violating his obligations is a grave offense, exposing the seducer to serious legal consequences. This is so even though the seducer did not force the contracted party to violate the contract. But in the case of marriage, the Court reasoned (aping the sexual revolutionaries' religion) that if it's not rape it can't be wrong, or at least not legally objectionable. This line of reasoning reduces marriage to a temporary sexual lifestyle choice that binds only because the individual, whenever he is presented with a temptation, chooses again to be bound. Rather than forming a new legal person, inviolable by outsiders, this new version of marriage forces each spouse to retain his own sovereignty, social and sexual, doomed to a stubborn separateness, not one flesh but two restless spirits.

In June of 1993, the Texas supreme court overturned a law that presumed a woman's husband was the father of her child, thus allowing another man to sue for paternity rights. "The right to be heard doesn't cease," the court said, "merely because the mother is married."[3] Thus the court declared that violating a marriage was so trivial an offense that the violator should not only not be presumed to lose the rights to children carelessly conceived in such a violation but that he should be allowed to violate the marriage all over again by the humiliation of a public trial.

For teens, the law has redefined sex as a public health matter, thus severely limiting the power of parents who subscribe to traditional marital and sexual codes to govern their children's sexual education. Schools and medical personnel have been empowered to teach novel sexual ethics, distribute condoms, and refer minors for abortions without parental permission or even notification. Here was a one-two punch to the heart of the old marriage ethic: First, the law declared sex private and so struck down puritanical laws that tried to restrict sexual behavior or even just nudge it into marriage. Second, the courts, by declaring sex a public health issue, justified state intrusions into private morality, but with this proviso: Only traditional moral standards were placed in legal hazard, forbidden from being upheld by private action, even within a family.

The law now forbids private individuals from distinguishing between married and unmarried couples in many cases. For example, many landlords and home mortgage companies, for a host of sound business as well as social reasons, once showed a certain favoritism for married couples and intact families. But with the rise in divorce rates, legislatures and courts established laws forbidding discrimination in housing or credit on the basis of marital status. This was done from a legitimate concern to protect the rising crop of newly divorced women and their children. Today, however, the laws prevent landlords, banks, and other private institutions from distinguishing between married and unmarried couples, as well.

Such rulings are part of a growing trend to grant marital or family rights to individuals in relations that are the "functional equivalents" of marriage. In the eyes of the law, marriage is increasingly reduced to a mere body count. Two bodies are two bodies. Whether they have legally pledged to have and to hold till death do them part or simply promised to share the washing-up makes no difference so long as they happen to inhabit the same space. Landlords, for example, may freely choose to limit the number of people living on their property. They may decide to rent only to single individuals, or to two individuals, or to four individuals. What they are not legally permitted to do is to notice that there is any difference between a spouse and a sex partner or, for that matter, between a family and a frat house. In 1990 the New Jersey Supreme Court actually declared ten college students living together the "functional equivalent" of a family, for the purpose of zoning laws.[4]

The most prominent example of this urge to merge marriage with other relationships is the growing popularity of "domestic partnership" laws. The energy behind this idea may be coming from gay activists, but for the most part these ordinances are carefully orientation-neutral. Anyone, gay or straight, can sign up to get at least some of the benefits of marriage without incurring its liabilities. In fact, such efforts to blur the boundary between marriage and unmarriage usually come wrapped in sexually conservative rhetoric. In New York City, for instance, then-Mayor David Dinkins described the new policy as a "major step" in granting "close and committed relationships" the same rights as "individuals bonded through the traditional concept of the family,"[5] the implication being that lovers who at least demonstrated some stability, and implicitly some degree of commitment and caring, and who presumably were avoiding the bathhouses ought to be encouraged. When Cambridge, Massachussetts, became the nineteenth community to grant domestic partners marital rights (including fringe benefits such as health insurance), City Councilwoman Alice K. Wolf maintained, "I feel these relationships that act like families, it's important to support them. Let's support love and commitment where it is."[6]

Thus in a reversal of the old-fashioned custom of frowning, however faintly, on those who shack up (and thus impersonate the married), the governments of New York, San Francisco, Seattle, and other cities now offer singles special privileges, if and only if they solemnly swear they are living together out of wedlock. But what commitment are these "close and committed" couples making to justify their new privileges? Marriage entails both rights and responsibilities. A husband can extend his health insurance to his wife, but he can also be bankrupted by her medical debts. By contrast, for domestic partners the commitments are optional while the benefits are guaranteed.

The activists cast their arguments in terms of equal protection: It is a violation of civil rights, they say, for the law to treat married and unmarried people differently. Thus, for example, they argue that laws or policies that permit an employer to extend employee benefits to spouses, while not extending them to live-in lovers, violate the principle of "equal work for equal pay": "Employment policies that provide family health care, bereavement leave, family sick leave, and other benefits only to married employees, while denying these life-saving benefits to unmarried ones, constitute blatant employment discrimination," proclaimed Paula Ettelbrick, legislative counsel for the Pride Agenda in a January 4, 1995, letter to the *New York Times*. "Employers should not be in the business of determining which employees are *worthy or moral enough* to receive rightful compensation, but rather are required by law to treat all employees equitably" (emphasis added).

In taking this view, proponents of domestic partnership mistakenly portray the legal benefits of marriage as a kind of Good Housekeeping Seal of Approval handed out by the government for special sexual merit. Such a misconception reflects a much wider loss of understanding of the origin and nature of the rights (along with the concomitant responsibilities) that constitute marriage. Government's purpose of allowing husbands to extend health insurance to their wives was not to indicate, "Here, we like how you have sex, have some tax subsidies," nor even to convey a warm fuzzy official approval of family or family-like feelings. There are many family members to whom employees were never entitled to extend insurance benefits—their mothers or siblings, for example—however much they might need it.

Family insurance benefits arose out of recognition of the tremendous costs that childbearing and child rearing impose on women. The intent of such favoritism was to protect women in their roles as mothers. As families have grown smaller and sexual customs have changed, the extent to which motherhood impinges on a woman's ability to compete in the market has no doubt dwindled. But motherhood still puts women at an enormous competitive disadvantage. Most mothers still withdraw from the labor force at least for a period of time, either partially or wholly.

Society attaches benefits to marriage because the married have undertaken crucial social responsibilities; those benefits help to carry them out—chiefly the legal, moral, and economic responsibilities to care for each other and for the children of their marriage. The Supreme Court, in a series of decisions beginning in 1968, has developed a curious blindness to these public purposes of marriage.

One of the least controversial but potentially most damaging series of cases has effectively barred discrimination between legitimate and illegitimate children. In the 1972 case of *Weber v. Aetna Casualty and Surety Company*, the Court said, "Imposing disabilities on the illegitimate child is contrary to the basic concept of our system that legal burden should bear some relationship to individual responsibility or wrongdoing. Obviously, no child is responsible for his birth and penalizing the illegitimate child is an ineffectual—as well as unjust—way of deterring the parent." In *Trimble v. Gordon* (1977) the Court ruled that states must treat legitimate and illegitimate children identically for the purpose of inheritance. And in *Gomez v. Perez* (1973) the Court ruled a state may not grant legitimate children a right to support from their fathers while denying the same to illegitimate children. These decisions conform to an overwhelming and admirable public sentiment that it is wrong to visit the sins of the fathers upon the children. In three other cases in the seventies the Supreme Court ruled that public policy must extend the same benefits to legitimate and illegitimate children—disability, social security, and welfare benefits.[7] But the purpose of distinguishing between legitimate and illegitimate children is not to punish either the child or the parent, but to protect the marriage.

As a private association of two individuals, marriage may have as many meanings and as many goals as there are private individuals. But as a public institution, marriage has one overriding purpose: to create an environment in which it is safe to have children. The rebellion against the notion of legitimacy is premised, in effect, on the idea that we do not need marriage to do that job. The abolition of legitimacy is the offspring of a prodigious cultural effort to make all environments equally safe for childbearing. It was born out of the optimism of elites who became convinced that, with proper government subsidies and the abolition of "archaic" laws, single mothering could be made as adaptive an institution as the so-called traditional family. In a properly designed society, marriage could be made strictly optional, a lifestyle decision about which the law, custom, and society could afford to remain perfectly neutral.

In the ensuing thirty years, despite numerous efforts at child-support reform, and child-care and welfare subsidies, we have not been able to make unmarriage as safe as marriage. But in the pursuit of this false dream of equality, we may succeed in deconstructing marriage to the point where it is almost as unsafe as other environments for childbearing.

The goal of abolishing illegitimacy, for instance, may be to raise the status of the natural child. But the real result is to raise the status of the mistress. And we cannot do that without lowering the status of the wife. A married man has explicitly assumed the obligation to support any children who may ensue from the marriage. To give, as the law in theory now does, the woman who sleeps with a married man the same right to child support as his wife, is to lessen the wife's rights in the marriage.

I do not mean to argue that married men have no obligations to children conceived outside the marriage. Throughout history, men have acknowledged such moral obligations and the law has sometimes enforced them. But never, until the present, have the legal obligations created inside and outside of marriage been held to be equal; in no civilized society has the fact of marriage been held to be irrelevant. Until today. Today our legal system holds that a married man's income is available equally to his wife and to his adulterous sex partner, provided she conceives a child. The only way to create such equality, since money is not infinite, is to take money out of the family.

Moreover, in practice, abolishing the distinction between marriage and unmarriage has raised the status of children conceived outside of wedlock in only the most nominal way. Certainly, it has not significantly improved their material condition. Barring a few widely publicized celebrity cases, the children of such sexual disunions are no less likely to be poor than they have ever been nor less likely to be ignored by their father or abused by their mother's live-in boyfriend. As a body of legal doctrine, however, such innovations form a practical bar to efforts to discourage illegitimacy or to define and enforce marital obligations.

In 1978, for example, the Supreme Court in *Zablocki v. Redhail* struck down a Wisconsin law that required a single or divorced person to comply with court-ordered support payments before he could marry.[8] Here, as usual, the Court wrapped its essentially radical decision in conservative-sounding rhetoric about the individual's fundamental right to marry. Using an unusual analogy, the Court wrote that "the woman whom appellee desired to marry had a fundamental right to seek an abortion of their expected child.... Surely a decision to marry and raise the child in a traditional family setting must receive equivalent protection." The actual effect of *Zablocki v. Redhail*, however, was to bar the state of Wisconsin from enforcing even the most rudimentary marital obligation—the obligation to pay child support after the marriage dissolves. It ruled instead that a man has a constitutional right repeatedly to acquire new marital obligations without actually being obliged to live up to any of them—to gain for himself all the lifestyle benefits of marriage without accepting its responsibilities.

The same body of constitutional opinion hamstrings current efforts to reform welfare so as to discourage illegitimacy. Congress or the states will find it very difficult to establish policies that differentiate between married and unmarried mothers if legal distinctions based on legitimacy are held to be violations of the Fourteenth Amendment. Unless the Supreme Court reexamines its stance, any law limiting or withholding cash welfare for young unwed mothers could be struck down.

Social policy is now shot through with rules and regulations weakening the privileged status of marriage as a child-rearing institution. In adoption and foster-care placements, the law no longer necessarily gives preference to married couples, and it often treats race as more important: Single black prospective adoptive or foster parents are given legal preference over married white couples. In an increasing number of cases, unwed mothers have discovered that their babies are being transferred not, as they assumed when they agreed to give up the babies, to a married couple, but to another single mother. In another example, until the sixties cities were free to set their own criteria for public housing; in some cities, including New York, city policies favored married low-income working families. Then in the late sixties the federal government offered major public housing subsidies, but with strings attached: Henceforth, public housing would have to eliminate this preference for married families over unmarried families. Since the best predictor of crime is the prevalence of single parents in a given neighborhood, predictably, the policy had the effect of turning projects into dangerous slums from which married working families fled.

By taking away the traditional supports of marriage or even forbidding private citizens and institutions from favoring families, we undermine the only institution ever shown to be capable of raising children well or civilizing the erotic drives of men. By sharing the benefits of the married, such as the tax subsidy for health care, with pseudo-marriages, we encourage the disastrous illusion that such liaisons can perform the same social purposes. By voiding the obligations of marriage, as we do when we convey the rights of the married to the unmarried, we turn marriage into an empty shell devoid of specific meanings—or worse, into a fraud backed by empty promises. But the courts and the legislatures have done even worse than that. They have made marriage illegal.

11

UNILATERAL DIVORCE

IN 1970 MARY, A NICE CATHOLIC twenty-something California girl, tried to commit an illegal act.

She and her boyfriend Jim decided to wed: They had blood tests and got a license; they engaged a priest to preside at the ceremony. The bride donned a white satin gown, the groom a tuxedo, and they exchanged vows. Afterward, she took his name. To all outward appearances, Mary and Jim were married. Everyone said so.

But 1970 was the year the state of California created no-fault divorce. With that act, and with no fanfare and little public debate, California quietly outlawed marriage.

Mary did not find this out until nearly a decade later when her husband flew off to Los Angeles on a business trip, never to return. Mary received a letter in which Jim explained he had married too young and needed to "find himself." She was left with two kids, $12,000 from the sale of the house, and $300 a month in child support.[1]

When Mary agreed to live with Jim, to accept his financial support and offer her own labor (paid and unpaid) to the household and to sleep in the same bed and bear his children, she did so because she thought she was married. Had Jim asked her to do these things for him without marriage, she would have undoubtedly slapped his face. Mary knew what marriage meant. The example of her parents and the teaching of her religion made the unspoken concrete: Marriage meant two individuals became one flesh, one family. It was a lifetime commitment.

But the state of California later informed her that she was not allowed to make or accept lifetime commitments. No-fault divorce gave judges, at the request of one-half of the couple, the right to decide when a marriage had irretrievably broken down. The state decided that, by and large, wanderlust would be protected by law, while loyalty was on its own. In a cruel display of raw judicial power, the state of California made Mary a single woman again, without protecting her interest and without her consent.

What happened to Mary in California in 1970 happened to many other people in many other parts of the country as state after state feverishly jumped on the no-fault bandwagon. By the early eighties, the revolution was complete: Eighteen states had eliminated fault grounds for divorce altogether; almost all the rest offered a no-fault divorce option. Unlike many European countries, which attach waiting periods as long as five to seven years before a man or woman may obtain a no-fault divorce against an unconsenting spouse, American legislatures opted for quick and easy spouse disposal. Why wait to bury a dead marriage, they reasoned? Most states require less than a year's separation for a no-fault divorce.

No-fault legislation was supposed to permit a couple to get a divorce by mutual consent. No longer, reformers promised, would a perfectly amicable divorcing couple have to pretend the husband was a cruel philanderer to get the courts to give them a divorce. But what no-fault laws actually did was something dramatically different: Under the guise of making a merely technical adjustment to the legal mechanics of divorce, the legal profession radically transformed the legal and moral basis of marriage. It created a new beast: not *no-fault*, but *unilateral* divorce. Today, while it still takes two to marry, it takes only one to divorce.

Divorce by mutual-consent divorce is rare. Over 80 percent of divorces are now the unilateral choice of one partner.[2] Americans were given the freedom to sever the marriage tie at any time and for any reason and so lost the ability to make a permanent, binding commitment. We gained the right to divorce and in the process lost the right to marry.

And this is the remarkable thing: No one noticed.

Rings and vows were exchanged, garters thrown, cakes cut, households set up, and children born. People continued to use the same word—*marriage*—to describe this radically new social institution that had been created, a relation that, legally speaking, more closely resembles taking a concubine than giving oneself to a spouse.

Divorce reformers imagined that they could ease the passage of disgruntled individuals out of bad marriages and yet retain intact the institution of marriage. No-fault divorce, they said (and we believed) is only a humane way of disposing of dead marriages. It doesn't affect the vitality of the truly wed.

This reform is often portrayed as an increase in individual choice or freedom. But the legal changes that constitute the divorce revolution can more accurately be described as *a shift in power:* from the married to the unmarried in general, from the spouse who wants to stay married to the spouse who wants to leave, from the person who wants to commit to the person who wants the right to revoke his or her commitments.

The reformers did not calculate what would happen once the message contained in the new marriage laws sank in. They never pondered what it would be like to get married and yet know that one's spouse not only could leave at any time, but also had an absolute right to do so. They never contemplated the anxiety that burdened young men and women who consider betting their futures in a game heavily weighted in favor of the unfaithful, the immature, the betrayer.

The spouse who decides to divorce has a liberating sense of mastery, one of the key components of personal happiness. He or she is leaving, breaking free, reaching for the exhilarating headlong embrace of change, which, with its psychic echoes of the original adolescent break from family, can boost self-esteem.

But being divorced reinforces exactly the opposite sense of life. Being divorced does not feel like an act of personal courage, for the simple reason that it is not an act at all. It is something that happens to a spouse and over which, thanks to no-fault legislation, the spouse has no say at all. The spouse who leaves learns that love dies. The spouse who is left learns that love betrays, that he or she has no control over the terms of marriage. Neither the culture nor the courts will enforce any commitment. The only rule is, He who wants out, wins.

Ten years after divorce, 10 percent of middle-class "couples" are better off.[3] The legal transformation of marriage from a key public institution to a private consumption item is a remarkable story. In a single generation, marriage has been demoted from a covenant, to a contract, to a private wish in which *caveat emptor* is the prevailing legal rule. It is surely an irony of history that at the same time that the law has increasingly rejected the age-old notion that employees are terminable at will, it has embraced the idea that marriages can be terminated at the will of one party. We now live in a society where it is legally easier and less risky to dump a wife than fire an employee.

Society chooses to protect those relations it deems most important. A anthropologist from Mars (to borrow a phrase from Oliver Sacks) surveying our legal system and our cultural mores would surely conclude that "consumer" and "employee" are our most valued and irreplaceable roles, around which society builds (for better or worse) legal and social protections. Meanwhile, relations such as "husband," "wife," and (to a lesser extent) "mother" and "father" are treated as less important roles, bit players who can be safely left to the workings of chance and the unprotected sexual marketplace.

The murder of marriage is a particular atrocity because it was mostly the act of a small and narrow elite. As difficult as it is to believe, the historical record is fairly clear: In the early seventies marriage was radically transformed and the traditional marriage commitment outlawed in a way that has endangered the economic and emotional well-being of millions of women and children, largely to please lawyers.

In 1966, before the no-fault revolution, only 13 percent of

Americans believed divorce laws were too strict.[4] As Harvard professor of law Mary Ann Glendon notes, "Discontent with fault-based divorce seems to have been felt more acutely by mental-health professionals and academics than by the citizenry in general."[5] It was not an anguished public, chained by marriage vows, that demanded divorce as a right. The revolution was made by the determined whine of lawyers, judges, psychiatrists, marriage counselors, academics, and goo-goo–eyed reformers who objected to, of all things, the amount of hypocrisy contained in the law.

Fault-based divorce, they believed, forced couples who wanted to split to fabricate evidence of adultery or mental cruelty in order to get a divorce. Lawyers were forced to manufacture, and judges were forced to pretend to believe, fabricated evidence, thus undermining the public's respect for the legal profession.

Has no-fault been a success? If you ask divorce lawyers, judges, and legal scholars, they'll say, Yes, certainly. And if the purpose of our legal system is to create better working conditions for lawyers, then they are right. Every survey of family court judges and divorce lawyers reveals that the legal profession remains immensely satisfied, that the no-fault divorce revolution has achieved its goals: eliminating "hypocrisy," raising the social status of divorce lawyers, and reducing acrimony around divorce—or at least the amount of acrimony to which judges and lawyers are exposed. An Iowa evaluation concluded, for example, that according to "the satisfied majority both of judges and attorneys" no-fault divorces resulted in "a more honest and civilized approach void of… fraud, perjury and abuse." A poll of Nebraska judges found that two-thirds agreed no-fault laws had lessened animosity between divorcing parties. These judges also acknowledged the laws had introduced unilateral divorce, but they seemed unconcerned by the fact.[6]

The chorus of approval for no-fault divorces was amplified by initial studies that nearly unanimously concluded that these changes in the law had little effect on the divorce rate. For ten years these studies, which confirmed what the intelligentsia wanted to hear, remained the unchallenged conventional wisdom: The law, we were told, was utterly impotent to influence people's behavior. You can't legislate morality.

But evaluating the effect of the law on divorce rates turned out to be tricky. Not only do state statutes vary, but different states changed different aspects of divorce law. Some states merely added no-fault to other grounds for divorce. Others abolished fault altogether. Still others cut waiting periods.

Many of the earlier studies assumed that all the changes lumped under the no-fault rubric had the same effect on divorce rates. Moreover, in many cases, states officially passed "no-fault" laws only after judges had already effectively changed legal practices to ease divorce. This made it difficult to assess the effect on divorce rates of statutory changes that largely codified what judges were already doing. To add to the confusion, many other states were suddenly labeled *no-fault states,* not because the law had changed, but because they were included in a catalog of no-fault jurisdictions assembled for a 1974 listing in an influential journal, *Family Law Quarterly.*[7] Since many early researchers relied on this listing as definitive evidence of when states adopted no-fault divorce (when in fact the law had not changed or had changed much earlier), it called into question their conclusion that changes in the law had no effect.

Two recent studies, however, using different methods of analysis independently concluded that some of the changes in divorce law did increase the divorce rate in at least some jurisdictions—and by as much as 20 percent and 25 percent.[8] At least one researcher found that no-fault divorce increased the divorce rate among certain families with children, in particular.[9]

Which legal changes appear to have the most effect? Apparently changes in timing, such as reducing waiting periods. When divorce is made quick and easy, as well as nonjudgmental, more marriages fail. Such has also been the experience in Canada, as one researcher noted, "After falling for several years the [divorce rate] rose to an all-time high following passage of the Divorce Act of 1985, which allows divorce after one year's separation, regardless of the cause."[10]

The bad marriage and the good-enough marriage are not always static or easily distinguished things. Many, if not most, marriages fall on hard times, go through bleak periods, and endure angry interludes. Like old age, marriage is not for sissies. But when law encourages the urge to flee, more marriages suddenly "irretrievably break down." As one man put it, "I believe I got a divorce too quickly and too easily. Our state has a no-fault divorce law, so we were able to end a seven-year marriage in less than four months. Now I really wish we had worked harder to save it."[11]

The sudden collapse of marriage is not a historical inevitability. It is not merely the result of blind social forces that we do not understand and over which we have no control. To a much greater extent than most social critics have been willing to acknowledge, a 50 percent divorce rate is something we do to ourselves, to each other, and to our children.

Try this thought experiment: What would happen if courts treated property and business contracts as we now treat the marriage contract? What if American law refused to enforce business contracts and indeed systematically favored the party that wished to withdraw, on the grounds that "fault" was messy and irrelevant and exposed judges and attorneys to unpleasant acrimony? What if property were viewed, as marriage increasingly is, as a strictly private matter, so that when disputes arose, thieves and owners would be left to work things out among themselves, because after all, one cannot legislate morality? If the corporation were required to operate on the same legal principles that govern our marriage laws, the economy would collapse. It is not surprising that under the same regimen, marriage is on the verge of doing just that.

Today all of us are children of divorce, however happy our own or our parents' marriage. We have seen what happened to an aunt, a neighbor, a brother, or a friend. People are afraid to invest in a relationship in which they know from hard experience what the law teaches: The one who leaves, wins.

The law now treats divorce as a private decision, the unilateral lifestyle preference of one partner. But divorce is not merely a private problem because marriage is not solely a private good. Those who remain securely married provide enormous benefits to society, for which society need never directly pay, while those who abandon wives and children create an enormous public burden, which we all share.

There is another, more powerful sense in which marriage is not just a private good. Although marriage confers vast benefits on those adults who enter into it, and those children who issue from it, people cannot create it for themselves. Worshipers of contract, conservative and liberal, tout the sanctity of the private agreement privately negotiated. But even in the most libertarian society, the law shapes private bargains; indeed, makes them possible. It would make no sense to crow about legal contracts in a world without the legal right to private property. It makes far less sense to talk about private marriages that are unsupported by laws binding parties to their promises. It makes still less sense to do so when children appear, whose consent to the deal was never asked.

In *Man and Superman*, George Bernard Shaw wrote: "Nothing is more certain than that in both [America and England] the progressive modification of the marriage contract will be continued until it is no more onerous nor irrevocable than any ordinary commercial deed of partnership."

He was wrong. In America we have diluted the marriage contract until it is much less binding than the average business deal. Marriage is one of the few contracts in which the law explicitly protects the defaulting party at the expense of his or her partner.

The semblance of marriage, its outward forms and ceremonies, continues because, as Mary Ann Glendon put it, the kind of marriage imagined by our current laws is not the only kind of marriage imagined by our people. Other stories of loyalty and devotion, of commitment and courage, of the wild daring leap of faith implied in binding oneself to another human being for life remain—camouflaging the stark, brutal invitation to faithlessness contained in our marriage laws. Our erotic ties remain much stronger than the weak words of contract the law leaves us to describe.

Yet slowly, inexorably, the story contained in the law is becoming the dominant story our culture has to tell about marriage. Because, for an increasing number of people, the story contained in the law has become the story of their lives.

The very least a free society must do is offer us an option to marry. In creating the marriage relation, society gives us an opportunity we cannot create for ourselves. Love cannot create marriage. A family generates affections, but affections alone cannot generate a family. What makes family ties unique is that they are not merely voluntary, as friendships are. Families are places where love binds itself, where it freely chooses to set aside choice. Your lover is your lover only as long as you both love. But your brother is still your brother, even if you don't like him very much. A father must provide for his son, even if he considers him a snot-nosed punk.

Marriage is not merely a "public affirmation of love," as so many like to say. If it were, there would be no need or reason for it to be a legal or public institution. Lovers throughout history have publicly affirmed their love in various ways, from exchanging locks of hair to running off to Monaco. What makes marriage the ultimate declaration of love is that it is risky: We pledge our lives, fortunes, and sacred honor to another human being. Thanks to no-fault divorce we can now do so *safely*, with two fingers crossed behind our backs.

Many fine and important relationships are created by private feelings. Through affection, people become friends, comrades, and lovers. And it is a great thing to have a friend, a comrade, a lover. But none of these relations is marriage.

Marriage exists not to punish people but to help them transform love from a fleeting emotion into a permanent bond.

To re-create marriage we must rethink our approach to the law of marriage. The old marriage contract, we are told, was oppressive. But imagine if today's marriage licenses set down the new contract state legislatures have written for us, warning that marriage is a strictly temporary relation that neither party can depend on. If we were handed this new marriage contract, how many of us would sign? Is this what we want in marriage? Is this what we mean when we say "I do"?

People enter marriage with a variety of expectations. For many, children, family, and the future may not be at the top of the list. But while men and women are entitled to proclaim their love and not make a family, they are not entitled to demand that society restructure the institution of marriage to suit the fancy of lovers while destroying the foundation of families. Couples who define marriage as long-term intimacy don't need a piece of paper; their own hearts must show them the way. Two unrelated individuals who wish to create a new family do need the law; indeed, they need all the resources that history, tradition, law, and religion can provide. They need the right to surrender the rights of lovers and take up the heavier and much richer burden of lasting, committed love.

12

THE CULTURE
of COURTSHIP

THE SEXUAL REVOLUTION IS OVER. Sex won.

Or did it?

Sex is everywhere—in movies, TV, advertising, novels, college campuses, and grade school classrooms. A whole generation of adults only dimly remembers a time when young men and women were embarrassed to admit to their parents they were having sex outside of marriage. Though their dreams of a new political order proved utopian, kids of the sixties were remarkably successful in swiftly overturning the sexual mores of a millennium.

From 1963 to 1975 the proportion of adults who believed that sex outside of marriage was wrong dropped from 80 percent to 30 percent (before rebounding somewhat to 46 percent by the mid-eighties).[1] And yet everywhere, despite the widespread acceptance of premarital sex, cohabitation, and the growing respectability of adulterous liaisons (witness Jackie O, American princess, and Marla Maples Trump, media queen), many American women betray signs of unease with the new sexual order.

Free sex is everywhere; free love remains more elusive. Anita Hill tapped a deep vein of resentment in women from all parts of the political spectrum. We call it *sexual harassment,* and we believe our only objection is that it interferes with women's careers. But many women have responded most fiercely to a remembered sense of sexual helplessness, a sense of becoming sexual prey. Naomi Wolf's *Beauty Myth,* which bemoaned the pressures on women to be sexually attractive, struck a responsive chord and was a runaway bestseller. Her next book, *Fire with Fire,* a virtual recantation, flopped. Feminists like Andrea Dworkin and Catherine MacKinnon joined forces with Christian fundamentalists to wage war against pornography, against indiscriminate male lust.

In one Atlanta school 84 percent of teenage girls, when asked what they most wanted from sex education, begged for adult advice: How does one say no without hurting someone's feelings? Meanwhile, plaintive self-help books like *Women Who Love Too Much* made it clear that even many educated sophisticated American adult women would do anything, take anything, accept anything from a man in exchange for love.

What is sex? What does it mean? What place does it fill in our lives? Sexual revolutionaries would have us believe that sex is just a pleasure.

It never was true, even for the revolutionaries. In the sixties sex outside of marriage was a political act, a wild declaration of generational independence, a statement of existential freedom, a rejection of the bonds of centuries. A generation later, sex no longer packs this punch. The taboos have crumbled the revolution is over. We haven't yet come to terms with picking up the pieces. The old certainties are gone. But no satisfying new answers to questions about the meaning and purpose of sex have emerged to fill the vacuum.

Although close to half of all Americans continue to believe that sex outside of marriage is wrong, the old religiously based vision of sex's place in life has nonetheless been firmly shunted to one side, reduced to cultural marginality. Those who attempt to bring the old sexual values to bear in the public arena—in their schools and communities—are relentlessly stigmatized as religious zealots who are old-fashioned and out of touch with today's youth. At worst, they are fanatics; at best, old fogies. Their sexual values are no longer considered realistic or desirable by most educators, judges, and journalists. In short, the old religious sexual values are no longer *respectable.*

By the early nineties the most influential discourse on sex was taking place between the traditional Left and the new Left: between allegedly "neo-Victorian" feminists such as Andrea Dworkin and Catherine MacKinnon who believe that much of sex is coerced, and a new group of mostly younger feminists who want to shout from the rooftops that sex is good, more sex is better, and sex without a lot of depressing moralizing political ideology thrown in is best of all. *Esquire* magazine recently lumped together this group of mostly younger women as "do-me feminists."

Neo-Victorian feminists like to think of themselves as champions of the oppressed, speaking for women brutalized by unrestrained male sexuality. Do-me feminists prefer to think of themselves as *feminist fatales,* wild women daring to do what no woman has done before—which they seem to believe means having lots of sex and talking lots about it. As Naomi Wolf put it, "It's up to us to saturate the airwaves with our millions of erotic truths."[2]

The poles around which this respectable sexual debate revolves— intellectually, legally, morally, and culturally—are Andrea Dworkin's infamous dictum, "All intercourse is rape," and Wolf's, "We need sluts for the revolution."

In other words, the main question about the nature of sex and its role in the good life is, as *Esquire* put it: "When *Hungry Girl* fanzine asserts 'SLUT. Yeah, I'm a slut. My body belongs to me. I sleep with who I want,' is that 'sexual empowerment' or an unwitting expression of 'patriarchal colonization'?"[3]

This stunted sexual dialogue makes it even more difficult for many women to express, even to themselves, their own profound sexual alienation. This surely is one reason the language of rape is frequently being introduced, by and on behalf of women, to express a sense of violation for which we have lost any other language. It was a crucial achievement of the sexual revolution to replace the language of love in sexual relations with the rhetoric of contract. Henceforward, the culture declared, no sex act could be wrong as long as it was a voluntary transaction between mentally competent adults. As the renowned sexologist William Masters (of Masters and Johnson) put it, our prevailing sexual ethic "is that any sexual practice taking place in private between consenting adults is acceptable."[4]

In other words, if it's not rape, it's not wrong. And so some women, struggling to find words to express the sense of violation in becoming, in the act of love, an object of use, essentially reversed the formula: It feels wrong, so it must be rape.

They are right about the violation but are wrong in allowing sex to be circumscribed by the language of contract and consent, language unequal to either the power of sex or the pain of modern women. Since the sexual revolution, to talk about sex and to be taken seriously (that is, to be *respectable*), you have to adopt one of two positions: either the sexologist or the pornographer, the rationalist or hedonist, Dr. Ruth or Hugh Hefner. The goal of sex is either personal development or pleasure. Either way, in either view, the aim of sex is the self.

Some feminists have tried to escape this mundane dichotomy, insisting, as Andrea Dworkin has written, that "sexual intercourse is not intrinsically banal."[5] But because orthodox feminism is also a creature of the sexual revolution and because its central theme is a relentless search for autonomy and independence, it too has succumbed to this central debilitating delusion that all sex is essentially masturbatory.

The effects of this stunted conception of sex can be seen and felt everywhere, but especially in the changes in our "culture of courtship," the rituals and customs by which people come to be married. We do not think very much about the culture of courtship today, probably because the customs by which people do come to be married now occur almost accidentally. In contrast to almost all previous civilized societies, which have had a courtship culture whose acknowledged and indeed designed purpose was to produce enduring marriages, the sexual culture in which young men and women are initiated today is deeply hostile to erotic love, and so to marriage. The new sexual culture (one can hardly call it a culture of courtship) is governed by the perspective of adolescent males (whose experience of sex is primarily masturbatory), who are often deeply ignorant of even their own best interests, not to mention those of women, children, or society at large. It is deeply, profoundly, and intrinsically hostile to female sexuality. Young women raised in this culture learn that femaleness is problematic.

The sexual revolutionaries taught us there was a paradise out there—not only of pleasure, but also of exploration of sexual identity, of conquest and discovery... a whole universe of sexual meaning. But the new sexual culture taught us there is one important barrier standing between us and this utopia: the female body, which unfortunately, as an unpleasant side effect of sex, happens to produce babies. But not to worry, say teachers, sex educators, and the voices of reason, civilization, and adulthood: say, we can fix your body up so that it works just as well and is just as convenient and as free of side effects as the male body.

Sexual liberation, first and foremost, means separating sex from marriage. For women, that requires separating sex from babies. But since the care of children is one of the primary reasons for which society establishes marriage, once children are separated from sex it is extremely difficult to reattach sex to marriage when we discover that is what we want. The culture of courtship is replaced by the dating game, a permanent culture of the temporary. When that happens, an extraordinary number of women end up childless and single or in marriages that are little more secure than extended affairs.

Adult society no longer conspires to marry off the young, who now must fend for themselves. This is extraordinarily difficult to do in a culture in which having a succession of temporary sexual partners is socially acceptable; indeed, it is the social norm. To let it be known one is seeking a husband is a grave *faux pas*, an unseemly expression of feminine desire in an age where femininity has become the new taboo.

Today most American women grow up repeatedly experiencing (despite birth control and legal abortion) that tiny moment of dread as the end of the lunar month draws near. Have I been caught by my body, or am I safe? The tension builds. Then, whew!—it subsides. Not this month. This month I got lucky. Again.

This little drama is a monthly reminder for us and for those men who claim to love us that pregnancy would be a disaster. Living a life in which our femaleness is our greatest enemy, we live in fear that our bodies will betray us, and him, and the limits of the love we make.

What effect does this tiny, dreary epiphany, repeatedly experienced and repeatedly shoved aside, have on today's young women? What happens when for years female sexuality and maternity have been shrouded with anxiety, objects of fear? With experience, women learn to separate themselves from their troublesome bodies, their plague, their cross. In this alienation from our bodies, we are schooled to think of ourselves and our sexuality in strictly male terms (men being the barren sex), an education almost as narrow and constricting as the haute Victorian tendency to insist that well-bred young women had no sexual feelings at all.

The consequence of this sexual reeducation may not be felt until many years later, when women are surprised and disturbed by the intensity of their maternal feelings and the power of their desire not to be separated from their babies. Unprepared women find themselves unable to give themselves or their babies what they most long for: time together, the brief precious period of union, the culmination of eros— before the ways of the world and the separation of identity begin to drive the inevitable wedge between mother and growing child.

Unprepared, they may not look for men willing to support them as mothers, even temporarily. They may find themselves unable to ask for male support after years of preaching strict androgyny to boyfriends and husbands. Or they may have made large financial commitments, such as buying a house, based on a two-worker income that they cannot now easily afford to reduce even temporarily for those few fleeting months between birth and childhood.

Today men's and women's early romantic experiences ill-prepare them for marriage. They no longer learn to assess their romantic partners as possible marriage partners. Women, like men, require less from a sex partner than from a spouse, and thus, in their formative years, young men's and women's sexual episodes lead them astray. Men learn that nice guys don't get the girl. They learn to believe the androgynous lessons their girlfriends constantly throw up at them, lessons that serve well in young adulthood. But these lessons strip women of power and choices inside of marriage, relentlessly force women out of the home, family, neighborhood, and community so they can devote most of their energy instead to the corporation, which will support them if their husbands or lovers will not.

By age fifteen, one-quarter of all girls have had sex; by seventeen, one-half had. And yet, 83 percent of sexually experienced urban teens said the best age for first intercourse was older than the age at which they actually began.[6] In a 1986 Harris poll, 73 percent of girls and 50 percent of boys said social pressure was one reason teens did not wait to have sex. The partners of girls who first have sex in their teen years are, on average, three years older than the girls themselves, which in the case of the fifteen-year-old girls would make their partners young adult males. In 9 percent of the cases, the girls' first sex partner was twenty-three or older. Of white girls under the age of fourteen who were no longer virgins, two-thirds were forced to have sex.[7]

Why are young people, especially girls, launching into sex too early? The answer is not merely biological. Teenagers have always had hormones. At least some of the research showed that the onset of sexual maturation (which varies considerably among individuals) had very little effect on when kids began their dating career; social pressures, not biological ones, determined when kids started dating, and early entry into dating was strongly related to early entry into sex.[8] And although teen boys' sexual desire and behavior may be strongly affected by hormone levels, for girls it seems that though hormones influence their level of sexual desire, their behavior is determined not by raging biology, but by social context.[9]

Teenagers, especially teen girls, are begging for adult authority and direction on sex. What they get instead is insistent sexualization, not just from their peers, or Madonna, or the consumer culture, but from alleged voices of reason as well—from experts and from schools. The people who indoctrinate young men and women in the new, stunted, and imprisoning culture of sex are not just pop culture icons; they are the schoolmarmish voices of authority.

There is both an official and an unofficial sex culture. The former is embodied in sex and "relationship" experts. The latter exists in story and song—movies, television, and music. The difference between them is this: The unofficial sex culture teaches young men and women that sexual desire is an uncontrollable passion. The official culture teaches that sex is an appetite and therefore capable of being rationally directed toward the goals of appetite: maximizing pleasure and minimizing pain.

Like all moralizers, the doyens of the contemporary sex culture paint pretty pictures for the young in bright primary colors. The National Guidelines for Comprehensive Sexuality Education published in 1991 by SIECUS, a leading sex education group, recommended teaching youngsters this about sex: "Adults kiss, hug, touch, and engage in other sexual behavior with one another to show caring and to share sexual pleasure."[10]

Oh, really?

This is a sexual ideology as prudish in its own way as the Victorians': a cleaned-up, truncated, prettied-up, shallow, *adulterated* version of sex fit for children or talk-show hosts. There is no hint here of any of the deep reality of eros, of its grandeur or cruelty, ecstasy, longing, or the humiliation of losing oneself in another human being.

Nor is there any hint that men and women "engage in sexual behavior" for any bigger or smaller reason than pleasure. No hint of the terrors of loneliness, or the urgency of lust, or the need to prove one is a man or a woman, or the even more urgent desire to break through the bounds of flesh, to give oneself, to take another. No hint of passion, or love, or frailty, or longing, or hatred—no hint of the moral and emotional intensity that gives sex the power to create and to destroy.

Under the mistaken impression we are making girls and boys more "comfortable" with sex, adults now teach the young that sex can be safe, that Eros is a tame god; thus, they have released youngsters to face the onslaught of sex with no protection. For many, the result is very uncomfortable indeed. Girls who should be worrying about their math exams are worrying about sexual performance and sexual compliance (who will love me if I am not good in bed?), pregnancy, disease, and abandonment. By the time these girls get to college, they do not believe that sex is a sacred act of union, the making of love, nor even a simple pleasure, like chomping into a good steak (what fool could believe that?). Instead many believe, as they have been taught by the new AIDS abstinence curriculum, that sex equals death.

Why is it that girls' academic confidence, previously as high as boys, begins to plummet after junior high school? If gender bias were the answer, then girls in second grade ought to feel just as oppressed and as awkward and uncertain as high school sophomores. It is far more likely, however, that girls are responding to the fierce sexual pressures unleashed not just by puberty, but by a society in which adults are no longer willing to take the trouble to provide moral and emotional guidance and create sound social mores for teenagers. In the name of some bizarre rite of sexual liberation, American girls are being thrown naked into the sexual marketplace, where the only rule is *caveat emptor.*

Parents are strongly discouraged by authorities from trying to interfere too much with their children's sex lives. In New York City, for example, a pamphlet paid for with federal dollars and distributed in some New York City public schools outlined a sexual "bill of rights" for teenagers, including, "I have the right to decide whether to have sex and who to have it with." Parents, as John Leo notes, "were surprised to learn that all children had the inalienable right to sleep around, and wondered who, exactly, had bestowed it."[11]

Parents who seek to reestablish the connection between courtship and marriage, even in the gentlest form, get a rude comeuppance from expert opinion, which is virtually unanimous in insisting that the good parent is "nonjudgmental" about sex.

Sometimes parents who try to pass their sexual values on to their children are openly scoffed at. At a recent school board meeting, a mother stood up to voice her objections to the condom education program. "Parents like you are the reason we need this program," she was told abruptly.

More often this opposition to parents' authority is cloaked in conservative rhetoric.

A Holbrook, Massachusetts, mother writes in anguish to Dear Abby that her fourteen-year-old daughter had just confessed she had been having sex for more than a year. "Everyone I talk to about it sympathizes, but they tell me that this is how it is nowadays—most youngsters 13 and 14 are having sex." (Actually, as mentioned, one-half of all seventeen-year-old girls are still virgins.)

Dear Abby sympathizes too, but tells her only: "You, as the parent, must educate your daughter and help her set limits and make wise choices." But above all, "Please don't be judgmental."[12]

One of the experts' favorite clichés is that, since parents cannot restrain their teens' sexual activity, the best they can do is be supportive and help the kids avoid or escape some of the consequences of sex. The power of sex makes this plausible, but the experts are mistaken: Talking to your children can influence their sexual behavior—depending on what you say. Parents who are most successful at keeping their teens off the sexual merry-go-round are those who are "moderately strict." Teens who perceive their parents as "too strict" have somewhat higher levels of sexual activity, whereas (unsurprisingly) kids whose parents are the least strict are the most sexually active.[13] Parents with traditional sexual values who talk to their teen daughters succeed in discouraging sexual activity, while daughters of more liberal parents and daughters of traditional, silent parents are more likely to have sex.[14]

Cultural and community attitudes have a profound influence on teens' behavior, even under otherwise adverse circumstances. A 1989 survey of inner-city youths in New York City found, even in these poor neighborhoods, that only 30 percent of young Hispanic women were sexually active compared to 71 percent of young black women. In similar testimony to the power of culture, a 1987 survey of college students found that Mexican American students were more sexually conservative in their attitudes toward premarital and extramarital relations than their Anglo counterparts.[15] Despite the allegedly irresistible power of peer culture, one study of Canadian college students discovered that the "sexual permissiveness" of parents was far more influential in determining whether young people would cohabitate than the attitudes of their peers.[16]

Yet most parents and other adult community leaders have bowed in submission to the authority of the sex experts, or they have merely despaired. Now-discarded social customs, such as forbidding dating until age sixteen or later, insisting on double-dating, separate—rather than coed—sex education classes, and even separate-sex schools, were part of a concerted effort on the part of parents and the community. They hope to delay the onset of sexual pressures until children were closer to marriageable age (or at least adulthood), to protect girls and admonish boys, and to reassure both that sex had a human place and a human meaning, that these urgent impulses threatening to overwhelm them were not senseless, random outbreaks of appetite or insanity, but a call to love—a desire they might ultimately fulfill and find fulfilling and fruitful in all senses of the word.

Today all too many parents have abandoned any attempt to create a cultural meaning for sex and thus regulate the sexual behavior of teens. When sex educators insist on coed sex classes and graphic sex education films to replace those boring textbooks, parents and the community obediently comply—as obediently in wealthy as in poor neighborhoods, and sometimes more so. In some affluent urban neighborhoods, young teens are inviting each other to coed slumber parties—why wait for college to enjoy coed dorms? Parents, uneasy and perplexed, go along out of an unconscious desire to obey the baby boomers' great unwritten commandment: *Thou shalt not be uncool.*

They have failed, of course, these ever-rational sex experts, to make sex into what they pretend it is. (Do they believe it? Can any man or women really believe it?) Most sex education programs do not succeed even in their stated goal of reducing teen pregnancy.[17] Pregnancy and disease rates have risen along with sex education everywhere. In the rural backwaters of Arkansas, after years of Joycelyn Elders' sex tutelage, the teenage pregnancy rates rose significantly.[18] In swank suburbs such as Falmouth, Massachusetts, after the 1991 adoption of the most "progressive" sex education curriculum, the number of babies born to teenage mothers jumped almost 30 percent in one year.[19] Ellen Hopkins, a journalist who interviewed sex educators for *Parents* magazine, discovered that, "other than those who teach in abstinence-based programs, none of the educators interviewed for this article could provide proof that their programs were keeping teenagers healthy and chaste (or, at the very least, childless)."[20] "Asking if sex education *works* is almost a meaningless question," explained Martha R. Roper, a sex educator from Manchester, Missouri. "We didn't develop our course with the purpose of reducing teen pregnancy," maintains Robert Selverstone, Ph.D., who teaches sex education in a Westport, Connecticut, high school. "We are trying to promote healthy sexuality in young people by giving them the skills they need to help them make responsible sexual decisions."

The official sex culture seeks to rationalize sex by reducing it to a manageable appetite. Only by "breaking through fantasy and emotional barriers," as two sex educators recently put it, and putting students through a series of "rational... behavior sequences" offering "negotiating skills" and "explicit scripts," will young men and women be brought to a state of sexual health.[21] In Falmouth, the program emphasizes "sexual decision-making skills" and "information," according to the school health coordinator Helen Ladd—part of the rationalist fantasy about sexual hygiene.[22]

This peculiarly American attempt to tame Eros, to demote him from a god to a kind of domestic good-luck charm, has a very old lineage in American thought that stretches back to the progressive sexual hygiene movement of the Victorian era. Nineteenth-century feminists sought "to rationalize sexual desire, to detach it from an excessive individualism, to domesticate it, to make it harmless and beneficent."[23] Most nineteenth-century sexual hygienists, however, sought to tame Eros by restraining sexual desire—teaching men sexual restraint and consideration for their wives. We, on the other hand, prefer the Oscar Wilde approach: The best way to get rid of temptation is to give in to it.

The official, sanitized sex culture has nevertheless failed to tame the unofficial sex culture in which teens actually participate. It is easy to see why. However irrational, episodic, and degraded the teen sex culture may have become, it is not nearly so degraded as that of the sex experts. The unofficial sex culture at least acknowledges the power of sex, though it fails to create for it a story or an end to give it meaning. However degrading the unofficial teen sex culture may be, it does not urge kindergartners to yell "penis" and "vulva" in school or pretend to teach fourth and fifth graders about sex by having them unroll condoms onto bananas. By the seventh grade the official sex culture is prepping young girls for their future love lives by having them rehearse shouting "No Glove, No Love!" on the first date. Even so-called conservative abstinence curricula, capitalizing on the AIDS scare, tend to promote not sexual virtue, but sexual fear.

Dana Mack visited one health issues class on the subject of date rape. After viewing a scary dramatization of date rape, students were asked what "attitudes" might lessen their risk of being raped.

"Never be alone with a boy?" one wiry brunette girl suggested tentatively.

"Bring a gun on dates," ventured a red-haired, freckle-faced fourteen-year-old girl.[24]

Through most of human history, and in our own culture until quite recently, courtship bore some relationship, however fragile, to marriage. Today, we no longer court each other for marriage; instead, we court each other for sex. Marriage is what may happen if the relationship "works out." To separate courtship from marriage in this way is to sever sex and love, because marriage is the incarnation of sexual love. All other attempts at commitment are limited, wrapped in self-protective mental reservations: I may love you but I'll keep myself separate from you.

Marriage is the embodiment of sexual love because it attempts to create a true union, to make sex not about the self, but about the joining of two selves. The new culture of courtship is not only indifferent, but also deeply hostile, to marriage. The lesson it insistently teaches is that we should believe in love. Looked at long distance, from the vantage point of marriage, dating and mating is a repeated exercise in failure, a training ground for learning how not to love too deeply or at too great a cost. In the dating and mating version of love we learn to hedge our bets. We learn, subconsciously yet inevitably, what our divorce courts now teach more explicitly: The one who leaves first, wins.

Stephen Carter, author of the 1987 bestseller *Men Who Can't Love*, in 1994 published a sequel, *He's Scared, She's Scared*, about women's new inability to take the plunge into marriage. "Commitment terror," he calls it. Diane Zelcher, thirty-two, knows about commitment terror. She dreamed of love and marriage and a house in the suburbs and babies, but when her boyfriend proposed, she panicked: "I felt something pressing against my heart, almost like a door slamming on the rest of my life," she says. "I didn't want to lose my newfound love, but the pangs of doubt refused to go away. Finally I had to say good-bye just to save my sanity."

At support groups around the country, Carter claims, more and more women doubt they'll ever be able to bring themselves to say "I do." "Now the first generation of children of divorce is coming of age, and young women are questioning seriously the value of marriage as an institution." Therapists, says clinical psychologist Nancy Molitor, are treating an increasing number of women for behaviors characterized as "intimacy problems": women who choose inappropriate or unavailable men and conclude "all men are jerks."

In part these young women's fear of marriage is probably due to the spectacle of their parents' divorces. Yet their own experience in the dating culture is at least as discouraging. "I never thought I'd still be single at thirty," says Nicolette Barber. "But so many of my relationships have ended in disaster that I've all but given up."[25] Young women who eschew marriage and become unwed mothers have far more negative attitudes about relationships with men, attitudes born of their observation of their parents' troubled marriages (they are disproportionately children of divorce), but also of their own repeated experience of sexual exploitation. Stephanie Schamess, who studied teenage unwed moms, noted that "girls reared by single mothers are significantly more likely to become sexually active in their teens than are those raised by two parents," and that, longing for their absent fathers, these girls become "particularly vulnerable to involvement with men who would treat them badly."[26]

Even men and women from good families become schooled in the art of putting down shallow emotional roots. With time we learn that love, which at first seemed omnipotent, is easily overwhelmed—by time, distance, anger, boredom. We become timid, half-hearted lovers because we cannot stand being taken in, being taken advantage of. In the dating culture, fear triumphs over love.

The ultimate expression of this new erotic timidity is cohabitation. This may come as a surprise to the modern, sophisticated young woman who often views getting a man to move in with her as a superlative proof of love. At last he's taken the plunge, he's committed, though exactly to what is necessarily left vague and open-ended. Spelling it out in black and white (as in, say, a marriage contract) might make closing the deal impossible.

Over the past generation, cohabitation has become more bourgeois than bohemian. Between 1970 and 1991, the number of cohabitating couples jumped from 500,000 to 3 million, a 600 percent increase. As of 1988, although only 5 percent of women ages fifteen to forty-four were currently cohabitating, one-third of all young women had done so sometime in the past. Nearly one-quarter of white women and one-third of black women had lived with their first husband before marriage.[27]

The widespread emergence of cohabitation is, in one sense, a refutation of the hedonist dictum that sex is merely about pleasure. Quite apart from all social pressures and institutions, human beings continuously struggle to make a story out of sex. They do not want to experience their sexuality as a mere promiscuous appetite. They seek relations in which this most urgent drive has a meaning, preferably the meaning of love. Quite apart from religious command or moral principle, men and women seek to make sex an act not just of pleasure, but of union. In this sense, cohabitation is evidence of an innate impulse toward marriage.

Yet cohabitation thwarts as often as it satisfies the impulse to marry. Cohabitation comes wrapped in the language of commitment, but at its core it is about anxiety, commitment with fingers crossed. In this sense, like the hedonist ethic, cohabitation seeks to reduce sex, to make it more about the self and less about the union with the other—to keep the self more contained and therefore safer. Cohabitation is what lovers do when at least one of them does not dare to marry, to love without a net. It is yet another confirmation of the triumph of fear over love—and perhaps the most destructive one.

Cohabitation is far more threatening to marriage as an institution than mere promiscuity could ever be. Merely having sex, even with a man one loves, is not at all like being married. And so premarital sex does not blur the line between marriage and unmarriage nearly as much as cohabitation. Cohabitation apes marriage and thus creates the external appearance of a union of lives without creating the internal, moral, legal, or emotional reality of such a union. The result is highly destabilizing not just for marriage as an institution, but for the young men and women who mistake a substitute for the real thing. Thus not only are most cohabitors who hope for marriage ultimately disappointed, but cohabitation itself appears to make cohabitors who do marry more likely to divorce.

This is a piece of news almost no one, not even conservative or profamily scholars, wishes to hear, so much do we want to believe that cohabitation is merely an imperfect form of marriage rather than a subversive substitute for it. Even such a prominent profamily scholar as David Popenoe recently went so far as to recommend that cohabitation be built into the social "script" for young adulthood, to discourage early marriages (likely to end in divorce) and presumably as an alternative to more promiscuous habits: "From society's viewpoint, the most important reason why people should be encouraged to marry relatively late in life is that they are more mature.... We should anticipate that many of these years of young adulthood will be spent in nonmarital cohabitation, an arrangement that makes more sense than the alternatives to it, especially living alone or continuing to live with one's family of origin." In a footnote he adds, "I am not implying, much less advocating, sexual promiscuity here, but rather serious, caring relationships which may involve cohabitation."[28]

Similarly, when New York City Mayor David Dinkins signed a bill granting live-in lovers some of the same rights as married couples, he described it as an effort to give "close and committed relationships" the same rights as "traditional" families. In the name of honoring commitment, New York City now joins a growing list of at least twenty-five other cities and counties from Seattle to Minneapolis that legally celebrate shacking up. Part of a growing trend among family experts who equate cohabitation and marriage, two researchers recently argued that the growth of cohabitation was proof that Americans were not retreating from marriage. "If we expand our notion of 'marriage' to include legal marriage and cohabitation, there has been little decline in the institution of marriage in the United States."[29]

For years, sexual rationalists argued that in a sexually free society in which sex outside of marriage was not only common but publicly approved, couples would marry for more profound reasons than mere lust and that more sexual experience would make both men and women more adept at choosing a lifelong sexual partner.

If men and women would live together before pledging themselves for life, the argument went, they would be able to choose spouses more rationally, with much more information, and the result would be longer, stronger, and more enduring and satisfying marriages. "Contrary to the thinking of traditionalists," two sex experts confidently predicted in 1989, "living together before marriage contributes to more stable relationships later on in life."[30]

We believed it. Mostly, we still do. More than 80 percent of those who plan to cohabit say living together allows couples to make sure they are compatible before getting married.[31] Even Dear Abby says so. And in December of 1994, at a National Press Club luncheon in Washington, the duchess of York, when asked what advice about men and marriage she would give her two daughters, Princess Beatrice, six, and Princess Eugenie, four, replied: "Get to know them, perhaps live with them a bit. Really get to know what's going on."[32]

It made perfect sense but it proved to be perfect nonsense. Once again we have conducted a great social experiment, and the results are in: Cohabitation not only undercuts marriage, but it also produces less stable marriages. In 90 percent of cohabitations, at least one of the sex partners expects the arrangement to end in marriage. Almost half will be disappointed.[33] William G. Axinn and Arland Thornton found that "cohabitating experiences significantly increase young people's acceptance of divorce."[34] Larry L. Bumpass and James A. Sweet found that first marriages that begin with cohabitation are almost twice as likely to dissolve within ten years: 57 percent of marriages that begin as cohabitating unions fail in that time span compared to 30 percent of all first marriages.[35] Their research confirms other studies in Sweden and Canada that find "marriages preceded by cohabitation are more, rather than less, likely to end in divorce."[36]

Washington state sociologist Jan E. Stets analyzed data on more than ninety-six hundred American households and concluded that cohabitating before marrying reduces the happiness of married couples. Stets found that married couples who lived together first had reduced relationship quality, less stability, and more disagreement, and spent less time together. Moreover, one unsuccessful cohabitation appeared to reduce the happiness of future cohabitations.[37]

The sexual rationalists were right: People learn from experience. What people learn from the experience of cohabitation, as they do from divorce but more frequently, is that love ends and lovers cannot be trusted. They define relationships as short-term commitments, and this definition often becomes self-fulfilling.

Cohabitation, the ultimate expression of the current culture of courtship, not only lowers an individual's chance of a happy marriage, but it also undermines marriage itself. Marriage is a state with privileges and responsibilities. If its privileges are gradually dissipated in the name of diversity or individual choice, and only its responsibilities remain, individuals become more reluctant to marry. When its responsibilities also begin to dissolve, then marriage itself begins to disappear. It is no accident that cohabitation emerged as a widespread phenomenon at exactly the same time marriage was being demoted from a permanent commitment, severable only for cause, to a temporary, fully revokable arrangement, terminable at will of either spouse.

Perhaps as social scientists now suggest, cohabitation can be just like marriage. But only if, as we shall see, marriage has first been demoted into something just like cohabitation.

13

THE GREAT
TABOO

STEVEN MINTZ, A DISTINGUISHED PROFESSOR of history at the University of Houston and author of *Domestic Revolutions: A Social History of American Family Life*, shares a theory with many other Americans:

> The rising divorce rate has grown out of the refusal of women and men to submit to empty, loveless or abusive marriages.[1]

Shimmering behind this simple cheerful theory of divorce is an equally widespread sentimental theory of marriage. Marriage is about love, or rather about a particular aspect of love—emotional gratification. Indeed, as sociologists Frank F. Furstenberg, Jr., and Andrew J. Cherlin recently put it, "Emotional gratification has become the *sine qua non* of married life."[2] Under our refined modern notions, marriage is an ethereal thing of the heart and soul. To bring any consideration, particularly any materialistic consideration, to marriage is a kind of secular profanation.

Thus for all our surface radicalism and openness about sex, our modern notion of marriage is as highly spiritualized, and above all as disembodied, as any Victorian's. The difference is that while the Victorians were embarrassed by sex, we heirs of Victorian culture are embarrassed by other material needs: For us, money has replaced sex as the great unmentionable in love.

If money in any way holds a marriage together, we believe, then the marriage must be bad, vulgar, cynical, untrue. The theory is so often propounded that we've come to accept it as a given. The divorce culture takes it a step further. If money is what is holding a marriage together, then it would be better to make other economic arrangements and allow the marriage to fall apart.

"For many women, greater economic independence meant that they did not have to remain in an unsatisfactory marriage,"[3] note two researchers casually, almost as an aside. "It may seem unconscionably cynical to say that wives stay in marriages because they cannot support themselves outside them, but our data show there is some validity to this,"[4] agrees another pair. "The increasing employment of women makes divorce more likely by reducing a woman's dependence on her husband's income, making it easier for her to leave an unhappy marriage," chimes in a third.[5]

Sentiments like these are routinely expressed by both pop and academic pundits in response to one of the most consistent social science findings with regard to marriage: Money matters very much indeed.

Who are the divorce prone? Three decades of research have produced a consistent answer: the socioeconomically disadvantaged. Lower education, lower income, very young age at first marriage, and broken homes are all associated with higher divorce rates.[6] In general, the more money, the more social status and the less divorce.

Poorer families are far more likely to divorce than more affluent families, with one exception: Families in which both spouses work full time are far less likely to be poor, but also far more prone to divorce than families where mothers do not work or work part time.[7]

"There has by now been an abundance of such studies relating income to divorce," notes Rutgers sociologist David Popenoe, "and nearly all have reached the same general conclusion. It has typically been found that the probability of divorce goes up the higher the wife's income and the closer that income is to her husband's."[8]

So consistent is this finding that Andrew Cherlin recently pre-dicted, "The increased labor force participation of young married women ultimately will be seen as the most important stimulus to the... [rise] in divorce after 1960."[9]

For those interested in rebuilding marriage, this fact poses something of a conundrum. On the one hand, the strong influence of economics on divorce suggests one avenue by which public policy may have helped destabilize marriage. In the past several decades, the government has acted powerfully to push women into the workforce, both by manipu-lating the tax code and child-care programs in favor of two-income fam-ilies and by extending affirmative action programs to include women. This suggests that the government might help restore marriage by reversing these policies. On the other hand, the strong preference cul-tural elites have for encouraging women to work full time, combined with the prevailing reluctance to accept that there is any legitimate rela-tion between money and marriage, leads even those concerned about the collapse of marriage to despair of making such changes.

Meanwhile, the fact that the more equal wives' and husbands' incomes, the more likely marriages are to fail, merely proves to divorce cheerleaders that those marriages ought to break up. This line of reasoning suggests that a 60 percent divorce rate is not too high, but far too low: Many of the married mothers who work part time or not at all, this argument implies, are undoubtedly trapped in mar-riages they would dissolve if they had jobs.

Only in bad marriages, according to this common way of think-ing, might a husband's ability to offer his wife and children a good income play any role in sustaining the unions. Marriages in which money matters are presumed to be marriages that are better off dead. But marriage is a peculiar hybrid institution. Like man himself, it is part angel and part animal—an emotional union of two hearts and souls and a rather earthly and often uncomfortable junction of two bodies and two bank accounts.

Our contemporary embarrassment about money, about the material needs of love, is profoundly destructive to any attempt to create a true marriage. Perhaps all marriages should be (and certainly some marriages are) held together only by a heroic moral commitment, with no eye to gratification or reward. But given that most people are neither heroes nor martyrs, marriage as an institution will be strong only when society is arranged such that marriage holds rewards for both men and women. Marriage has a body as well as a spirit, and in a healthy society (as in a healthy individual) the body cannot be disdained or ignored or separated from or opposed to or mistaken for the spirit.

Our embarrassment about the relation of money to marriage is all the more acute because to explore it we must violate the other great taboo subject: the sex role.

Our society recoils at the very idea of sex roles. Not just the sex role as it was defined in the fifties, which many women found too confining, but the idea of the sex role itself. We rebel against any explicit attempt to create for gender a story or purpose—a socially shared meaning. We view social roles as imposed by society on people. They restrict and confine us. Sex roles, in particular, perpetuate unfair and unequal distribution of power, money, and influence between men and women. We are reluctant to acknowledge or to describe our behavior in terms of sex roles, except in a pejorative sense, as a prelude to their final abolition.

But in reality, whether they know it or not, people like roles in life for the same reason they are drawn to them in movies, sitcoms, novels, plays, and even sporting events: Without roles, there can be no plot. Artists, intellectuals, journalists, academics, and sports heroes create character types and story lines that we enjoy vicariously and later use to flesh out our own life plots.

Drawing on resources and materials that culture provides, people are constantly creating, demolishing, modifying, and re-creating roles that define their lives, because roles in life—as on the stage—help transform random and chaotic experience into a story, a purpose. Without stories our lives make no sense, and thus we cannot define success, nor know how to act well or what it means to do right.

Many women who recoil at the mention of sex roles enjoy very much playing other roles: the avant-garde revolutionary, say, or the hard-driving corporate careerist, or the sexually wild woman. They may also enjoy playing more conventional roles: devoted mother, playful aunt, good neighbor, caring friend, citizen–activist.

The current intense distrust of sex roles grew out of the circumstances of a particular generation of American women, which saw both a tremendous surge in affluence and a huge increase in the number of women (and men) with college educations, at the very same time that sex roles began to take a particularly strong and, for some women, oppressive form: Just as many women acquired the money and skills to move beyond domestic pursuits, child experts began to insist that mothers be available to their children nearly constantly or risk psychological damage. Many elite women found the disparity between their desires and the range of roles offered to them too great. They rebelled, not just against the particular 1950s vision of sex roles, but against the idea of the sex role itself—which is to say against the idea that society and culture should attach any importance, or ascribe any set of meanings, to gender.

Each individual man or woman is now supposed to define for himself or herself what it means to be a man or a woman; he or she is to be the architect of his or her own sex.

When I was eighteen, such a breathtaking challenge seemed exhilarating. As I grew older, I began to suspect that we are never so deluded as when we imagine we are creating ourselves out of nothing. Such people, far from being authentic, self-made originals, are usually merely caught up in great waves of culture of which they remain studiously unaware—blinded by the sight of themselves posing as independent thinkers, while their ideas and ideals shift every five years, or ten, with every shifting current. They sail with the tide, and they never know they are at sea.

Now I wonder: Does it make any more sense to ask people to define their gender for themselves *ex nihilo* than it does to ask a man to figure out on his own—without education, apprenticeship, or direction—what it means to be a good carpenter? To be sure, such self-defined carpenters would have ample scope for personal innovation. But would their houses stand?

Social roles emerge because there are jobs that need to be done; the roles contain much of the information the individuals need to perform those jobs well. Sex roles per se came under attack when we lost the notion that sex had any important function. When sex was redefined as a recreational sideline—a hobby, like model trains or watching sports, which may have intense meaning for a private individual, but is without social significance—the notion of sex roles was redefined as an intolerably oppressive infringement of individual rights.

Sex roles are not fixed, in the sense of being unalterable. They do change in different cultures and in the same culture at different times in response to changing circumstances. Within certain limits (almost everywhere, men specialize in violence, and also in protection from violence, while women have the main responsibility for the care of babies), there is in sex a certain magnificent diversity.

But because sex is not merely a personal but a transcendent desire, because in sex the opportunities for drama are (to put it mildly) greatly magnified, because sexual culture plays such a large part in shaping the culture as a whole, because sex is *not* just a personal pastime but a social force, and above all because sex does produce babies on a regular basis, the sex role in some form regularly emerges in all cultures. Sex difference evolves but never dissolves.

Even today, at the heart of marriage is an unacknowledged exchange of sexual gifts: the promise by a man and a woman to care for each other and for any children that ensue from their union. Less so today, perhaps, than in the past, but still to an astonishing degree, in marriage men and women diversify: Women divert at least some of their energy to caring for children; men redouble their work efforts in order to permit women to do so.

Children, when they arrive in marriage, affect men's and women's work patterns differently. In general, men work more and make more after they become a father, while mothers, on average, work fewer paid hours and earn less.[10] Working fathers with children under six are more than four times as likely as working mothers to work at least fifty hours a week.[11]

Today's great sexual wage gap is not between men and women—single men and women make equivalent salaries—but between married men and singles of either sex.[12] Married men make 70 percent more than a single of either sex.[13]

What explains this huge gap? Is it merely, as some argue, that more successful men are more likely to marry? Or does marriage itself, by giving men's work a new meaning—in other words by giving men a sex role—make men more productive?[14] A recent study by economists Sanders D. Korenman and David Neumark sought to discover why "married men earn substantially more per hour worked than men who are not currently married." Married men, they found, experienced faster wage growth for the first ten to twenty years of marriage, and this growth could not be explained by location, union membership, changes in labor market experience, number of dependents, or occupation. Moreover, marriage increased "by almost 50 percent the probability of recent hires receiving one of the top two performance ratings," even after controlling for education, location, and prior experience. The researchers concluded that "marriage per se makes workers more productive" (or at least male workers).[15] Other studies have found a reverse effect for divorce: Women become more committed workers and men less committed workers in the aftermath of divorce.[16]

In recent decades, the greater amount of time women rather than men have devoted to child rearing has been construed mostly as an exercise in dependence. Marriage, according to the now-conventional wisdom, was structured to benefit men at the expense of women. Thus in 1971 Germaine Greer denounced marriage for creating "the prison of domesticity." Andrea Dworkin excoriated a system in which "every married man, no matter how poor, owned one slave—his wife." And Susan Brownmiller announced that marriage and rape were so entwined that it was "largely impossible to separate them out."[17] Jesse Bernard, a distinguished sociologist, argued with great success that there are two marriages—"his" and "hers"—and that of the two, his is much better.[18] And recently two influential experts maintained, in a typical sentiment, "With all its supposed attributes, the traditional family more often than not enslaved women. It reduced her to a breeder and caretaker of children, a servant to her spouse, a cleaning lady and, at times, a victim of the labor market."[19]

If this conventional wisdom were correct, American wives should be much happier than before. The old sex roles have been, if not abolished, at least diminished. Between 1982 and 1992 the proportion of families that met the strict test of "traditional"—married-couple families in which the husband works and the wife does not—plunged from 43 percent to 24 percent of all families.[20] In 1960 only 20 percent of all mothers with children under age six were in the labor force. Today 60 percent of mothers with young children work, at least part time.[21]

But this liberation of women from marital dependency has not increased the happiness of women, especially younger married women who are most likely to find themselves in such liberated circumstances. As noted in chapter 8, "The Bad Marriage," the percentage of younger married women who describe themselves as "very happy" has dropped dramatically. Between the early seventies and the mid-eighties, the proportion of married women ages eighteen to thirty-one who said they were "very happy" unexpectedly plummeted from 44 percent to less than 35 percent. Meanwhile, the happiness rates of single men in this age group almost tripled, soaring from 11 percent to 31 percent in the same period.

Moreover, despite the erosion of the breadwinner role, the flood of women into the workforce, the decline in patriarchal authority, and the increased risk of divorce (much of it initiated by women), the proportion of married men who say they are "very happy" has not changed at all. As Norval Glenn notes, "It appears that recent changes... have led to a distinct decline in the happiness of women, but have had no net effect on the happiness of men as a whole."[22]

Not only are marriages not happier as a result of the divorce and the gender revolutions, they are, on average, distinctly less happy for one sex—and not the sex the experts would predict. According to the data on marital happiness, it seems that we are restructuring our social institution to benefit the least productive and most dangerous element of the population—single men—at the direct expense of younger married women.

This is less surprising when we note that the recent massive influx of women into the workforce for the most part did not stem from personal choice. For some women, of course, a career undoubtedly represents a devoutly sought-after choice. But for many other women, these same statistics of rising labor force participation by young mothers are not signs of freedom and progress, but indicators of constraint and decline. For the first time in our history, regardless of their wishes, millions of middle-class married women with very young children are being turned out of the home and thrust into the marketplace.

And these stressed and distressed mothers are not a small group of women. Only one in three mothers who work full time believes she can spend "the right amount of time" with her family.[23] A majority of working mothers say they would prefer to work part time or not at all.[24] When asked whether they personally would prefer to be part of a two-earner couple or a one-earner couple, Americans opt for the one-earner couple by a margin of almost two to one—54 percent to 31 percent.[25] As Stephanie Coontz, no cheerleader of the traditional family, notes, "The percentage of women who say they would prefer to stay home with their children if they could afford to do so rose from 33 percent in 1986 to 56 percent in 1990."[26] And that preference has proved surprisingly enduring. In the most recent prestigious Roper polls, 53 percent of women said they would prefer to be at home.[27]

Perhaps it is no accident that women's love affair with the workforce ended just as working mothers ceased to be unusual. When mothers first entered the labor force in large numbers, they were doing more than holding down a job—they were advancing a revolution. The career woman was interesting and different. Professional work was a distinguishing mark, a mark of unusual ambition. Women had an intriguing new role to try out.

Today's women cannot envision their work in this exciting way— they are not transforming the world, they are pulling down a desk. And it turns out that many jobs (from computer clerk to corporate lawyer) are a lot less interesting than advertised. Like their husbands, today's working mothers do it for the money.

The usual interpretation of the higher divorce rates among two full-time working spouses is that work enables women to escape unhappy marriages. This happy explanation of the relative fragility of two-career marriages is, I think, overly optimistic. For one thing, the rise of working women has not eliminated the fundamental economics of divorce. Working women who divorce still face a substantial drop in their standard of living. After all, if you needed two incomes to make ends meet, you are unlikely to feel very happy about your standard of living with only one income.

Part of the relative instability of two-career couples may be due to self-selection: Wives with less traditional attitudes may be more likely to both work full time and divorce. But there is another explanation that has been mostly ignored: Full-time working women, especially women who are working against their wishes, may be more prone to divorce because they *get less* from marriage.

A woman at home (part or full time) who chooses divorce must give up her entire way of life. By contrast, a wife who works full time and divorces can simply continue to do what she is doing anyway. Life may get a little harder—or even a lot harder—but for a wife with a full-time job, a change in her marital status does not seem to entail a radical transformation of her day-to-day lifestyle.

It may seem odd to think of full-time working wives as *getting less* from marriage than homemakers. But there is considerable evidence that many women see it just that way. Even for many mothers who choose to work, the choice is driven not by desire, but by fear.

Elaine Stassen, a young wife who, in her late twenties, left her job to care for her infant son, is typical. Though her marriage seemed sound, she was afraid of being abandoned and so returned to graduate school to prepare herself to earn a better salary. "I got my degree so I could feel that if anything happened I could survive and take care of Jamie."[28] Work was supposed to be a route to power, autonomy, and independence. Instead, for many women like Elaine, the decision to work is increasingly impelled by a pervasive anxiety. Whatever sense of control they might gain from work, they lose from living in a society that no longer upholds and sustains marriage, a society in which their most important relationship is no longer dependable or under their control.

Not infrequently the younger women with whom I spoke were practicing a kind of "defensive" careerism, working "not because they wanted to but because they were afraid not to," comments Catherine Johnson.[29] This is just one of many unhappy synergisms driving up the divorce rate: As the divorce rate rises, more and more women, out of anxiety for their own and their children's security, choose to work. But the more women in the workplace, the more the divorce rate rises, creating a vicious cycle in which all women end up, not with more economic security, but with less and less.

Today the young woman who contemplates dropping out of the workforce to care for her own baby, even temporarily, must fight strong cultural forces that seek to keep her tied to the workplace. In the wake of our rebellion against sex roles, many husbands are no longer willing to make the sacrifices—financial or leisure time—that would allow their wives to stay at home. Sometimes the strongest objections come from the women's own mothers. "You are your only security," one mother (herself happily married for over thirty years) warned her daughter. Mothers who trusted their own husbands for many years have witnessed the changes and no longer trust their daughters' husbands to care for them.

Although the new stereotype paints housewives as bored or depressed, research literature tells a different, more complicated story. What matters most to the well-being of mothers and their children is neither working nor not working. What is important is real choice. The least depressed women are those who work because they prefer to and those who stay home because they prefer to. Conversely, the wives most likely to succumb to depression are those who are employed against their wishes or those who have no job, but want one.[30] Similarly, one of the most consistent findings of day-care research is that when women are happy to be working, kids tend to do fine; but when mothers are forced to work against their wishes, their children suffer.[31]

An inordinate fear of the 1950s' sex roles has blinded us to this simple equation: If work is to be a choice, women must have husbands willing to support them, financially or emotionally, in that choice. It is sex roles, albeit in a modified, flexible form, that set women free. When husbands are able and willing to be primary breadwinners, women have more options, not fewer. Unlike their husbands, women may choose to devote themselves to more interesting, rather than more lucrative, work. With good provider husbands, they can shape their work lives around the family if they wish, rather than being forced to make their families bow to the needs of the corporation. They can choose to devote their talents and education and energy to the rearing of their children, the nurturing of family relationships, and the building of community and neighborhood. They may even have the leisure (unknown to full-time working mothers) to cultivate artistic, cultural, and intellectual interests.

If all married mothers are all working because they want to, then there is nothing the government can or should do about it. But if middle-class, married mothers are now working because they must, new questions emerge: Why is our generation of women so much poorer than our mothers', with no choice but to work? And what, if anything, can be done about it?

14

THE BODY
of LOVE

IN 1965 CARYL BRACKENRIDGE MADE A BIT OF HISTORY: She became one of the first eight women to graduate from the Harvard School of Business.

In 1994 Brackenridge, along with her classmates, was interviewed by *Forbes* magazine. What had she been doing in the ensuing thirty years?

Rearing children mostly. Volunteering in her community. Recently she has devoted her time and expertise to the Washington Township land trust, which seeks to preserve farmland and restore an eighteenth-century grist mill.

She was not alone. Among this group of elite, ambitious women, carefully groomed for success in the corporate world, "Only two of the eight followed a traditional career path.... Most of the others, faced with the conflict between a traditional woman's role and a career, chose the former."[1]

In 1965 a woman with a Harvard MBA undoubtedly faced more career obstacles than women graduating today. But Caryl Brackenridge, like most of her classmates who faced similar decisions, expresses no regrets. "I'm not sure I didn't do more for our society than a woman who earned a salary," she says.

Michelle Turnovsky, whose own career was similarly constrained by her decision to follow her husband during his many job transfers, is similarly without bitterness. She is now a senior lecturer at the same university at which her husband is a tenured economics professor. Does it bother her that her husband has climbed farther up the career ladder? "Oh, no, not at all," she says. "I've really enjoyed taking care of my kids." Aware that her attitude is considered politically incorrect, she quietly added, "Maybe I shouldn't admit such a thing."[2]

In 1990 Maria Shriver told NBC she did not want her previous role as anchor of *Sunday Today* and NBC's weekend evening news; she asked for and got a part-time position running a series of four prime-time specials so she could spend more time with her baby daughter. Meredith Vieira asked that her part-time arrangement with *60 Minutes* be renewed; when CBS insisted she work full time, she declined to renew the contract. Connie Chung similarly asked her network to allow her to rearrange her career for family reasons.

When women like these discover that the corporate world is somewhat less enthralling than advertised, or that babies are rather more, they have a myriad of options. Some have made fortunes; most are married to men who are also Harvard School of Business graduates, or the equivalent. They can comfortably afford what is fast becoming an upper-middle-class luxury, the luxury of raising one's own children. They can enjoy what for most women has always been the greatest reward of a stable marriage (though these days we are not allowed to admit it): the opportunity to throw themselves with abandon into loving and raising their children. The loss of this greatest gift of marriage for women—the giving of which has always been for most men the deepest psychological and spiritual reward of marriage—is devastating not just to individual mothers but to the entire society, for when marriage can no longer provide the rewards for which it is most prized, then it will begin to collapse across society.

The hunger for family time is not confined to successful, prominent women. But the options increasingly are. Ever fewer middle-class women can financially afford to put their children first. It is perhaps the most common grief of American women today and the truest loss to American children. Yet to date, no prominent women's group has devoted any time, energy, or political muscle to helping women regain the choice to care for their own babies. Instead, concern for a woman's desire to mother her own children has been allowed to become a solely right-wing issue, painted by the women's movement as the preserve of alleged fanatics who want to "oppress women" or "turn back the clock."

The feminist elites steadfastly refuse to recognize a problem exists or to honestly face the solution. *New York Times* columnist Anna Quindlen, for instance, has tirelessly urged working mothers to lobby for more and better child care. She acknowledges that work is, for most mothers, not an exercise in self-fulfillment, but a financial necessity: "Few of us are working to fulfill ourselves anymore. Most women are working to fulfill the banks, the telephone company and the public utilities."[3]

Quindlen's position is typical. The recognition that more and more middle-class married mothers are forced to work continuously, against their wishes, is almost always a preface to a call for more day care—never a more radical call to restore the economic base of the American family nor to give women any choice but the one to work.

In the passage of a single generation, the average American woman has become too poor and too vulnerable to have as many children as she would like or to spend as much time as she would like raising them. The unasked question is, Why? Why is it that we, as a generation, are so much poorer than our mothers? And why is it that the economic pressures forcing young married mothers into the workplace have yet to emerge as a political problem in need of political solutions? Why has the economic strangulation of motherhood been accepted as inevitable?

Richard Easterlin has shown that if the wives' labor force participation had remained at its 1968 level, family income would have fallen about 8 percent between 1968 and 1982.[4] Over the past two decades, it appears a great many women have, against their wishes, effectively doubled their workload to produce relatively small (but perhaps crucial) increases in family income.

The distress of these women and their families, and the ensuing social costs, have been largely ignored. Instead, the flood of mothers into the workforce in the seventies and eighties has been treated for the most part as encouraging evidence of women's progress, or by the Reaganites as a wondrous reaction to supply-side tax incentives when, in many cases, it is merely a sign of the deteriorating economic position of American families. The huge increase in the labor force participation of women is, as we have seen, one of the strongest underlying forces pushing up the divorce rate. The story most experts have constructed around these statistical truths is a simple, happy Disney tale of liberation: More money has given women the freedom to leave unhappy marriages. But even if their optimistic interpretation were true, what about the 50 percent of full-time working mothers who would prefer to be working less or not at all? For these women, frustrated in their desire to devote more time to family and community life, marriage may falter precisely because it is increasingly failing to provide the benefits expected. These women's marriages are vulnerable, not because they now have more choices, but because they have fewer. Thanks to the deteriorating economic conditions, millions of American women and their families are simply getting far less from marriage than they want, need, or deserve.

Rather than addressing the economic decline of married mothers and their families, social policy has focused—determinedly and single-mindedly—on a different goal: equalizing the earnings of men and women. The stagnation of men's wages has been viewed not as a social problem but almost as a blessing because it has allowed women to achieve something closer to statistical parity with men.

Statistical parity is less liberating in real life, however, than it appears in theory. If women could buy their way out of the feminization of poverty with their labor, then African American women should now be no more likely to be poor than their male counterparts. For although a racial gap remains between the wages of black and white Americans, the gender gap between the wages of black men and women has been erased. Since about 1940, the proportion of black single women who work has remained fairly stable. Among those who do work, however, "black women's wages have risen dramatically relative to those of black men."[5] Between 1947 and 1984, the median earnings of black women rose from 34 percent of the earnings of black men to 80 percent. And by 1984 black women who work full time year-round made 86 percent of what their male counterparts made. Today there is some evidence they may make more.[6]

As black women's pay approached parity with black men's, poverty ought to have become a gender-neutral phenomenon. Growing equality in the workplace ought to have produced, according to current theory, greater economic protection for women. Instead, something surprising, perverse, and unintended happened: The feminization of poverty intensified. The more women's wages approached parity with men's, the poorer women got.

From the late sixties to the early eighties, the proportion of black women with children who were poor for the long term rose from 17 percent in the years 1967–1972 to 24.2 percent in the years 1980–1985.

"Inequality grew," notes Christopher Jencks, "because fewer black mothers were married."[7]

In 1970 three out of five black women ages twenty-five to twenty-nine were married and living with their spouses. By 1987 only one out of three black women in that age group were married. "Indeed, by the late 1980s, black women 25 to 29 who had never married far outnumbered married black women."[8] Those who do marry are far more likely to end up divorced because, as Mare and Winship point out, "The higher a woman's earnings and the greater her permanent commitment to the work force relative to her husband's the less likely she is to remain married."[9] Moreover, the data suggest that one of the primary reasons for this retreat from marriage was the failure of black men's wages to keep pace with rapidly increasing black women's wages. "Marriage patterns during the past two decades appear consistent with the presumption that women consider marriage only if a prospective husband earns more than some minimum threshold."[10]

Yet because of the retreat from marriage, instead of becoming more economically secure as they became more statistically equal wage earners, black women became rather less so. Because of declining male wages and, even more, because of the decline in marriage, the average black teenage girl who (as President Clinton would put it) "played by the rules"—did not have an out-of-wedlock birth while a teenager and graduate from high school—experienced a precipitous drop in future income compared to her counterpart a generation earlier. Around 1970, the girl who played by the rules would find herself, at age twenty-five, enjoying a family income of $26,000 a year (in constant dollars). By the early eighties, that same girl playing by the same rules would, at age twenty-five, enjoy a family income of just under $18,000, a drop of 30 percent.[11]

Equal pay for equal work is simple justice: When men and women work at the same job, they should receive the same wages. But historically, men and women do not work the same jobs. Men who are the primary support of families place a higher premium on wages; they avoid jobs that, however powerful or prestigious, do not produce high incomes.

Women's labor force patterns are more complicated and less uniform. Women tend to cluster in occupations that more easily combine with mothering; they enter teaching or nursing or computer programming because it is possible to work part time, part of the year, or from the home. Other women make different choices—different from family-centered women, and different, too, from men. Take, for example, two glamorous, influential professions: publishing and television. A generation or two ago both were heavily male. But lately, both publishing and entry-level television reporting, where jobs bring low salaries and long hours but interesting and potentially influential work, are becoming almost entirely female professions, populated by eager Ivy League and Seven Sisters grads who are seeking access to power and fame perhaps, but consider money optional. "In entry-level positions in television," Don Fitzpatrick, head of a national television reporter headhunting company told the *New York Times*, "it's 9.5 women for every 0.5 men."[12]

Even ambitious young women demonstrate that for them money matters less than it does to their male colleagues. Among well-educated professionals a woman who makes only a moderate salary is not for that reason any less attractive as a dating or marriage prospect. But a man who makes little money is less sexually attractive as a potential mate—a fact of which men are very much aware. High male wages are an erotic attraction for many reasons, among them the fact that well-paid men are more personally and sexually confident. But high wages attract potential wives also because it is male labor—men's willingness to serve as the primary breadwinner for their families—that gives women choices, whether the choice is to stay home with their children or to choose interesting, rather than lucrative, work.

If the new economic strains on the family were the result of chance or inescapable economic forces, then the narrow array of options promoted by orthodox feminists—subsidized day care or a six months' parental leave—might be the best we could hope for. But to a large degree the economic pressures ripping apart families and women's lives are the result of government action, or inaction, on two fronts: falling male wages and rising taxes on families.

For the first time in American history, a whole generation of men is making less than their fathers did. From the fifties to the early seventies, the income of full-time male workers grew steadily: Between 1955 and 1973 (when men's wages peaked), men's income jumped by nearly two-thirds, rising from $17,000 to $28,500 (in constant 1985 dollars). Suddenly, the growth in men's wages stopped and launched into a gradual decline, dropping to $25,000 a year in 1980. By 1985, writes David T. Ellwood, "the income of the typical full-time male worker was below the level it had been in 1970."[13] The averages disguise an even greater drop for younger men—the emerging generation of husbands and fathers. Between 1973 and 1986, as Frank Levy discovered, the average annual earnings of men ages twenty-five to twenty-nine (prime marrying years) plunged 20 percent.[14] Moreover, the evidence suggests the drop in male wages has yet to bottom out. A 1994 study by the Center for National Policy found that over the past decade men's median pay dropped by about 5 percent.[15] The most recent data show that even college-educated men, who were previously immune, are beginning to experience the same decline. Between 1989 and 1993, according to an Economic Policy Institute report, the median wage of a college-educated man fell at the same rate as that of a high school graduate. Since 1990, even the earnings of men with postgraduate degrees have begun to fall slightly.[16]

And yet, with so many people preoccupied with illusory statistical equality, this ongoing drop in male earning capacity has sparked hardly a political protest. As astonishing as the decline itself is the lack of public response to it: To date no party or ideological faction has raised the declining wages of men to the status of a serious social and economic problem deserving of a serious search for possible solutions.

Such a search would undoubtedly reveal that the decline in men's wages has many causes—some strictly economic, like the decline in blue-collar union positions and the rise in the service industry. But this decline is also likely to prove both a partial cause and a partial consequence of the decline of marriage. When women are forced into the workplace because of inadequate men's wages, marriage ties weaken and fewer marriages form. Meanwhile, men who do not marry or who divorce and do not remarry tend over time to make less money. Thus part of the decline in men's wages may be traced to men's growing unwillingness (or inability) to assume the responsibilities of marriage. Between 1970 and 1985 the proportion of white males ages twenty-four to twenty-nine who were never married jumped from 21 percent to more than 40 percent. (For black men in that age group, the proportion who never married similarly rose from about 28 percent in 1970 to 56 percent in 1985.)[17]

Cause and effect appear to run both ways, creating a vicious cycle of declining marriage rates, which brings on declining wages and marriageability, which, in turn, brings on still greater declining marriage rates. As men as a group become less able to marry and support families, they become less willing to do so as well. Marriage rates among men appear to be strongly (though not exclusively) influenced by wage rates, as two researchers recently noted: "Men's earnings... fell by 20 percent between 1972 and 1989. Marriage rates followed a roughly parallel course."[18] Mare and Winship found that a $100 increase in the weekly earnings of black men raised the odds of marriage by about 30 percent for young men ages twenty to twenty-three and by about 20 percent among older bachelors ages thirty to thirty-nine. "The employment and earnings effects for white men were remarkably similar to those for black men in every age group," they discovered. "For both races, these effects were large."[19]

Thus for younger white men the sharp drop in earnings since 1970 has produced a corresponding reluctance or inability to marry.

Over time, men who believe they are unable to support families find marriage less attractive and are less able to attract mates. Moreover, once married, they may be far less willing to support their wives and children. One-third of young men now say they would be "not at all willing" to marry a woman who lacks a good income.[20] Many of these men may be found eschewing marriage in favor of living with the ultimate inexpensive, undemanding woman: Mom.

Men and women are, as one *New York Times* reporter recently noted, "reacting very differently to the soft job market and soft marriage market."[21] In 1990, according to the Census Bureau, single men in their prime marriage years were almost 50 percent more likely than single women to be still living with their parents. Indeed, almost one-third of all single men ages twenty-five to thirty-four were still in the nest, compared to about one-fifth of single women in that age group.[22] Just twenty years ago, men and women were equally likely to spend part of their twenties living at home. Today some 45 percent of men spend at least part of their twenties living with their parents, compared to just 35 percent of women, and the gap appears to be widening.[23] Between 1980 and 1990, the proportion of all men in this age group—married and single—who lived at home jumped by half, from 10 percent to 15 percent, while over the same period the percentage of women who lived at home rose only slightly, from 6 percent to 8 percent.[24]

The men who live with Mama come in all types: divorced men on the rebound, men experiencing temporary economic difficulties, and men with long-term drug habits. One thing many have in common is that, in sharp contrast to their own fathers, they feel little pressure to become responsible family men. Faced with the shock of realizing they cannot reproduce their father's standard of living, many young men are responding by turning the paternal home into a new kind of bachelor pad, complete with maid service. The money they save on housekeeping is spent on bachelor toys that (unlike marriage and family) increase a man's status.

"I come and go as I please and dinner's always ready when I get home," says Ed Mastoloni, a $35,000-a-year financial analyst who lives with his parents in Greenwich, Connecticut. Mastoloni says he could afford to move out if he had not recently splurged on an expensive jeep and jet ski.

"Everything's always done—the laundry, the food," concurs Jeff Seaman, a deputy sheriff in Cincinnati who makes $19,000 a year. "And I drive a Corvette, not a rusted-out Ford Escort."[25]

Danny Baldassano, like many of these new bachelors-about-Mom, could afford a place of his own, but the expense would seriously cut into his lifestyle. "I could make it on my own," he says, but he'd have to cut back on his four-night-a-week pub crawls, $35 concert tickets, and $1,000 Las Vegas jaunts with friends.[26]

The fathers of these aging teenagers are often aghast. One, a San Francisco garbageman, has two sons ages twenty-five and twenty-eight still living at home. One son was recently laid off as a housepainter, the other has a drug problem. He gets infuriated when he comes home "dead tired" from a midnight shift and finds his grown sons lounging about the house. If they can't find the $18-

an-hour construction jobs they want, he says (speaking from an earlier era, when work and independence and being the head of household defined manliness), they should "wash dishes and deliver newspapers." Recently, he complained, his son bought "a Chevy muscle car instead of four-cylinder Honda," and "now he's choking on the payments."[27]

Herman Specht, supervisor of a zinc smelter, is angry at a son who returned after a divorce and job loss to live in his parents' home. "He can't keep a job and he can't keep a wife," he grumbles. "The only thing he can keep is his mother and father."

"My husband thinks back to what he was doing at that age," contributes Mrs. Specht. "He doesn't understand that the economy today isn't what it was then."[28]

When parents are divorced, the relationship between the parent and child may be less exploitive and more clearly a functional substitute for marriage for both mother and son. Eva Farris, a divorced mother, lives with her twenty-five-year-old son, Mike, an auto mechanic. Mike makes some financial contributions to the household and also does Eva's yardwork and car repair. "Plus, I run off her boyfriends on occasion," Mike says.[29]

"Moms of this generation," agrees a *Wall Street Journal* reporter, "many of them divorced, seem mostly glad to have their sons back in the fold. The guys keep them company and help out with chores men often handle, such as mowing the lawn."[30]

But this "marriage" between mother and son, while it serves the immediate needs of both, does not serve the larger social purposes of a real marriage: rearing and nurturing the next generation.

Sons "married" to divorced mothers are withdrawn from the marriage market. They feel little social pressure to become the kind of man who can support children, emotionally or financially. They have cars instead of kids, sex partners instead of wives. They are the suburban counterparts to the inner-city men who live off women on welfare: living shallow, episodic, stunted lives, unavailable to women and children, accountable to no one. Their numbers are growing rapidly as the social pressures on men to marry—and then to become the kind of man women want to marry—dwindle.

Once again a vicious cycle seems to be at work; a culture in which marriage is fragile and dangerous produces yet more young people disinclined to marry. Two sociologists who investigated "the returning young adult syndrome" identified a number of social and economic developments that fueled that trend, including "reticence to marry." Professors Allan Schnaiberg and Sheldon Goldenberg view postponed marriage as "an adaptation to rising marital disruption rates in their parents' generation, as well as among their married siblings or friends." They note: "These young adults have a good deal of experience with divorce and its costs."[31]

How do we raise boys to be dependable men, reliable husbands, and responsible fathers? A complicated question, but to start, we have to stop telling men that they are optional.

When we tell our girls that becoming a single mother—through divorce or failure to marry—is a perfectly acceptable lifestyle choice, we forget that our boys are listening too. And this is what they hear: Men aren't necessary. Women can do it alone. Women and children are usually better off without men. Breadwinning oppresses women and children. Marriage and breadwinning can be hard. Why do it, if you are only oppressing the ones you love?

So we should start by admitting the truth. Women need and want men who are capable of supporting families. Romantic love is a fine thing. We want it for ourselves and our daughters, preferably within a secure marriage. But few marriages can be secured by romantic love alone, especially when the romantic image of a strong male protector is transformed into an underemployed boy eagerly agreeing women should work overtime. The failure of men and women to care for each other, either because they are unable to do so—or because the culture has taught them they need not or should not—is a failure not just of economics but of eros. To provide for and protect, to have and to hold, are the most tangible expressions of the language of love, and the most credible. If we set up marriage or the economy (or rewrite the sexual constitution) so that men and women can no longer fulfill their wedding vows, neither love nor marriage will survive. Marriage is the *embodiment* of love, that mundane human institution that makes the imperatives of Eros, the rigorous commands of romance, sustainable by two beings who bring body as well as spirit. We cannot long sustain any venture in which body and spirit are opposed.

Once we admit that the growing inability of men to support women and families—and the damaged culture of masculinity this failure spawns—is a serious problem for women, children, and, in the long run, men themselves, what do we do about it?

Those who look for European solutions to American problems miss the point. Working American moms, like other Americans, display a characteristically American aversion to bureaucratic, centralized programs touted by experts. According to a 1993 study by the Families and Work Institute, only 29 percent of working mothers consider day care licensing to be "very important" to high-quality family child care.[32] Most will go out of their way to avoid day care altogether, often preferring to cut back on work hours or to work different shifts in order to keep the kids out of day care, especially when the children are young. Today, the majority of preschool children whose mothers work are cared for by family members, while only 23 percent are in child-care centers. Twenty percent are cared for by their fathers, 23 percent by other relatives, and almost 9 percent are cared for by the mother herself.[33] Most important, more public day care will not give women what they most want: more time for their kids, more choices for themselves.

Day care tax breaks and subsidies inevitably funnel public money exclusively to two-income families, which are, on average, considerably more affluent than one-income families. In 1990, married-couple families in which the wife worked (full or part time) had a median household income of $47,000, more than 50 percent higher than the $30,000 median income of married-couple families in which the wife did not work.[34]

Part of the reason for the ongoing self-destructive infighting between mothers who work and mothers who stay home has been created by badly designed family policies such as those that unnecessarily pit career women against both homemakers and working women who choose familial rather than market care for their children. The upper-middle-class professional woman who chooses center-based day care gets a tax subsidy. The middle-class woman at home, or the working-class woman who works nights so her husband can care for the kids, does not.

The result is family policy narrowly crafted to benefit a small, relatively affluent sector of the population. In 1988, 77 percent of the federal Child and Dependent Care Tax Credit went to families making more than $30,000 a year; 43 percent went to families making more than $50,000.[35]

Under the Bush administration, Congress attempted to remedy these inequities by expanding the earned income tax credit for working families. The result counterbalances some of the inequities of the day-care tax credit, but not consistently and not necessarily in a pro-marriage fashion. Earned income tax credits are a form of guaranteed annual income, which research has shown tends to drive up the divorce rate,[36] probably because once again such guarantees tend to make marriage seem less necessary economically (even if often breaking up, the ex-wife finds life apart much more difficult than she imagined).

Falling wages are just part of the explanation for the deterioration in men's ability to provide for families. Just as men began to make less and less, the government began to demand more and more of married families' income, dramatically shifting the tax burden away from single persons and onto families with children. The dependent exemption, which in 1948 shielded three-quarters of the average family's income from federal taxes, now protects less than one-quarter. Since 1948 the proportion of income that the average family pays in taxes has increased 800 percent. The amount the average family now loses in federal taxes would more than pay the cost of financing the average new family home.[37] In fact, the increase in the tax burden on families is so large that it dwarfs the effects of men's declining wages. Tax policy is directly in the government's control, and by simply restoring to families the tax code they enjoyed a few decades ago, the financial condition of the average family would be sufficiently altered to allow a substantial portion of working mothers to work less or not at all outside the home.

Much of the decline is due to erosion in the value of the dependent exemption, which today is worth less than one-third of what it was in 1948. But equally important and frequently neglected is the huge rise in payroll taxes that took place in the eighties, even as marginal income tax rates were being cut. Lawrence Kudlow has pointed out that, "as a result of repeated payroll-tax increases in the 1970s and 1980s, middle-class wage earners shoulder a higher tax burden today than they did in the 1960s." In fact, between 1985 and 1994 the overall marginal tax rate (income tax plus FICA, minus the earned income tax credit) for a person earning $30,000 a year jumped from 20 percent to more than 30 percent. For the $50,000 earner, the tax rate leapt from 25 percent to more than 43 percent. Thanks largely to payroll increases, and despite the Reagan tax cuts, a man earning $50,000 a year—just slightly more than the average family income—saw his after-tax purchasing power decline "a whopping 24 percent."[38]

Neither political party is doing much to restore the economics of marriage. Almost all Democratic family initiatives concentrate on helping women quickly return to the corporation, where they belong; day care tax exemptions and credits, and brief unpaid family leaves may help ambitious women facilitate their careers but do nothing to support women or their choice. Republicans support "family values" with rhetoric, saving almost all their political capital during twelve years of power for "important" causes, defined in traditional male terms: defense and individual and corporate tax rate cuts. These causes encouraged overall growth in the economy but did little to roll back the family tax burden.

Love is spirit. But we make love with our bodies. We sustain love by our bodies, by the sweat of our brow, by the pains of our labor.

Marriage thrives when men and women need each other, financially and sexually. The more we value independence over interdependence—in sex, love, or money—the more fragile and unhappy our marriages become.

Restoring the body of the love may be a simple task, but it is not an easy one. It will require a major reordering of political priorities, a new burst of energy that will happen if (and only if) married men and women begin to view themselves as a political class (as senior citizens or farmers do) and vote accordingly. Or when intellectual elites recognize that the creation and maintenance of the norm is at least as important a task as the support and sustenance of the disadvantaged.

Because as private social institutions like marriage begin to systematically fail, public institutions—from schools to the welfare office—are swamped and overwhelmed by the consequences.

15

THE DIVORCE
ADVOCATES

STROLL DOWN THE BOOKSTORE AISLE. Notice something peculiar? The catalog of words that we utter fearlessly has expanded. On the long shelf there are books about love, of course. There are books about coupling and uncoupling. There are books for children of divorce, and parents about to split up. There are sex manuals galore. There are many, many books on "relationships." Even lesbian and gay couples can get advice on everything they always wanted to know about sex, money, psychology, intimacy, and the law. The love that once dared not speak its name now won't shut up.

We can talk about anything these days. Well, almost anything. Because while there are a great number of books about how to meet your mate, or how to get rid of him, few or none will tell you what it means to be married to him. Everywhere there is advice for "partners" and "couples." Husbands and wives, on the other hand, may have ceased to exist. Marriage has all but dropped off the bookshelf, to say nothing of the magazine rack and the checkout counter.

The trouble started not in the pop-psych section of the bookstore, but in the academic literature. More than two decades ago Jesse Bernard, an influential sociologist, was already looking forward to the time when marriage would be but one ill-defined subset of a much broader category: "relationships." She predicted, "We may one day arrive at the idea not of an all-or-nothing marital status, or an either-or one, but one of degrees of being married. 'How committed are you?' we may ask, rather than merely 'What is your marital status?'"[1] Another scholar, writing in the *Journal of Family Issues*, argued that family should be reimagined as just one particular kind of the more general category, "close relationship situation."[2] In her first popular book, *American Couples*, an exhaustive study of marriage, cohabitation, and gay and lesbian relationships, Pepper Schwartz, a sociologist at the University of Washington, referred throughout to participants in all these various pairings as "couples," a "destigmatizing" term ranking marriage as just one among many different types of couplings.

These are just a few examples of a ubiquitous phenomenon. As Barbara Defoe Whitehead noted in her review of the academic literature, around 1970 the weight of expert opinion shifted decisively against traditional marriage and toward being in favor of divorce and other alternative lifestyles. A large part of that shift amounted to a fascination with the notion that marriage could and should be knocked off its pedestal as the uniquely preferred context first for sexual love, then for family making, blurring the line between marriage and unmarriage. As Whitehead said, "[I]t is hard to convey, without seeming to exaggerate or distort, the nearly voyeuristic focus in the literature on 'marriage alternatives' such as 'swinging,' group marriage, open marriage and the like." Moreover, "Reading through the journals and textbooks of the period, one can't help but note the dwindling use of the word 'marriage.' Marriage becomes just one form of 'coupling and uncoupling' or one possible 'intimate lifestyle.'"[3]

The opinions of such experts "drawn from the ranks of sociology, psychology and the therapeutic professions," Whitehead pointed out, have become decisive in our society, and "are treated as authoritative by media and policy elites. Even religious opinion increasingly draws upon social scientific teachings and insights. Talk of 'roles and relationships,' 'singlehood,' and 'gender identities' not only fills the pages of the *New York Times*; they are also the stuff of Sunday sermons and inspirational bestsellers."⁴

The experts' demotion of marriage influenced Americans directly—through the work of lawyers, therapists, and counselors—and indirectly—through women's magazines, bestselling books, and media images. By the early seventies, divorce began to be portrayed not just as a sometimes necessary evil, but as a positive good, a type of freedom, an exhilarating choice, a lifestyle alternative. Divorce, which had always existed in American society as a safety valve for certain extreme situations, began to be viewed as a normal, even salutary act. On the contrary, a refusal to divorce in the face of some personal unhappiness, began to be portrayed as a kind of masochism or, at best, a failure of nerve.

One medium for importing the experts' view of the proper status of marriage into daily life was the burgeoning number of courses in sex and family life from grade school through college. New York University psychologist Paul Vitz, after reviewing virtually all the leading texts used in such courses, found that few had much to say about marriage, and even fewer had much to say that was positive or useful. Most textbooks, he found, did not denounce marriage. They did something far worse: They marginalized it. Marriage is the center of most people's lives, but it occupies a small distant corner in the world of textbook writers.

Sexuality experts were among the most egregious offenders. Take, for example, one of the leading standard college texts, *Human Sexuality Today*. The authors, distinguished academic sexuality experts, who have taught more than twenty thousand American college students, have a clear set of priorities. Birth control rates a whole chapter, of course, as does the biology of reproduction. Sexually transmitted disease also merits a chapter, along with homosexuality, sexual abuse, and gender identity. Love and relationships (with much talk of couples but none about spouses) are similarly honored. There are extensive subchapters on anal stimulation, paraphilias (ranging from obscene phone calls to bestiality), pornography, and prostitution.

Where does marriage fall in this extensive catalogue of human erotic experience? It is condensed into just two paragraphs sandwiched between "Living Together" and "Extramarital Sex."

And what do these two paragraphs tell today's young adults about marriage? "The frequency of sexual intercourse usually decreases over time in a marriage"[5] is the first thought to greet them.

The student influenced by experts like these will have much to say about every possible human sexual combination except for marriage, the one around which most people center their lives.

But it is not that the writers of such books are reluctant to assert moral standards. The experts have a very firm sexual ethic, which they are delighted to impose on their students. Young readers are told quite sternly, for example, that homophobia is wrong. As one chapter in *A Guidebook for Better Sexual Health* put it, "It's Not Okay to Be Antigay." "Society is making progress," the authors note encouragingly, "though many myths prevail. Many people still think that homosexuality is a sin."[6] Students are firmly informed: "Fancy names for perversions are exhibitionism, masochism, sadism, fetishism, voyeurism, necrophilia, and bestiality. There is nothing wrong with any kind of sex between consenting adults in private, if each partner is non-exploitative and the act is voluntary."[7] Today sex textbooks are constantly moralizing on everything from masturbation (everyone should) to having a baby (not everyone should). But about marriage they exhibit a peculiar, deafening silence.

While social scientists claim that the mantle of objectivity requires them to treat marriage as one of a number of equally acceptable options, they do not scruple to do a little stigmatizing themselves from time to time. The objects of stigma have changed, of course, from those who divorce to those who display any disapproval (however mild) of divorce or any preference for marriage over other sexual arrangements. One recent researcher, Constance Ahrons, in her book, *The Good Divorce: Keeping Your Family Together When Your Marriage Comes Apart*, went so far as to maintain that (in 1994, no less!) it is not divorce, so much as social disapproval of divorce, that is harmful: "[a]ll language that is nuclearcentric, causes immeasurable harm to children of divorce.... The negative language so common to divorce imprisons millions of families by making them feel that they are somehow bad and unacceptable."[8]

Other divorce advocates have taken the opposite tactic to make us all much more comfortable with divorce: Marriage, they assured us, was not really breaking down, only changing in ways that will revitalize and strengthen the family. They have reassured us that the apparent breakdown of marriage was not really happening.

For more than two decades (until the early nineties, which saw a very modest counterrevolution in expert opinion), expert discussions of the state of marriage were dominated by certain divorce myths trick of speech: Concerned about family breakdown? Open any professional journal, scan any respectable op ed page, read any widely reviewed book on the subject of marital breakdown, and you would see the same twin messages: Marital decline is inevitable (so why not just lie back and think of Madonna?); and marital decline is good (people are freer, happier; children are healthier; and marriages are better because we divorce or fail to marry). Eventually these two circumlocutions produced a third: Marital decline is not happening at all, because marriage never was what we thought it was (which is why the decline of what turned out to be our illusions about marriage was inevitable).

In December 1993 *New York Newsday* ran an editorial page forum on the family that perfectly captured this logical progression. For an entire week, readers of "Redefining Family: A Series About the Many Ways We Raise Our Children" were given the expert treatment to massage away any lingering, irrational anxiety that family "change" might have excited. In the first installment, Steven Mintz, a historian and co-author of an important book, *Domestic Revolutions*, surveyed the history of marriage in Western society, from Rome to Boston, and emerged with this important lesson: "Families have never been more stable or harmonious than they are today," and "[t]he only constants in the history of the family are change and diversity."[9] In another,

Melvin Konner, an anthropologist at Emory and the author of *Childhood: A Multicultural Approach*, took us on a tour of the marital practices of Polynesians, Bushmen, Eskimos, and Nayars, and concluded that "to continue sounding a hysterical alarm about the devastating psychological effects of divorce without stronger evidence is irresponsible. It has made millions of parents feel guilty—not to mention perpetuating some very bad marriages. And as a society, we might as well realize that whether we support the process or not, it will go right on happening."[10] Further installments went on to explain that what was often called "family breakdown" was simply the welcome development of American society becoming more open to the many permutations of family life that mankind had witnessed through the ages.

Such reasoning is not confined to editorial pages but pops up with distressing regularity in scholarly books, journals, and tracts. "If we expand our notion of 'marriage' to include legal marriage and cohabitation," two scholars recently noted, "there has been little decline in the institution of marriage in the United States."[11] Yes, and if we expand our notion of law and order to include larceny, murder, and rape, then there has been little increase in crime over the past thirty years.

Thus in soothing tones the experts speak down to us from a great height. Sociologists, anthropologists, historians—the discipline changes but the message remains the same: *Don't worry, be happy.* Academics spend their lives brilliantly manipulating abstract symbols, and they believe passionately in the efficacy of their incantations: Change the word, and you change the reality. Poof! The family is not breaking apart. Poof! The family is merely in the process of being *redefined*.

And who could be better qualified to take on the task of redefinition than they themselves, the masters of the logos? This godlike business of naming is, after all, the intellectual's parlor game par excellence: We can change reality by changing the way we talk about it, from which is just a short jump to wishing can make it so.

As divorce rates rose, the public reverence once reserved for marriage began to shift gradually to divorce, and our intellectuals and opinion leaders began to reinforce the notion that divorce or unmarriage might often be morally superior to staying in a struggling marriage. Ph.D.-laden dispensers of advice began urging women, in particular, to get rid of their husbands.

One of the high points of this genre was a 1993 book charmingly titled *Get Rid of Him* by Joyce Vedral. Here the modern divorce story was told in its most pristine form: "Two people get together and it works—because at the time, in many ways, they are on the same level.... As time goes by, people evolve.... Often this natural evolution is what causes a previously comfortable relationship to become no longer tenable." To punctuate her point, Vedral provided scads of stories of women who dumped the geek and lived happily ever after. Ms. Vedral, herself happily divorced, urged readers to "take inspiration from the women in this book, some of them still in college, others in their sixties, who listened to the voice inside that said, 'Get rid of him.'"[12]

Particularly revealing is the chapter called "Get Rid of Him If You Are Bored to Death with Him," in which those who fail to divorce are characterized as timid, boring people who haven't the guts to go for the gusto. "The women you will meet in this chapter were frightened of change. They were tempted to cling to the known, to stay on the sure road, but instead many of them called for every ounce of courage within them and took 'the road not taken.'... Others have chosen the more comfortable road—the path of least resistance and some of them are wondering what would have happened if they took the road less travelled."[13]

As this idealization of divorce continued, the experts' words, phrases, and ideas echoed far and wide throughout the culture. The *New York Times Magazine* actually published a scathing column denouncing *The Bridges of Madison County*—an innocuous, sentimental novel that has become the sleeper hit of the past few years—because in the end the wife did not leave her husband. The same prejudices stamp those most powerful popular moralists of women's culture—women's magazines and television shows. These are an underrated social force. Elite women tend to be alienated by their lowbrow quality, and men, elite or not, generally ignore them. But it is here that the postmarital culture can be seen at its clearest.

Women's magazines especially (as opposed to men's magazines) are relentlessly and patronizingly moralistic. They are constantly telling women what they ought to do: what to eat, how to dress, how to make love, whom to marry, when to divorce, what perfume to wear, what laws to support. In fact they do little else. And for more than two decades now these magazines have idealized divorce, peddling the experts' advice to a broad, general audience. Most women's magazines have become as skittish about using the M-word as any academic journal. Though most women are married, there is no longer a single prominent, nondenominational women's magazine explicitly addressed to married women. Instead, we also find such carefully ambiguous and ambivalent terms as *couples* and *partners*, which embrace a range of relationships from last Saturday's date to a second husband and thus seem to imply they are all very similar.

Having a lover, of course, is nothing like having a husband—a fact equally well-known to dissatisfied wives and to single women anxious to turn the former into the latter. But in a postmarital world, the female elite that produces middlebrow women's culture is curiously reluctant to acknowledge what everyone knows and is determined to continue blurring the lines. Call the February 1993 issue of *Redbook* Exhibit A of the postmarital culture.

Here, unlike in some other magazines, the M-word is freely used. But marriage is put in its proper place. An article called "Why We Need Passion," for example, promises to tell women "how to keep it alive in your marriage." Instead, the author compares her relationship with her former husband of twenty years to that with her most recent lover, and waxes ecstatic over the latter. In her first sentence, the author explains, "I spent 21 years in a marriage that didn't lack love but did lack passion. I'm not doing that again." She had cheated herself, she tells us, by remaining in a less than sexually ecstatic relationship. In her new postmarriage relationship, "[w]e have such fun, such creative combustion, and such awe and reverence for what has happened between us that sometimes it scares us."

Another article in the same issue, "Love Behind Bars," tells the true tale of Kay and Ron, a modern love story. Kay, a happily married mother, has an affair with Ron, a convict, and when he gets out of prison she eventually marries him. "I don't regret that... I divorced my husband and married an ex-con," she says, as the moral to her story. "Ron and I are in love." Thus the romantic love story, long a staple of women's literature, is augmented by a new genre, the romantic divorce story. A woman will do anything for love, even cheat on and then dump her husband. To cap off the issue, we hear from one of the new generation of family experts, a Julie Rigby, who "writes frequently about parenting issues." What is Julie's point of view? "Dad's Gone, We're Fine: So we don't have a man in the house. So what! My child may grow up better for it."

In 1962 a sample of young, white, married middle-class midwestern mothers was presented with the following statement: "When there are children in the family, parents should stay together even if they don't get along." Fifty percent agreed.

Fifteen years later, when these same women were interviewed again, less than one woman in five agreed.[14]

In 1966 Americans were more than twice as likely to say they believed that divorce laws were "not strict enough," as to say they were "too strict." This opinion had remained stable since 1945. By 1968 (in response, perhaps, to a new wave of liberal divorce laws) public opinion was even more adamantly opposed to divorce: more than 60 percent of Americans maintained that divorce should be *more* difficult to obtain, with fewer than 20 percent called for easier divorce laws.

But by 1974, just a few years later, the public was no longer so sure. The proportion of Americans who thought divorce should be easier to get had risen by 15 percentage points, and the percentage who wanted to make divorce more difficult to get had dropped by 21 percentage points.[15]

Somewhere between the early sixties and the mid-seventies Americans replaced their tattering marriage ethic with a robust, new postmarital one. The fierce protectiveness once directed toward the institution of marriage was transferred to divorce. This dramatic shift in the public's attitude tends to be treated by experts as a kind of natural phenomenon or at most a result and not a cause of the rise in divorce. But it seems increasingly clear that the experts themselves played a key role in transforming American mores. As we see every day, recasting by academics of our sexual ethics has seeped down into the popular culture. But their influence has also been more direct, since we have given over the care of marriage in America to the same social scientists and professional practitioners trained and influenced by them.

In the mid-seventies, Sue and Robert were unhappy in their marriage. Eager to work through their difficulties, this couple decided to do the right thing—what all the experts from Dear Abby to Dr. Joyce Brothers recommended—seek a marriage counselor.

At their first session, the counselor listened to each spouse tell his or her story. Then he made his pronouncement, "You two have nothing in common. What are you doing married to each other?"

Fortunately, this couple, determined to improve their marriage, decided to switch counselors rather than mates. By the mid-seventies, however, their experience was far from unique. Dr. Richard Gardner, a professor of psychiatry at Columbia University and author of the influential seventies' divorce manual, *The Parents' Book About Divorce*, confirms that inappropriate therapy "is surprisingly common.... [T]herapists... have caused many divorces that should never have taken place."[16]

During the seventies divorce counseling emerged as a separate therapeutic specialty, and marriage and family therapists were directed, as one academic textbook noted, "to reexamine their roles in relation to divorce": "Whereas traditionally the primary purpose of the therapist had been to preserve a marriage... divorce was now to be seen as a viable option."[17]

Marriage counselors, thus liberated, not surprisingly discovered that it was much easier to break up the marriage of two very angry people than to fix it. What if, these experts pondered, we dropped our outdated notion that the goal of marriage counseling was to help the marriage and instead concentrated on helping the individuals in the marriage? In many cases, it appeared, at least one individual would be better off outside the marriage. Why not help that individual to realize his or her full potential? If counseling failed to produce a happy marriage, might not a counselor still help a client to a satisfactory divorce? And if divorce were considered as successful an outcome of therapy as a happy marriage, marriage counselors would soon have a whole lot more successes under their belts.

Even without hidden motivations (including the normal human desire to feel successful), the counselors' newly acquired neutrality between marriage and divorce tended to slide toward divorce. Whether or not one should divorce depends on what standards one applies. But a counselor who applies no standards tends to imply that there aren't any. As Dr. Gardner puts it: "Even when therapists are successful in maintaining a strictly neutral role, the partners may attribute to them motives that are genuinely not theirs. For example, a husband may conclude that the therapist's failure to condemn his wife for an affair served to sanction it.... Or a wife may interpret the therapist's neutrality as support for her decision to separate."[18]

When marriage and divorce are considered morally equal options, the result is not "neutrality" but the first step in the creation of a divorce culture. Love, commitment, patience, and faithfulness are hard. Unless a good-enough marriage is seen as an achievement worth struggling for and (if not absolutely always) generally preferable to divorce, why should struggling spouses bother?

The therapeutic community's tilt away from marriage was made easier by certain preexisting attitudes toward family life among therapists. Whether because people from troubled family backgrounds are disproportionately attracted to the helping professions, or because therapists' work immerses them daily into troubled families, or both, therapists tend to have a much different and somewhat darker view of normal family functioning than other groups. In particular, while families place great emphasis on what therapists term *cohesion* and what normal people call *togetherness,* therapists tend to view close family ties with suspicion. (This may be because in dysfunctional families this cohesion tends to prevent individuals from escaping the destructive family influence.)

One study of therapists found that, "in general, therapists' perceptions of normal family functioning appeared to be skewed toward less well-functioning families." In contrast to other groups (families with young children, college students, and grandmothers), therapists tended to see low cohesion within a family as normal and "appeared to see normal families as functioning less well than did other groups."[19] Another study compared the attitudes toward family of four groups— therapists, disturbed families seeking treatment, healthy families not in treatment, and Catholic and Baptist clergy—and came to similar conclusions. Families seeking treatment differed very little from families not seeking treatment in their definition of healthy family life. Both groups placed a great deal of emphasis on togetherness, or cohesion, while therapists placed more emphasis on communication and adaptability and were often suspicious of too much cohesion.[20]

Suspicious of family loyalty and committed to their clients' individual well-being, "[m]ost therapists don't see their role as that of marriage savior, not even 'for the sake of the kids,'" as one reporter noted.[21] The therapists tended to agree.

"It isn't divorce that causes long-term negative effects on kids," said Chris Rosenthal, a licensed mental health counselor. "It's living in a dysfunctional environment."[22]

"The goal is not to let the divorce of husband and wife influence the roles of mother and father because that's where the harm comes for the children," said another marriage and family therapist.[23]

"I don't think it's my job to decide whether it's a good marriage or a bad marriage, so I can't decide whether a couple should stay in it," is how another licensed marriage therapist in Florida put it. "My job is to help each of them see what they do that limits them or prevents them from getting what they need and want." Couples who stay together for the kids "teach children to be extremely insecure and lacking in the skills to be intimate and caring," she opined.[24]

Next to marriage therapists, the professionals who probably had the greatest influence spreading the new postmarital ethic, glorifying the position of divorce, were lawyers. Under the new divorce laws, lawyers have begun to function (whether they like it or not) as moral philosophers conveying the new postmarital ethic to shocked spouses.

When Martha's husband left her and her two kids after seventeen years of marriage for a younger woman, Martha was devastated. Her lawyer, however, was blasé. "That's not relevant," he said when she tried to tell him about her husband's adultery. "That's not relevant," he repeated, when she tried to explain she and her husband had agreed she should stay home with the kids. "You'll get temporary maintenance. Start thinking now about your future."

Get over it, lawyers tell their clients who persist in backwardly thinking that right and wrong, guilt and innocence, should affect who wins and loses in the divorce settlement. They are merely doing their job, dispensing technical advice. But in the process lawyers are inevitably heralds of the new postmarital ethic contained in our weakened marriage laws. It is through Martha's lawyer that Martha, her kids, and all her friends and relatives will come to learn what, or rather how little, marriage means in our society—how trivially regarded are the standards we thought spouses were expected to live up to. "Probably one of the hardest things for a client to understand," one attorney put it, "is the fact that if your wife had seven lovers in your bed at one time doesn't mean she gets a penny less than if your wife goes to [*sic*] a novena every night to pray for the return of your soul."[25]

The divorce advocates, purveyors of the new postmarital ethic, are all drawn from professions—the social sciences, the law, the therapeutic community, journalism—that, either by long tradition (the scientists) or recent fashion (the lawyers and therapists), are avowedly committed to a deep moral neutrality about the subjects of their work. But, on the subject of marriage and divorce, that neutrality is a mere superficial convention. Make no mistake: The divorce advocates are fierce moralists, painting visions of the good and denouncing the evil that men do with all the uncomplicated vigor of a country parson or a failed seminarian. On one point they are especially zealous: Though often professing a high regard for enduring love, the divorce advocates often show undisguised scorn for sacrifices people make to sustain marriages.

Some of the most passionate of these advocates have dropped the pretense of being anything but preachers, which is where the border between the therapeutic profession and the human potential movement disappears. Again and again in the human potential movement, those who stay married because they believe in marriage are held up as shameful examples of failure. John Bradshaw, a modern guru of faithlessness, writes at one point: "I thought of some of the people I knew who had been married a long time. I remembered how members of my family used to point to these long marriages as examples of what marital love was all about. I remember thinking how unhappy and lonely such and such a couple look."[26] Unhappiness is the new mark of the coward.

Since many, if not most, married couples experience at least some period during which the moral commitment of marriage, rather than its emotional delights, is what holds them together, the effects of this new set of morals on the married cannot be underestimated. Just at the time when moral courage is most called for, when love is an act of will and not a mere spontaneous emotion, we are told, repeatedly, that kind of courage is only a form of cowardice. Where once we feared becoming the kind of person who could abandon a husband or wife, we now fear becoming the kind of person who needs a husband or wife or, worse, stays with a spouse even after our need has passed.

16
THE RISE *of*
ROMANTIC DIVORCE

IT IS A STORY AS OLD AS THE HILLS YET, to the protagonists, never stale: A young woman fell in love with her boss, an older married man. He was a brilliant, kind, accomplished, assured mentor. And yet, touchingly, he needed her.

His wife didn't adore him. At home with the kids, she didn't seem to notice or care that her husband was a Great Man. Maybe she loved him, in a way, but it was a petty, grasping way, full of resentment and need, dragging him down.

John was no sexual liberal. A religious man, he believed strongly in the importance of marriage; a political conservative, he embraced family values. But there she was, with pale skin and dark hair tumbling to the waist. A girl's face with a woman's body—beautiful, fresh, talented.

So for the next seven years they played hide and seek, engaging in a tumultuous, passionate, frustrating, secret affair. After seven years, he could no longer bear living a double life. After seven years, he put an end to his dead marriage and brought his Rachel home.

"I decided I had a right to be happy," said he, adopting the therapeutic ethic. She explained her feelings differently.

"I loved him too much to help myself," said she, explaining her headlong rush into romantic adultery that prompted an equally romantic divorce. The fact that she couldn't help herself was proof that she loved. If she could have refrained from helping herself to another woman's husband, it would have suggested she was shallow, incapable of deep feeling.

Thus we make our faithlessness a testament to our love.

The story had a tiresome moral: A little while later she found her love, though equal to adultery, was not up to marriage; she abandoned it and him.

And yet in both her faith and her faithlessness, she was not alone. For roughly a thousand years, Dennis De Rougement noted, Western civilization held that marriage and romantic love were incompatible. The natural end of romantic love was death. It was a Platonic truth: We want only what we lack. Desire ends with death or with its satisfaction—which is to say, its extinction. Then in the eighteenth and nineteenth centuries, novelists and essayists began to demand not just that husbands and wives love each other, but that they be and remain "in love." By the early nineteenth century, English-speaking literature was replete with stories warning girls not to give their hands without their hearts. Elizabeth in *Pride and Prejudice*, for example, is shocked and disgusted when her clever friend Charlotte agrees to marry a silly, pompous clergyman out of a desire for a position. "She could not have supposed it possible that when called into action, she would have sacrificed every better feeling to worldly advantage… And to the pang of a friend disgracing herself and sunk in her esteem was added the distressing conviction that it was impossible for that friend to be tolerably happy in the lot she had chosen."

Certainly by 1830, if not earlier, "romantic love was fast becoming the necessary condition for marriage in the American middle class."[1] According to this new notion of romantic marriage, there was one— and perhaps only one—person in the world who would complete you, a union with whom would produce ecstasy. Moreover, only this kind of union was a true marriage. Of course, sometimes you may discover that your spouse is not the one who will complete you. The logical implication—that some apparent marriages were not true unions, but rather "dead marriages," mere legal corpses—began to be articulated fairly frequently in the nineteenth century, as the ideal of romantic marriage reached its zenith. Unarticulated was the corollary that romantic marriage would demand romantic divorce. In the nineteenth century, and for much of this one, divorce was held in too great disrepute for it to be explicitly associated with romance. But as the status of divorce rose to that of a sacred right, and as the status of marriage fell correspondingly, we became less timid about stating our ideals.

"Sometimes a well-adjusted secure woman can meet a man and know in her heart that she must go with him, no matter what the risks or consequences," so one woman's magazine urged the cult of romantic divorce in an article entitled "The Man You'd Leave Him For."

"You're happily married, or so you think. But when he comes along, all bets are off."[2]

It is a formula of a hundred romance novels, but with a twist. In this women's magazine the happy ending for romantic love is not a wedding but a divorce. There followed tale after tale of real-life married women who ditched their husbands under an irresistible romantic impulse.

Suzanne, a thirty-nine-year-old lawyer, fell head over heels for a handsome married man seated next to her at a dinner party. For two years, she could not "muster the nerve" to leave her husband because he was so good to her and loved her so much.

"Yet the day came when the pain of staying outweighed that of leaving," and so off she went. The two ditched their respective spouses, married, and reputedly lived happily ever after.

Lindsey, a thirty-three-year-old computer programmer who dumped her husband of six years for a man with a wider variety of political interests, was also afflicted by a strange cowardice. Because of her five-year-old daughter, "it took months for Lindsey to summon the courage to end her marriage."

"I'd say to myself, How can I do this to her?" Then fortunately Lindsey remembered the magic words for dissolving all erotic conflicts of interests: "Finally, though, I realized that she'd be much happier if *I* were happy."

(Funny how this magic formula never works in reverse. No one contemplating divorce ever looks at the child and says, "I'll be happy if only she's happy.")

In many respects the collapse of the social, moral, and legal status of marriage over the past several decades is undeniable. And yet the rise of romantic divorce points not so much to a devaluation of marriage but to a bizarre idealization of it. Romantic divorce is a necessary outgrowth of the extreme romanticization of marriage, as if we believe so much in an ideal vision of marriage that we think we should keep trying until we get it right. We marry or we break up marriages when we are swept away by a love so overpowering nothing can contain it. In a faithless time, when it seems no bonds are unbreakable and love always fails, we strive to experience love as powerful by making it break the only fragile bond left, the bond of matrimony. Ironically, breaking the bonds of marriage thus becomes an affirmation of marriage's sacred status. We think so much of love and, indeed, of married love that we can't actually stay married except when we feel in love. Many people feel married love is just so sacred they have to divorce. And sometimes they think so highly of marriage, they just can't bring themselves to do it.

JoAnne is thirty-nine but looks ten years younger. Fair complexion, dark hair cut Cleopatra-style across her large dark eyes. High cheekbones and a swan neck.

She and Ralph, the baby's father, moved in together the day Rebecca was born.

She sees herself staying with Ralph for Rebecca's sake. "I don't want to deprive her of a father or a real family," she says. How long does she plan to stay with Ralph? "Until Rebecca turns eighteen," she says. But she is very ambivalent about marrying him. She is not, however, ambivalent about marriage: "I have great respect for marriage. It's been around for thousands of years in every culture. I think it is very important." Asked whether she wants Rebecca to marry, and her answer is quick and unequivocal: "Oh yes. I want her to have everything I don't. I want her to do it right. I want her to get married first and have kids."

The concerns that make her willing to live with but reluctant to marry Ralph are not legal and financial, but symbolic and psychological. "I try to explain to my father: It's because I think so much of marriage that I don't want to marry him."

Marriage to her is not the ultimate commitment, but the expression of the ultimate commitment. It is a way of announcing to the world that you think so much of one man, you are willing to let him become a part of you. And frankly, JoAnne doesn't think that much of Ralph. She sees him as basically immature, not very ambitious, in key ways not her equal. She would be embarrassed, frankly, to have people imagine that she thought so well of him as marriage might imply. She is willing to be faithful to him, to bear his children, to share a bed and household and a bank book for most of her life. She is just not sure she is willing to make a public declaration of love.

JoAnne is the living expression of a nagging paradox: Americans express a high regard for marriage and a great willingness to end marriages. Marriage retains a powerful symbolic appeal that people are less and less able to translate into reality. Deep in her experience lies a subtle change in the meaning of marriage. Marriage is not an act of union, but a ratification of a union; not a commitment, but an expression of commitment. This is why today we are so willing to allow the unmarried, but "committed," to share in some of the honors and benefits of marriage. By any of the traditional structural or functional definitions of marriage—the nurturing of children, the protection of mothers while they do that nurturing, or the creation of an erotic link between men and their wives and children powerful enough to tie them to home and work—"gay marriage," for example—is not so much wrong as futile. But if marriage is primarily an expression of one's committed love, then it is wrong to deny it to anyone—as long as one feels committed and in love—or to hold anyone to it, once one has ceased to feel committed and in love.

Krista, an attractive twenty-three-year-old writer, has been living with Jesse, a twenty-year-old musician, for two years. Along with a group of similarly young, attractive, college-educated women gathered

220 The Abolition of Marriage

in my apartment, she struggles to explain why, although she is already committed, marriage still matters so much. She wants the world to know not just that she and Jesse are a couple, but that she is family, Jesse's family. "It bothers me, with his parents. I want them to have to acknowledge I'm somebody. I want them to recognize my place in Jesse's life. A wife is something a girlfriend is not. I just love the words 'husband' and 'wife,'" she says, shaking her blonde head almost ruefully. "I know the words are archaic, but I just love the whole idea."

She, like the other women in the room, lives with the omnipresent reality of divorce. They know that marriage is no guarantee of permanence. Sex and affection they already have. What is a young couple doing today when they agree to marry? Promising to care for each other as long as they both shall love. Krista and Jesse have already done that. So what do they need a piece of paper for?

Women like Krista absurdly, irrationally, long for the marriage bond. The words *I love you* have been drained, through frequent use, of all specific meaning. The act of love no longer speaks reliably of union. All that is left is this frail, eroding word, *marriage*, packed with centuries of loving, living, growing old together, in sickness and in health, until death do us part. Thirty years of the divorce culture have not yet undone the work of ages. It is the only word that still speaks.

In a culture in which people express love and make love with many different partners over the course of a lifetime, marriage occupies a singular position. Marriage retains a high expressive value, having not been drained of meaning by repeated use. *I've never married anyone else before*, we say to our new love—or, at least, *I've hardly ever married before*.

The perfect equation of marriage with romantic love, or rather with the expression of romantic love, often sounds idealistic, but it is actually profoundly self-protective. It makes not only the goodness of a marriage but its very existence dependent on its emotional satisfactions. If marriage is not a vow, but a public avowal of an internal emotion, then, as the emotions shift, the marriage itself fades away. A good marriage is wonderful. A bad marriage is a contradiction in terms.

One result for those who think about marriage in this way—or those who in bad moments are tempted to do so—is that a difficult marriage, one that just at this moment requires a great deal of work to stay with, becomes not just a burden, but something worse: a "lie." When marriage is predicated on an internal emotional state, then people are no longer simply married or unmarried, happily married or unhappily married. New categories emerge; marriages become true or false, live or dead. A marriage that appears to be intact may not be. John and Mary may be living together as husband and wife, but one or the other may be committing an awful fraud—pretending to be married when the marriage is actually dead.

Of course, most people do not philosophize about their marriages in this way, and when things are going well they might scorn the idea that during previous difficulties their marriages were dead. But when an idea as powerful as this is abroad in the society it is always there to tempt us at difficult moments, to make the steps necessary to extract oneself from a dead marriage far more easy to justify morally and emotionally.

Many a single woman justifies her involvement with a married man along these lines: It's not a real marriage (after all, if they were really married, he wouldn't want to sleep with another woman); he's just staying with her for the sake of the kids. The young lady imagines she is giving him the emotional and sexual sustenance a real wife gives; ergo, the woman he is married to is not really his wife. The marriage is an empty shell, a husk, a legal fiction.

Judges who issue divorce decrees, moreover, need not worry too much about the awesome changes they might be working in people's lives. In ratifying divorces, they are only doing the decent and obvious thing: burying the dead.

The scene is a cocktail party filled with upwardly mobile New Yorkers. A woman, secretly contemplating divorce, decides to do a little field research. Fearlessly, she approaches one guest after another and pops the question.

"How do you know when it's time to leave?"

The guests, well educated, middle-aged, cosmopolitan, oblige her with twenty or so different answers, varying in their degrees of difficulty: "When the other person bores you," "When you can't breathe any more," "When you fall out of love," and "When the thought of making love makes you sick."

But whatever the reasons they give, not a single person present, man or woman, distinguishes between leaving a lover and leaving a spouse. Incidents like these reveal a little-remarked change of huge cultural moment: For today we think and talk about marriage, argue for it, and define it exactly as the bohemian throughout history used to advocate free love.

For most of Western history people imagined that marriage created certain permanent duties and obligations that romantics, contrary to vast experience (though perhaps not their own), argued precluded love. Love, they said, can only be love when it is sustained in complete freedom, cleansed of any taint of duty. The remarkable thing is that we Americans have taken this vision of love as a purely and continuously voluntary association of individuals and imported it into marriage. We have managed, in other words, to make marriage indistinguishable from free love. This is a remarkable achievement, for historically free love was not marriage's twin but its great opposite. One way we know we are not far from the abolition of marriage is that we can no longer tell the two apart.

Free love got a bad name in the sixties, when it became synonymous with promiscuity, or sex without love. For a brief period even emotional ties came to be seen as too restrictive: to be free, love must cease to love. For centuries, however, free love meant not promiscuity, but naked fidelity: love that trusted itself so much it could dispense with bonds of any kind or a love that disdained the constraint of duty or the legal, social, and financial supports of marriage.

When Abelard offered to marry Heloise, she—pregnant and disgraced—refused. "Heloise," said Abelard, "argued that the name of mistress instead of wife would be dearer to her and more honourable for me—only love freely given should keep me for her, not the constriction of a marriage tie."³ Heloise, a nun, confirmed this: "The name of wife may seem more sacred or more binding, but sweeter for me will always be the word mistress, or, if you will permit me, that of concubine or whore… God is my witness that if Augustus, Emperor of the whole world, thought fit to honour me with marriage and conferred all the earth on me to possess forever, it would be dearer and more honourable to me to be called not his Empress but your whore."⁴

Elizabeth Cady Stanton voiced the moderate free-love position when addressing the New York state legislature in 1854: "If you take the highest views of marriage, as a Divine relation, which love alone can constitute and sanctify, then of course human legislation can only recognize it." Later, in a review of Caroline Dall's *College, Market and Court,* Stanton argued that the "sacred affections and delicate sensibilities of the Marriage Relation cannot be measured by the clumsy machinery of law. We only ask of it to act impartially by both sexes and to leave moral and spiritual relations to their own remedies and compensations." This exalted, romantic, superficially idealistic view of marriage was then, as it is now, tantamount to advocating its abolition, reducing married couples to the liberty of free lovers.

Fittingly, it was in a speech advocating the liberalization of divorce that Stanton most explicitly made the point when she declared, "We are all free lovers at heart although we may not have thought so…. We all believe in the good time coming… when men and women will be… a law unto themselves and when, therefore, the external law of compulsion will be no longer needed…. The element of legal compulsion is all that distinguishes marriage from those natural and free adjustments which the sentiment of love would spontaneously organize for itself."⁵

By 1920 these ideas, percolating for years among the intelligentsia, could also be found among some ordinary educated men and women. Especially women. In 1920 Rose Macman, a twenty-five-year-old Jewish schoolteacher, separated from her husband, Norman, a lawyer. When Norman tried to reconcile, she wrote him, proudly,

"You know that I am not the kind to live with a man because I am married to him or because the law says I am his wife. I believe I can live with whomsoever I please at any time provided I have sufficient love for him and I have no love for you. All is over between us. You do not fit my ideal of a man."[6]

A little blunt, perhaps. But romantic love has never been kind to the losers. Regardless of the quality of the poetry it may inspire, romantic love, when it is primarily defined by the current emotional state of the lover, is always ultimately about the self, the lover, and the rights he earns by the intensity of his feelings. The lover does not care for the beloved so much as he draws inspiration from her; one might almost say he consumes the beloved, although always to the highest purpose, or at least the highest purpose that the self, trapped in itself, can know.

17

CONSUMING
a SPOUSE

IN 1988, JOHN BRADSHAW PUBLISHED a book that was to be the capstone of his career. Based on the enormously successful PBS television series, "Bradshaw on the Family: A Revolutionary Way of Self-Discovery," the book sold more than 500,000 copies in hardcover and trade paperback.

The first sight to meet a half million eager book buyers' eyes was an inspiring dedication:

> To my wife Nancy, who is my best friend and the most gentle person I have ever known. Together we've shared a sometimes difficult and always exciting journey of family-making.

It was a moving testament not only to her but to his own journey: John Bradshaw had overcome an abandoning father, a toxic mother, a Catholic seminarian's indoctrination, and a descent into alcoholism. By championing his own inner child he had come at last to the ultimate prize: lasting love.

A few years later, Bradshaw published a new book, *Creating Love*. This time Nancy had disappeared from the dedication page and entered the text: Bradshaw confessed he and his wife had grown apart and amicably divorced. "When I woke up from my mystification, I saw how completely I had re-created my family of origin trance.... Our whole rhythm was out of step."[1]

> My original pain work culminated in a deeper and more loving relationship with myself. But it left me with a great uncertainty about how to be intimate and loving with others… I had to admit that *even after years of recovery and working on myself I still felt a baffling despair about love and fulfillment.* The reclaiming of my inner child was the beginning of learning to love, not the *end.*[2]

This time, however, he had gained true insight. This time he knew what had gone wrong. This time he had really attained the spiritual wholeness that is a prerequisite to a genuine marriage of hearts. First place in the personal acknowledgments in the new book now went to "Sissy Davis, who is my sweetheart and with whom I am creating love."

Bradshaw is the premier guru of the therapeutic/human potential movement, itself the current best expression of the relentless optimism of Americans. Other eras have seen other expressions, from Horatio Alger to Prohibition. In the age of therapy, the goal of work, marriage, love, and living is neither an improved net worth nor clean living, but *insight.* No experience that produces insight can be judged a failure.

One of the most powerful and necessary myths of a divorce culture is that divorce affects only the two people in the courtroom. In reality, of course, not only the frequency of divorce, but also the laws about divorce, and the ideas, morals, and mores that sustain those laws and protect the institution of divorce, transform what it means to be married.

Here is one of the biggest changes: a spouse has become a consumption item. Nowhere is this so evident than among the therapeutic elite, masters of the human potential movement, high priests of self-fulfillment, whose rhetoric has to an astonishing degree captured what used to be called the *caring professions*—from counselors to clergy. It has become the unexamined philosophical bedrock of the popular culture, mouthed by advice columnists, starlets, and discount philosophers everywhere.

Daphne Rose Kingma is not the most famous or the bestselling of the therapeutic gurus. But in her book *Coming Apart: Why Relationships End and How to Live Through the End of Yours*, she crystallizes the ideology in its purest form:

- "Now we live in a time when relationships exist to serve the deepest needs of the individuals in them... We enter into relationships to discover, foster, enhance, and sustain our individual selves."[3]
- "It is the creation of the self—living as exactly and wholly as oneself as we possibly can—which is our primary task as human beings. Because relationships assist us in accomplishing this purpose, I see their endings not as tragic but, although needled with pain, as potent opportunities."[4]

Opportunities for further growth. For self-enhancement. To complete new developmental tasks. What if your spouse doesn't see it that way? That is a sign he needs more personal development, because although "the reason we fall in love is to help us accomplish our external and internal developmental tasks," our "developmental tasks are our own responsibility."[5]

In this theory, there is not much difference between a husband and a vibrator. Which you choose depends on what developmental task you are trying to accomplish next. So if you, say, have fulfilled your needs to have a baby, and he hasn't gotten over wanting to be a live-in father, that's his problem. He will have to work it out in his next relationship.

Here indeed is a new habit of the heart. Love means getting what you want and getting out when you've gotten it.

The therapeutic ideal, by reducing love and marriage to means of personal growth, makes both temporary by definition. It is a rational, utilitarian, practical ethic, deeply American and consumerist. It encourages us to view marriage as a disposable spiritual consumption item and to view our spouses as particularly valuable vehicles for personal growth, to be traded in when they have served their purpose.

The therapeutic ideal—with its emphasis on the passing, if not fleeting, utility of marriage and other people generally—has consequently been an indispensable aid to replacing a culture of marriage with a culture of divorce. The problem with modern marriage, according to Kingma, is that we are unwilling to accept its inherently temporary nature. Too many of us cling to the "myth" that "love is forever": "Our marriage vows—'till death do us part,' are the public ceremonial expression of that myth. We don't say, 'I'll love you as long as it feels good,' or 'I'll love you until I find somebody else'.... We expect the person we choose to be our partner for our whole lives."[6]

These unrealistic expectations only set us up for unpleasant failures. "The truth," Kingma maintains, "is that relationships end. It is high time we explode the myth that love is forever so that when we end relationships, we can do so without such devastating crises in self-esteem."[7]

For the sake of our mental health and personal spiritual growth, we ought to accept a world in which no one will make or keep a promise to anyone except himself.

But to love is to surrender freedom—the freedom to flee, the freedom not to care. Love creates ties. Every effort to escape from that essential human dilemma, to reimagine love in such a way as to retain our primeval freedom, involves subordinating love to appetite—reimagining eros as a set of pleasing internal feelings, elevated feelings, perhaps, that promote our own development, but still essentially internal sensations. The result is that even in love we remain hopelessly solipsistic, self-condemned to eternal solitude, caged in our own flesh. What disappears in "love" imagined this way is the other person.

The therapeutic ideal, as Robert Bellah and company put it in *Habits of the Heart*, "proffers a normative order of life, with character ideals, images of the good life and methods of attaining it. Yet it is an understanding of life generally hostile to older ideas of moral order.... It enables the individual to think of commitments—from marriage and work to political and religious involvement—as enhancements of the sense of individual well-being rather than as moral imperatives."[8]

Yes, it certainly does that. But in a larger sense casting, as Bellah does, the "therapeutic" and the "moral" imperatives as opposites is not quite right. Surely the therapeutic ideology that proffers a vision of the good life and urges the steps necessary to attain it, is inescapably a kind of morality regardless of whether it acknowledges itself as such.

Such a set of morals and the mores founded upon it are, of course, profoundly destructive to marriage or any other social end. But the people who practice what the therapeutic ideology preaches are not particularly "selfish" in the common sense of the term. They are, often as not, caring, generous people who struggle hard to achieve their ideal in their marriage, and do not (as sometimes portrayed) abandon their spouse, on a whim. The disorders that ensue are not the result of a personality defect but of a defective ideal, indeed a destructive ideal.

The distinguishing characteristic of the therapeutic ideology is not that it is amoral, but that it allows the individual to imagine that all moral imperatives are directed toward a single, ultimate end: his or her own well-being. The self is a kind of trump card in any moral dilemma. Difficult, tragic moral conflicts between the self and others never arise because, in the therapeutic ideology, the self always comes first.

It is not a new ideal. By the mid-nineteenth century, many American intellectuals such as Caroline Dall, abolitionist, feminist, and cofounder of the American Social Science Association, saw the purpose of marriage as "self-development." "I do not feel that marriage is here an end," she wrote in 1859. "I think like other relations it is a means to growth."[9]

It may be easy to dismiss the therapeutic ideology as mere psychobabble. Whole chapters of Bradshaw read like products of that word game in which children shout out random nouns, verbs, and so on, which are later plugged into a story to make nonsense. Nevertheless, the therapeutic ideal has become so thoroughly saturated in our culture that, for the most part, we do not give it a second thought.

Intimidated by the weight of therapeutic opinion, even the clergy have become conveyors of the new notion of marriage as a consumer good and, thus, supporters of the divorce culture. One can see this trend clearly not only in the more liberal denominations, but in the more conservative as well.

The Catholic Church, for example, remains in theory unalterably opposed to divorce. But walk into any Catholic bookstore, and what books meet the enquiring Catholic eye? James Greteman's *When Divorce Happens: A Guide for Family and Friends* is typical of the genre. Divorce, as the title suggests, is a misfortune that happens to people, not a moral failure of their will to love. But just in case this random misfortune should befall you, this book offers "practical advice on how divorce can be converted into a process of personal growth." Another Catholic priest writes, "We don't get married to get divorced. We get married because we believe our lives will be intimately more satisfying if shared with another rather than experiencing life without a partner." Casually, uncontroversially, speaking with the authority of religion and social work combined, he regurgitates the conventional wisdom: that the love which propels us toward marriage is really about the self.

Nasty, poor, brutish, and short is how Hobbes described life in his imagined state of nature, where each person was a law unto himself, with his own good paramount, with lasting vows or alliances unknown, and with society no more than a war of all against all. The therapeutic gurus don't speak Hobbes' language. Quite the reverse, they are the sultans of schmaltz, the heroes of the hug—apparently in all sincerity. But by nurturing a moral code that effectively turns abandonment into a virtue and self-interest into the highest virtue, they create something like Hobbes' hell on earth in which, lacking any common good to appeal to in dealing with one another, we are driven instead to use selfishness as the currency of all exchange.

Many women, for instance, embrace the divorce ethic because they fear that without an escape hatch they will have no power—no power to keep their husbands, no power to protect their own interests. Many a wife threatens to leave her husband because she does not know any other way to get his attention. When love is acknowledged to be about the self, there is no alternative basis in marriage to ask for what one needs other than to threaten to leave. If love is a consumption item, then the only way to move one's spouse is to threaten to remove the object of his or her gratification—oneself. In this way, as in others, divorce permeates marriage, making marriage itself, as we have seen, a less satisfying, less productive, and less loving union.

It has reached the point that, for many people, all talk of happiness in marriage seems to be linked to a threat: Make me happy or I'll leave. No love can flourish in that emotional environment, no matter how anxious the spouses are to give or to receive love. In a marriage culture, women ought to ask for what she needs *because* she is his wife, not because she might become his ex-wife?

If the goal is the happiness of the individual partner, then the therapeutic love contract, or marriage, is inherently temporary. It lasts as long as both people perceive themselves better off together than apart. And because it is conceived as an affair between adults, the therapeutic marriage inherently subordinates the welfare of children to the welfare of adults.

Tremendous energy is aimed at camouflaging this basic reality. If love is therapy for the self, then the previous idealization of marriage must now be directed toward divorce. So the new breed of children's divorce manuals never confront children with the hard facts. Instead they are full of hopeful sugarcoated bromides, the better to make the divorce medicine go down. These manuals tell children that "Mommy and Daddy divorced each other, they didn't divorce you," but omit to mention that likely as not you're going to have to kiss your daddy goodbye. They are never told that, as the years pass and their father remarries, their relationship will more likely than not dwindle to something like the one most children maintain with a distant uncle or that when it comes time to go to college Dad may even explain, as a father of one acquaintance of mine did, that he had no extra money for her college that year because he had opened an education account for the new baby. The divorce manuals never mention that their mother's boyfriend may sexually abuse them. Discussions of sexual abuse are inevitably directed at the traditional intact family, the cradle of all Bradshaw's horror, more than 90 percent of which he diagnoses as dysfunctional.

Oedipus. Medea. Lear. Erotic conflicts within families are the oldest staple of tragedy. What is new is our American insistence on denying the tragedy, which we can do only by denying the conflict. The happy talk stems in part from the convenient conviction that happiness, not love, unifies. What makes one happy must (or at least should) make all happier. We stand with the victors in the race for happiness. Because they are happy, we say, what they have done is good; those who are left behind we either ignore or lie about (children) or blame (deserted spouses) for refusing to grow, for persisting in believing that we have injured them.

In *A Return to Love*, Marianne Williamson, spiritual teacher, lecturer, and bestselling author of *A Course in Miracles*, presents the therapeutic idea of love and marriage in its highest, most spiritual, most idealistic form. And as a woman of spirit she can set those abandoned spouses straight: "Relationships are assignments. They are part of a vast plan for our enlightenment, the Holy Spirit's blueprint by which each individual soul is led to greater awareness and expanded love."[10] For that reason, we would be wrong to consider divorce necessarily a failure. "But if both people learned what they were meant to learn, then that relationship was a success."[11]

Far from being a rhetorical excuse for abandonment, an escape clause like divorce is actually the deepest form of commitment, a way of saying, "'I love you so much that I can release you to be where you need to be, to go where you need to go.' This moment in a relationship is not about an ending. It's about the ultimate fulfillment of the purpose in any relationship: that we find the meaning of pure love."[12]

This is the apotheosis of romantic divorce (and a celebration of masochism): to reimagine divorce as an act of love.

One could proffer many arguments against the therapists' diminished vision of eros. But the simplest rebuttal takes place in every human heart at the moment it gives itself to another human being. Then we know that the therapeutic ideal—conceiving love as essentially solipsistic—fails to satisfy love's own urgent demands. When love ends, the solipsists' theory of love may comfort us at least by justifying our longing to leave. What it cannot explain is our desire to merge. It cannot explain the persistent longing for a union of two lives, two hearts, two bodies. It cannot explain, in a culture thoroughly imbued with the language, laws, and mores of therapeutic sex and therapeutic love, the strange stubborn longing for marriage.

This desire for union on the lovers' part is viewed suspiciously by the therapists and is construed as evidence of immaturity—an attempt to return to the pre-Oedipal state. Feelings of ecstatic union are seen as signs of immature love or psychological neediness. Real love, they chide, requires work.

So it does. But work toward what? The impulse of eros may not be its fulfillment. But is union of selves a mere illusion, as the therapeutic view suggests? Or is it rather an aspiration? And are we better off inquiring what the aspiration means, listening to what eros is telling us or ignoring the mystery in favor of comforting myths about a world in which love is as safe and tame as a new diet or a trip to the gym?

The therapeutic culture, after all, offers no inoculation against love's wounds. Love cannot be made safe, sifted of all tragedy. To love is to place a knife against one's heart, because contrary to all the gurus' promises, one cannot love alone. The open heart is a wound stanched by the lover. Withdraw, and blood flows. Marriage suffers from the defects to which flesh is heir, but if marriage is increasingly risky, unmarriage has proven no solution.

The gurus of the human potential movement are a strange lot. But what is most strange is how accurately they represent the distilled essence of the divorce culture. What they believe fervently, all the divorce advocates believe moderately. The message they shout joyfully from the hilltops is echoed in murmured approval by the responsible prodivorce academics.

Marianne Williamson has found a way to turn divorce into a sacrament. But even reformers who acknowledge the stress of divorce never attempt to create a new marriage ideal. Instead, they concentrate, as Arlene Skolnick puts it, on the need for a new "cultural model of the successful divorce and the successful post-divorce family—one that does the least harm to children and leaves them with good relationships with both parents."[13]

The fantasy the divorce advocates pursue is a world of ideal divorces, where spouses politely disengage from relations with each other while respectfully and enthusiastically cooperating in parenting, making whatever sacrifices of personal feeling are necessary to help their children prosper in their new postmarital homes.

It is an unlikely enough vision in any world inhabited by human beings. Whereas it is easy to break down taboos against divorce and illegitimacy, it is much harder to create this new world where unmarried and divorced men and women cheerfully coparent and make the idealistic sacrifices as parents they were unwilling or unable to make as spouses.

Instead of concentrating our energies on a world of ideal divorces, why not seek instead a world of ideal marriages, where husbands and wives get up every morning rededicated to the effort: to love one person well, making whatever sacrifices are necessary to make the family a safe, wholesome place for each other and for their children.

Ozzie and Harriet never existed. So what? Whatever we aim for, the arrow falls short. The ideal serves to make that for which we strive more visible and to collect the disparate moments of consciousness into a story in which we can find the meaning of our lives. The questions are, which are we going to idealize, and toward which ideal will we strive, and perhaps fail? Perfect love or perfect unlove? Ideal marriage or ideal divorce? One, experience has proved, is no more attainable than the other. So which will we choose?

PART THREE

❧

THE
FUTURE
of
MARRIAGE

18

HOW NOT *to* SUCCEED *in* REVIVING MARRIAGE

"Maybe we're just a thoughtless generation," a young woman muses. "Maybe we just keep making wrong choices, over and over again." She is not alone in so suspecting. The belief that the roots of the divorce crisis are individual, psychological, or personal has a long history in America. Faced with the seemingly relentless decline in the institution that is the center of our lives, Americans have wanted to believe that something so simple as more education, more knowledge, or more thoughtfulness can stem the tide. In fact, since the late nineteenth century, reformers have promised an American public disturbed about divorce that whatever program the reformers were pushing would also strengthen marriage and family life.

Education has always been a particular favorite. "[The] frequency of divorce in the United States," one nineteenth-century editorialist put it, illuminates the "thoughtless manner in which marriage is contracted.... What we need to correct some of the evils of marriage, is not the liberty to commit the same errors a second time, but the qualifications that will prevent us from making the mistake in the first place."[1] Similarly, essayist Marguerite Wilkinson argued that the cure for the "divorce evil" was the "right education": If young people worked and played and studied together, they would know each other better and make better marital choices than those brought on by "proximity or moonlit perfervid error."[2]

Elizabeth Cady Stanton argued that the solution to rising divorce lay in laws restricting who could marry in the first place. "They who can give the world children with splendid physique, strong intellect and high moral sentiment," Stanton wrote in 1869, "may conscientiously take on themselves the responsibility of marriage and maternity." The rest, she argued, should be legally forbidden to marry.[3] Thomas Higginson, addressing the American Social Science Association in 1873, stood up for coeducation as a solution, proclaiming that "if anything is certain in our school system, it is, that the sexes, once united in school, are united forever."[4] In 1890 Mary Livermore, writing in the pages of the widely read *North American Review,* insisted that the only cure to "restlessness and unhappiness in married life" was "legal equality."[5]

Then, as now, there was a general reluctance to think deeply about what makes marriage succeed. Reformers tend to embrace whatever nostrum is currently popular as the solution to all social ills and impute to it the magical power required to restore marriage as well. Thus at the Boston Radical Club in May of 1878, a Mrs. Wells argued that "unhappiness in married life is caused by women having children when they don't want them," a condition that has largely disappeared in modern life without appearing to alter much the possibilities of human unhappiness in marriage.[6] Similarly, sex education, androgyny, and a host of other notions were all at one time or another promoted as cures to what ails marriage.

One reason we are reluctant to think deeply about family and marriage is that the family does not fit into the intellectual categories with which we feel most comfortable and whose metaphors come most easily to the tongue—especially the market metaphors that so permeate the American culture. Lacking the language to articulate the family relation, we try, futilely, and destructively, to fit the family into the language of economics or management, blinding ourselves to who we are and how we actually live.

The market is the arena of the stranger. The marvelous genius of capitalism is that it allows strangers to coordinate their activities productively, and without coercion, to the greater good. Creating structures in which people who hardly know each other can work the commercial miracles of modern society is an achievement not to be underrated, which is why the metaphors of capitalism are so powerful. But it is not a model for what families do.

The opposite of the market, in one direction, is the bureaucracy. Like the market, the bureaucracy imposes a certain order on human relations, allowing strangers to interact in predictable ways. But unlike the market, the bureaucracy directs their interactions according to a master plan. The bureaucrat is the philosopher-king, his reign is the imposition of the abstract on the individual. Because it too coordinates the productivity in strangers, the bureaucracy has had its own share of human triumphs and its even more grotesque betrayals.

What the bureaucracy and the market share is the ability to simplify and standardize human interactions, which is why they can coordinate the activity of strangers. To anyone who has been to the Department of Motor Vehicles lately it may sound odd to speak of bureaucracy as simplifying anything. But that is the purpose of all those forms and procedures—to reduce the complicated to the routine so that all the participants in the process know that, if they follow the rules step by step, they will end up in the same place, albeit perhaps not quickly enough. The standardized nexus of human interaction in the bureaucracy is "the form." In the market, the nexus is even simpler: It is cash or, if some trust has been achieved, credit, which one might call the market's universal standardized forms.

But what is the nexus of human interaction in the family? We so deeply avoid the subject—especially when, as in a book like this, we discuss "serious issues" such as "the state of the family"—that it is almost unbearable to pronounce it. Its name is *Love*. Or if you prefer a slightly more all-encompassing and powerful term, big enough to capture all the variants of love, including its perversions such as hate, lust, envy, and pride, then *eros*. These are not so easily standardized.

The family cannot be organized around so coolly liberal a set of incentives as those provided by cash, because the family, alone among the major structures of our society, remains stubbornly preliberal. The family cannot be rationalized according to the forms of bureaucracy because it is not rational. Why pour out your sweat and blood, why shed your tears for this child and not that one? Oh, it was your sperm, you say? Are you mad? Yes, quite mad. No family policy that ignores this universal human madness can possibly succeed.

And yet almost all of them do. As more people of all political persuasions become concerned about the effect of the collapse of marriage on children, reform proposals have begun to circulate. Almost without exception the proposed solutions are timid, abstract, inhuman, afraid of or unaware of the need to confront or engage the powers of eros. A few might be minor improvements, but most are simply irrelevant and many would make matters worse.

We are approaching one of those pregnant moments in a nation's history. The effects of the divorce culture have become so widespread, the reality of pain and loss so evident, that the force of experience in our own lives or the lives of those we love might just triumph over the rigid liberationist ideology of our youth. There is a new hunger for family life and a new willingness to take risks to re-create marriage. The danger is that the tremendous political, moral, and intellectual energy that is gathering will be squandered, dispersed in mere rhetoric, or lost in side battles for counterproductive ideas. After all, there are many examples of government programs designed to support family commitments that have instead undermined and accelerated their decay.

Consider the case of Sweden. In the thirties the Swedish welfare state was consciously designed to support the family and, especially, to encourage a higher birth rate. Government supports aimed, as Alva Myrdal wrote in her 1941 book *Nation and Family*, "to strengthen the family, to alleviate its worst trials and tribulations, and to make possible harmonious living."[7]

Yet as Rutgers sociologist David Popenoe notes, after sixty years of the most extensive family support programs on Earth, Sweden now finds itself with "a high family dissolution rate, perhaps the highest in the Western world, and a high percentage of single-parent, female-headed families." Sweden also has "the lowest marriage rate and the oldest average age at first marriage, and the largest percentage of households in which unmarried persons of the opposite sex cohabit. In addition… almost half of all Swedish children are now born to unmarried mothers." Even the simplest goal of Swedish family policy—to raise the birth rate—has foundered. "Sweden continues to have one of the world's lowest birth rates and smallest average family sizes." And even in Sweden, which boasts all the panoply of government family supports now urged in the United States, children raised outside of marriage experience many of the same traumas and disadvantages as American children. One recent study of nine thousand Swedish families found that, even after controlling for parental education, teenagers living with only their mothers scored lower in educational aptitude and achievement than those with two parents.[8] It is difficult to avoid concluding, as Popenoe does, that "in a paradoxical way, the political actions of the Swedish welfare state designed to strengthen the family have probably contributed to its weakening."[9]

Why? The reasons are likely to be as complicated, personal, explosive, and difficult to articulate as eros itself. Does it not seem at least possible that when government makes it materially easier to be a father, by taking over so much of the responsibility for providing for mothers and children, that being a father becomes less erotically satisfying? Or to put it more plainly, isn't a father who glories in the knowledge that he is needed more likely to devote his life to his family than a father who has been made dispensable?

In this country every few years some new divorce reform, some way of compensating for marriage's increasing fragility, is proposed. Hopes—soon dashed—run high that finally some effective substitute for the intact family has been found.

Take joint custody. In the seventies, a few exceptionally cooperative divorced parents began experimenting with voluntary joint custody. Preliminary studies of these parents brought back glowing reports. Joint custody, the professors and the pundits claimed, would bring fathers back into the family, lighten mothers' economic and emotional burdens, and ensure children all the advantages of a good-enough marriage, while freeing adults to develop themselves unhampered by inappropriate marital bonds. Joint custody was the magic bullet that would allow us to re-create the stable family outside of the bonds of marriage, to place the family beyond the anguish and ambivalence of eros.

So for a short while judges, understandably eager to shed the difficult task of making Solomonic decisions between two good-enough parents, rushed to impose joint custody on divorced parents and their children. Now, a few years down the road, we find sadly that children in joint custody are doing no better, than children in sole custody. According to Furstenberg and Cherlin, "[j]oint *legal* custody seems to be hardly distinguishable in practice from maternal sole custody." The evidence for the effect of joint physical custody is less established (as the number of such families is quite small), but at least two studies also suggest that children in joint physical custody "were no better adjusted than children from the mother-physical custody families."[10]

Feminists such as Lenore Weitzman, author of *The Divorce Revolution*, were among the first to notice the devastating economic costs divorce imposes on women and children. They proposed another new way to reconstruct the postmarital family: Through stricter child-support laws the government would take a more active role in ensuring the well-being of children after divorce.

Actual child-support payments have been so low (official payments fathers are supposed to make have been low enough) that numerous efforts have been made to boost these numbers. In 1981 Congress authorized the Internal Revenue Service to withhold federal income tax refunds from deadbeat dads. The Child Support Amendment of 1984 required employers to deduct child support payments from delinquent parents' paychecks. The 1988 Family Support Act set guidelines for child support and increased enforcement. These and other programs made child support easier to collect, but, overall, bore modest fruit. The grand result: In 1990 about half of single mothers were awarded child support. Only half of these received full payments. The average amount actually received was just under $3,000, which accounted for about one-fifth of family income.[11]

None of these efforts has made a serious dent in even the material poverty of one-parent families. And new child-support laws, however good in themselves, will not give these children fathers, stable families, faith in love, or even the ability to compete economically with children from intact homes. The tremendous sacrifices of time and money married fathers routinely make for children are of a kind that cannot be legislated. There is no law that says married parents must mortgage their house or drain their retirement accounts to pay for their children's college. There is no law that says fathers (or mothers) must take two jobs to give their children new braces, a home in a better school district, or a shot at the Ivy League. Yet married fathers do those things routinely. And, as a matter of empirical fact, we have discovered that many of the very same men who, in the undivided loyalties created by marriage, will make such sacrifices for the children in their own home, simply will not do so for children who have become part of someone else's household, and that someone an ex-wife. At best, outside of marriage men will pay only what they believe they can afford—after their own household expenses are met. Deny or decry it as we will, inside of marriage child support is an erotic adventure, outside of marriage it is a tax increase.

More important, even for the best of men, the dissolution of marriage creates loyalty conflicts for which there is no easy solution, conflicts between their children and their stepchildren, their children and their wives, their first batch of children and their second. Not everyone can come first. Put the children first, the advocates say, and I agree. But can a culture that refuses to insist that men and women accept the sacrifices of marriage credibly insist these same people make large sacrifices for the sake of unmarriage?

The advantages of a good-enough marriage simply cannot be re-created outside of marriage, for they lie precisely in the union of economic, erotic, and emotional interests of children, mother, and father, that is, the essence of marriage. The energy that is being poured into trying to remake divorce and illegitimacy into a substitute for marriage is only distracting us from the larger, more ambitious, and more fruitful task of rebuilding marriage.

Such a restoration is not part of our political agenda because honestly acknowledging the power of eros is not part of our political etiquette. Instead, with the only metaphors available to us—those of the bureaucracy and the market—we settle for managing what we have persuaded ourselves is the inevitable decline of the family. The differences between the Democrats and Republicans come down to this: The Democrats are in the business of managing family decline while denying it ("these are just new kinds of families"); the GOP is in the business of managing family decline at the least cost to taxpayers.

As irrelevant as many of the standard Democratic/bureaucratic family support programs are, equally damaging is the GOP's cynical manipulation of the growing concern of Americans over the state of marriage. This reached its height in George Bush's losing 1992 campaign, in which "family values" was merely a rhetorical fig leaf covering up the lack of any real political agenda. By standing foursquare for marriage, the GOP hoped to avoid the necessity of summoning the political will actually to do anything about its collapse.

The danger is not that such cosmetic political efforts will backfire but that they may succeed. Recently, Republicans have shifted their attention to gay rights, and there is every sign the GOP will use popular unease on this issue as a substitute for any real effort to arrest family decline—a way to attract the votes of many concerned about the family decline without having to spend any political capital addressing it. Opposing gay marriage or gays in the military is for Republicans an easy, juicy, risk-free issue. Most of us are not homosexual, and we can decry homosexuality quite comfortably because such denunciations ask nothing of ourselves. For the GOP to succeed by placing such a marginal issue at the center of the political debate is worse than failure: For four years, or eight years, or twelve years, voters may have in the White House a president who maintains the status quo and utters "family values" while doing nothing to stop the forces ripping apart marriage as more and more people resign themselves to decay and despair.

Lethargy and despair are, after all, precisely what intellectuals and opinion leaders, including many on the Right, are preaching on this subject. The message—that at all costs we should keep divorce off the political agenda—is often disguised by the same rhetoric of realism that was used to justify the switch to no-fault divorce in the seventies: The law can't really do anything to slow the increase in divorce, which is the result of inexorable social forces, so we are better off not pretending it can.

Behind the "realism," one suspects, is political cowardice combined in some cases with a guilty conscience. Republican as well as Democratic politicians surely know that a very substantial portion of the electorate believes that divorce on demand is a fundamental human right. Everyone knows "you can't force people to stay married." And unwed mothers are still by and large poor and marginal, while there are millions of divorced men and remarried women who are firmly middle class.

Thus Dan Quayle, like Charles Murray and other conservatives, finds it far easier to denounce illegitimacy than to take even mild exception to divorce. In his widely publicized Murphy Brown II speech, he condemned the practice of having children outside of marriage but hastily added: "I am not talking about a situation where there is a divorce." As *Washington Post* columnist Richard Cohen rightly asked, "But why not? Divorce is the sundering of the sacred family.... To say this, though, would risk alienating millions of Americans, many of whom have decided to put their personal happiness ahead of what's best for their children."[12]

Call it what you will; as long as such "realism" prevails, there is no hope for restoring the American family nor even for arresting its decline. Politics and economy are a part of culture, not its opposite. Only a realist could believe that the spiraling degeneration of American society could be addressed without putting the collapse of marriage on the political agenda.

19

RE-CREATING
MARRIAGE

FOR THE FIRST TIME IN AMERICAN HISTORY, a whole generation of children appears likely to be worse off than their parents. Why has no serious political effort been made—or even proposed—to revive and stabilize marriage? Even in our minds we dare go no further than timidly considering how to take the edge off children's worst deprivations: Democratic policy wonks ponder which government policies can keep kids just this side of the poverty line, while their GOP counterparts merely add the proviso, and at the least cost to the taxpayers.

After canvassing the nation, a February 27, 1995, *Time* magazine cover story dramatically titled "For Better, for Worse: The Growing Movement to Strengthen Marriage and Prevent Divorce," could find no bolder proposal to combat the collapse of marriage than more counseling and waiting periods for marriage licenses.

Reforms like these amount to less of a crusade than a white flag of surrender. The results of our thirty-year experiment—demoting marriage from a key institution to a lifestyle option—are in; the damage the divorce culture has wreaked on our children, our society, and the national purse is increasingly difficult to deny or ignore.

The truth is, we can no longer afford the fashionable luxury of despair. Whether they are liberal sociologists blaming the collapse of marriage on inevitable historical forces or free-market conservatives waiting helplessly for a second religious "Great Awakening," the siren voices of apathy must be resisted. Especially apathy disguised as reform.

Faint-hearted efforts to manipulate government aid and child support may keep more kids above an arbitrary poverty line. But no social program can give divorced couples the economies of marriage. Nor can the law compel the kind of enormous sacrifices—from working overtime, to taking a second job, to mortgaging the house to pay for college—that married fathers routinely make for their children, but which divorced or unmarried fathers seldom do.

"What good is a piece of paper?" we children of the sixties asked. And it is in the lives of the children of the eighties and nineties that research has uncovered increasingly troubling answers. The good marriage is slipping ever further out of our grasp. Meanwhile, the ideal divorce remains even more elusive.

The next great American challenge is to get out of the business of merely managing the decline of the family and begin the process of rebuilding it. To recreate marriage, we have to step back from the angry couple and look at marriage in a wider context: What incentives are now in place, and what incentives does marriage require? How can we restore some traditional supports, and how can we come up with innovative ways to nurture marriage? People who wish to marry are attempting to do something—something more than merely living together until they drift apart. How can law, culture, and public policy conspire to help more Americans achieve their heart's desire?

Do not look for or expect easy answers—a single silver bullet to slay the divorce dragon. Piece by piece, the cultural, political, and economic edifice supporting marriage has been taken down, often only half-consciously by courts and reformers who sincerely believed they were expanding "personal choice." Reconstructing marriage will require taking a serious, unsentimental look at a wide array of public policy decisions in the light of a new understanding of what marriage as an institution requires.

Absent such a thoughtful and determined effort, marriage will not by some mystical process revive, and it may not even survive. The tragic experience of the African American family should warn us that it is indeed possible for marriage, as a durable child-rearing bond, to virtually disappear. The forces undermining the married family in modern society are many and deep: the decline in male wages, the deteriorating neighborhoods and schools, the graying of America and the consequent diversion of resources from children to the elderly, and the sexual revolution.

Above all, a 50 percent to 60 percent divorce rate—tolerated for a generation—in itself sets in motion a dynamic of decline that will not spontaneously reverse itself. In a divorce culture, anxious married couples sharply limit their investment in each other and in children. As the marriage contract becomes attenuated and unenforceable, fewer married women feel safe bearing children. And as fewer single women see any need to marry to have children, the illegitimacy rate soars. Meanwhile, their children—the children of divorce—are themselves at higher risk of divorce and unwed parenthood, a phenomenon that by itself fuels a dangerously downward spiral of marital decay.

To break the cycle requires first and foremost strengthening the law of marriage. The first step is to end unilateral divorce. Making divorce quick and easy at the discretion of one partner has led to a surge in the divorce rate everywhere it has been tried, for reasons obvious to anyone who has ever been married. Recent research suggests such changes in divorce law may account for as much as 25 percent of the increase in the divorce rate.

Reforming no-fault divorce is more than a tactical necessity. Simple decency requires that the law retreat from relentlessly favoring the spouse who leaves in no-fault divorces and place some minimal power back into the hands of the spouse who is being left. Imposing a five- to seven-year waiting period for contested no-fault divorces (as do many European jurisdictions) would serve the ends of both justice and prudence: raising the number of marriages that ultimately succeed, while at the very least ensuring that those who want a quick and easy divorce will have to negotiate with their marriage partner in order to get it.

Stabilizing marriage law also requires finding new mechanisms for making sure the marriage contract has legal force. One reason for America's seemingly relentless drift toward more and more lenient divorce laws is federalism: since states are required to recognize each others' divorces, divorce law has tended to be driven by the most permissive state. A New York husband who wants to divorce his wife can, after a quick trip to Reno, come back a free man, regardless of New York law. One solution is to make the marriage contract explicit, rather than implicit: give married couples a copy of the marriage contract now drawn up for them by state legislatures. Federal law should require that state courts recognize the validity of marriage contracts of other states, and should require the use of the written contract as the basis for divorce.

Finally, some legal avenue should also be opened for those who wish, in marrying, to make an enduring commitment. At the very least the law should support permanent marriage by giving people the option of making one. Prenuptial agreements are routinely used to protect the wealthier spouse in the event of a divorce. If the law can limit marital liability, should it not, at the very least, accommodate those who—out of love, longing, religion, or ideals—seek to extend it? A prenuptial covenant, permitting divorce only for serious cause, or even, if the couple wished, prohibiting it altogether, should be a legally enforceable option.

Other roadblocks the law has put before community efforts to sustain marriage must be removed. Federal statutes, originally intended to protect single and divorced women from discrimination, should be amended to make it clear that it is not illegal for private parties or local governments to distinguish between married and unmarried *couples* in housing, credit, zoning, and other areas. Putting landlords who don't want to rent to cohabitating youngsters in the same legal fix as bigots who won't rent to blacks is both insulting and self-destructive. It keeps neighborhoods from sorting themselves into varying codes of behavior and thereby prevents private society from doing what government can't do well: upholding community moral standards. For similar reasons, domestic partnership legislation, if enacted, should be explicitly restricted to homosexuals. Offering the legal benefits of marriage to those who have refused its legal responsibilities is both unfair and unwise.

In the area of adoption and foster care, the law should once more reinforce marriage as the child-rearing norm. In many states, such as New York, mothers who surrender their children for adoption or who lose their children through neglect and abuse are given an inordinately long time to change their minds or their ways. If, for example, a baby is abandoned in a hospital, what does the government do? In New York City, social workers track down the birth mother and offer her "services." For older children, who are already attached to their mothers, this hesitation on the law's part to take children from their families makes sense. Children love even very inadequate mothers, and this attachment deserves our respect. But when young mothers surrender their rights by abusing and neglecting infants, when babies are abandoned at birth or born addicted to crack, the law should step in more swiftly to give the child a real chance to become part of a loving married-couple family.

Welfare policy has been discussed extensively elsewhere. To that currently raging debate I would only add this proviso: The primary goal of welfare reform should not be to save money, but to reverse the trend toward unwed motherhood. Whether they admit it or not, the Republicans' approach to welfare hinges on curbing the skyrocketing illegitimacy rate. If welfare reform does not succeed in reducing out-of-wedlock births, then scaling back the federal financial commitment will have the Dickensian results its opponents prophesy.

As of this writing, Congress appears poised to pass the Senate's welfare package, avoiding a family cap and a ban on welfare to under-age mothers in favor of a five-year time limit on benefits, a requirement that half of welfare recipients work, and the transformation of

Aid to Families with Dependent Children (AFDC) from an entitlement to a block grant.

If the goal is curbing illegitimacy, the Senate approach has serious drawbacks. Workfare has been tried extensively and found to be both very expensive and only modestly useful in getting women off welfare. Pushing workfare is really part of the continuing and (I believe) futile attempt to remake the single-parent family into a functional substitute for marriage. If most educated divorced women regain their family income only through remarriage, can we really expect poor, uneducated, underparented young women to singlehandedly raise decent kids and pull them out of poverty?

For the purpose of ending a culture of dependency, a five-year time limit may be worse than useless. For the average teenager, much less a poor, inner-city kid, five years seems an eternity. The Senate proposal thus invites a vulnerable young woman to have a baby she cannot support and then cuts her off after she has made decisions (like quitting school or having another baby) that make it virtually impossible for her to become self-supporting. Similarly, while one can imagine asking her to give up for adoption a baby she cannot take care of, one cannot really ask the same woman, five years later, to ditch a preschooler just because she is poor.

Far more important is ending welfare for underage mothers. In 1993, 369,000 babies were born to unmarried teenagers, about 30 percent of all out-of-wedlock births.[1] If we aren't willing to tell these poor, undereducated unmarried girls categorically that they should not be raising children alone, we aren't serious about ending poverty or making a start on rebuilding marriage.

Instead of routinely giving custody of babies to girls too young to drive a car or sign a contract, the law should require that every baby born in America be under the guardianship of a competent adult. That adult will assume full legal and financial responsibility for the child until the minor mother grows up and demonstrates (through marriage or a full-time job) she is capable of providing her children with a home. If the girl's parents (or other friend or relative) are unwilling or unable to provide such a guarantee, the baby should be made available for adoption.

Welfare is not the only issue. Our bumper crop of children having children is in part the fruit of a 1972 federal law that made it illegal for schools receiving federal funds to expel students or restrict their participation in school activities because of pregnancy or parenthood. The law produced its intended result: The high school completion rate of young teen mothers jumped from 19 percent in 1958 to 56 percent in 1986, according to the Alan Guttmacher Institute's 1986 study. At the same time, the proportion of births to unmarried girls skyrocketed. A high school diploma has proved no substitute for marriage, either for babies or for their childishly young mothers. Indeed, as we saw, even a college degree does not innoculate youngsters from the disadvantages of growing up outside of marriage. The federal government should get out of the business of trying to make unwed motherhood a viable social institution: Using the power of the purse, Washington has done much to elevate unwed motherhood in the minds of youngsters from a moral wrong to a Constitutional right.   School districts should once again be permitted to require pregnant girls (and where identifiable, the boys who impregnate them) to attend special schools during the pregnancy. Such a policy recognizes that getting pregnant is not a pathological behavior, but a profoundly attractive human achievement, one that other girls are likely to envy and emulate, particularly in poor neighborhoods where neither marriage nor career appears to be likely possibilities.

At the same time, we should change the emphasis in school classrooms from merely combating teen pregnancy to discouraging out-of-wedlock births. This need not (and ought not) require stigmatizing children from broken homes. Children without fathers know better than anyone else the special strains of life outside of marriage. But in current health and family life textbooks, marriage is treated as a small footnote in the much larger and more important story of child abuse or of family diversity. Much of the small space devoted to marriage is taken up by dire warnings against that fifties' bugaboo, teenage marriage.

Surely there is something wrong with a society that can explicitly tell its teenagers not to get married but is afraid to warn them against out-of-wedlock births for fear of sounding overly moralistic. We owe our young people a well-grounded knowledge of the economic, social, health, and emotional advantages of a good-enough marriage. All federally funded sex education and family life programs should be required to focus on the value of a good-enough marriage for adults and children.

Moreover, transcending the welfare debate's narrow focus on changing the behavior of poor women, we must seek policies to stem the falling wages of men, particularly poor, black inner-city men. We need to reevaluate and reform current job-training programs, including workfare, that are available to or are successful with women only and relax federal regulations to permit local inner-city school districts to experiment with programs aimed specifically at vulnerable inner-city boys, including single-sex public schools.

The next step is to recognize that the whole underlying premise of our welfare system—reserving scarce public dollars for only the poorest, who inevitably turn out to be single mothers—may be self-defeating.

Norms are not self-sustaining. When government is as big and as powerful as it is in modern-day America, when it consumes so much of individual and national resources, then it inevitably plays a key role (whether we like it or not) in maintaining norms of behavior. When public policy refuses to recognize, reward, and reinforce norms, the norms begin to evaporate. Rearing children is arduous, time-consuming, and expensive. Single people have responded to the new erosion of marital supports by avoiding marriage altogether. Married families have responded by putting more and more family members in the workforce, laboring longer hours, cutting back severely on the number of children they have, and, in the ensuing distress, divorcing more often.

The illegitimacy rate is skyrocketing both because married people have so few children and because single mothers have more. Married couples can stop having children, or single women can start having them. Either way, the illegitimacy rate jumps.

Looking at the troubled state of the African American family, we must recognize that the relative childlessness of stable marriages is almost as serious a problem as the fertility of the unwed—at least insofar as the one or no-child family represents not the fulfillment but the frustration of the wishes of overworked, overtaxed, divorce-anxious married couples. Married families have been treated by federal policymakers as a kind of cash cow that can be relied on to generate tax revenues for any and all government needs. In economic terms, public policy now systematically discriminates against the married by taxing married families at unprecedented rates to provide a wide array of benefits available only to single mothers or to families of such low incomes that even working-class married couples do not qualify.

This pronounced public policy tilt against marriage was not always the case. Until the late sixties, for example, New York City public housing projects gave a preference to low-income married couples. But along with federal money came federal strings: Washington insisted that public housing dismantle this preference for the married poor. The result is not only an erosion in the quality of life at housing projects, but a dismantling of important supports for marriage in the working class. It is a measure of how far marriage has fallen from official favor that the Guiliani administration recently braved a controversy to bring back preferences—but only for "working" families, not necessarily for married families. (Meanwhile, in New York City public schools, children are taught that it is a violation of civil rights to "discriminate" on the basis of marital status.) Once again, Washington, D.C., using its immense financial leverage, effectively forbade local communities from supporting marriage.

Working-class families may need some public subsidies. Public housing projects, now obsessed with maintaining racial balance, would be far better off if the federal government permitted them to reserve a substantial portion of their slots for low-income married couples. To offset the marriage penalty working-class couples face, Congress should replace the earned-income tax credit with a "marriage bonus" administered through the tax code for all married families with incomes of less than 50 percent of the average married family.

But all married families need to be allowed to keep more of their own private income for the vital public purpose of rearing children. In recent decades, the economic basis of marriage has been allowed to erode, particularly in tax policy. Federal tax relief has been targeted at taxpayers in general and at low-income families, disproportionately single mothers. Meanwhile, the tax burden has shifted heavily onto married couples with children. To restore the protection that has been lost to inflation, the dependent exemption would have to be more than tripled, from about $2,500 to nearly $8,000 a year.

For low-income families, the recently expanded earned income tax credit helps offset tax increases. But the earned income tax credit, besides being subject to extraordinary rates of fraud, is another example of family policy aimed at incomes so low most married families need not apply. Less than 20 percent make under $25,000 a year, the approximate income cutoff for the earned income tax credit. By contrast, the majority of single moms makes less than $15,000 a year.[2] Policies like the earned income tax credit thus protect most single mothers, but relatively few married couple families. Even the proposed $500 child tax credit (which at this writing appears likely to be whittled down in the Senate) was designed to deliver disproportionate benefits to the lower middle class, ignoring the relative disadvantage now built into the tax code for all married couples with children. The question of fairness involved in the child credit or dependent exemption is not whether a couple with three kids making $100,000 should pay more taxes than a similar couple making $40,000. (They should and do.) The question is whether a family of five making $100,000 should be asked to pay the same taxes as a bachelor making $100,000 a year.

The theory behind the generous protections for the average family built into the fifties tax code is simple: Among the competing public interests of the nation, the needs of children ought to come first. Families must be allowed to keep all the income they reasonably need to rear children, before making other contributions to the national welfare. By allowing inflation to gut the dependent exemption, we have implicitly transformed children (and the marriages that protect them) from public contributions into private consumption items.

Probably the most straightforward way to stabilize marriage, without discriminating either for or against working mothers, is to restore the value of the dependent exemption to $8,000 per dependent (which happens to be almost exactly the amount the government estimates each child costs a middle-class family in out-of-pocket expenses) and index it to inflation. Such a policy would relieve the economic distress of many married families (who have been increasingly taxed as if they had the discretionary income of childless singles), provide more money for day care for those women who choose to work, aid families in which parents work in shifts in order to care for their own children, and help many other women withdraw from the labor force, perhaps temporarily or part time.

Allowing married families to provide for their own needs will be expensive. There are few short-term supply-side returns to family tax cuts, which is why economic conservatives tend to oppose them. Instituting them will require making politically painful choices in the federal budget. The returns come not in next year's revenues but in the long-range increase in productivity and social stability that will take place when a greater proportion of American children grow up under the protection that a good-enough marriage provides. The hidden crime tax, the ignorance tax, the drug tax, and the explicit taxes required to fund an ever-increasing welfare state all take a deep toll on the economy and an even deeper toll on American civilization.

For, above all, it is the collapse of marriage that has fueled the ever-increasing welfare state, and economic conservatives are fooling themselves if they believe they can do more than retard its political momentum in the long run, absent a revival of marriage. American self-reliance has ultimately been based not on rugged individualism

but on the mutual interdependence of husband and wife, the donation of the self in the service of children and community. Where after
all do the clients of the client-state come from? A decrease in the
divorce and illegitimacy rate would cut the ranks of the homeless, the
welfare dependent, the drug addicted, and above all the criminal class.

Changes like these are not small or cheap. They will happen only
when married families begin to view themselves (as senior citizens
do) as a coherent interest group or when society as a whole recognizes the central importance of marriage. Fortunately, there are
encouraging signs of the public's willingness to tackle the problems
of marriage as an institution. For example, since the late eighties,
according to Gallup polls, a majority of Americans once again say
that divorce should be made more difficult to obtain. Americans
want marriage. By a margin of 76 percent to 19 percent, or four to
one, Americans would rather live in a place "that strongly upholds
traditional family values" than a place "that is very tolerant of non-
traditional lifestyles."[3]

We may never return to the low divorce rates of the past century.
But surely it is possible, as a first step, to achieve one simple goal: to
create a society in which more marriages succeed than fail and in
which each year more children (rather than fewer) are born into the
relative safety of marriage.

It is so much easier to seek solace in the comforting clichés under-
writing the divorce cult: that marriages today are happier and more
loving, that women are freer and better off now that marriage is failing, and that our children will be happier only if we are "happy."
Above all, we cling to the comforting myth that "nothing can be
done" about the collapse of marriage. We find our despair comforting because it relieves us of the hard necessity of taking responsibility for our values and our actions, public and private—for the world
we are creating for ourselves and our children.

Law, economics, and public policy have all played a part in tearing
down marriage but they are not the sole villains. Escaping the divorce
culture requires an even more radical step: recovering the full meaning of marriage.

20

THE MEANING
of MARRIAGE

AT THE END OF A LENGTHY 1985 TEXTBOOK on marriage and family, sociologist Randall Collins makes this pronouncement: "Love has become more important, not less. People make their marriages more for love."

The divorce epidemic, he reasons, does not represent a failure of love so much as a sign of its increasing importance: "People are less willing to stay in a marriage without love," and, after all, "love is volatile."[1]

This has become the commonplace view, as frequently appearing on the boob tube or the cocktail circuit as in the scholars' texts. The alterations in our views of marriage are usually described as positive: people care less about money and more about love. "[e]motional gratification, therefore, has become a more central part of defining what is a good marriage."[2] Or, as Frank F. Furstenberg, Jr., and Andrew J. Cherlin put it, "[E]motional gratification has become the *sine qua non* of married life. It is the main glue that holds couples together."[3]

Marriages today are *better* than marriages in the past because marriages today are based on love. Our marriages are more fragile (we say, patting ourselves on the back) precisely because we care about love more than our parents or grandparents did. A 60 percent failure rate is the price we pay for basing marriage on love, because, after all, as everyone knows: "love is volatile."

Volatile. As in explosive, intense, ephemeral, ecstatic, and unreliable. Love is a cherub on wings launching surprise attacks with unseen arrows—fickle, imperious, and unpredictable.

Everyone knows that. Don't they?

There is another view of love, almost (but not quite) as old.
Love is patient, love is kind. It is not jealous, it is not pompous, it is not inflated. It bears all things, believes all things, hopes all things, endures all things. Love never fails.[4]

The foundation of marriage is love. The end of marriage is love. That is the consensus of Americans and, indeed, of Western civilization. As far back as we can record in American history, in the popular culture and in serious literature, from the pulpit and the philosopher's podium, expert and populist united in asserting that the only basis for marriage was love. To marry without it was to court disaster, for as the Puritans put it, "They that marry where they affect not, will affect where they marry not."[5]

But what is love?

This is hardly a new question. Early Christian thinkers, who created that uncomfortable synthesis of Judeo-Christian and Greco-Roman ideals that we call Western civilization, solved the problem by cutting love in half: there is eros and there is agape, the voluptuous Venus and the ascetic saint, the fickle cupid and the faithful mother. There is altruistic love—faithfulness, self-giving, loyalty, sacrifice. And there is romantic love—passion, desire, need, lust, ecstasy, union, delight. There is Mother Theresa, and there is Madonna.

The logic for cleaving love into these two parts has always been perfectly clear. What remains murky is not the difference but the sameness: In what sense are such polar opposites the same? In what way are the two loves both love? And thus what is this thing called *love* that we call upon in marriage?

Love naturally ends. Love never fails. People want to believe the latter when they enter marriage and the former when they leave it. But what do we believe in between?

The tendency among the purveyors of mores throughout most of

Christian history was to herd us toward agape. (Until the late sixties people imagined that Eros could pretty much fight his own battles.) But what if, in this, as in so much else, we are mistaken? What if the problem is not that we indulge erotic love, but that we ignore it: misrepresent and misunderstand our own stories, losing the narrative thread that gives meaning to our marriages and to our lives? What if, scorning eros, we literally do not know what we are doing when we love?

When John Adams settled down to write his political "*magnum opus*," *Discourses on Davila*, which sought to lay bare, in one biographer's words, "the emotional source of all political behavior," he began with a story: Once there was a starving pauper who had a dog. Save yourself, his friends urged, eat the dog's food so you may live. But the pauper refused, saying, "Who will love me then?"[6]

"In this '*who will love me then?*' there is a key to the human heart," maintained Adams, "to the history of human life and manners; and the rise and fall of empires." At the bottom of much behavior that appears to aim at wealth or power is another more basic passion, he argued, "the *passion for distinction*," a craving "to be observed, considered, esteemed, praised, beloved and admired by his fellows."

What Adams called the "passion for distinction" is one half of eros—the desire to be a good for another person: the beloved. This intense interestedness is what distinguishes eros from agape, which causes preachers and philosophers to look at it askance, is the desire to possess the beloved. Unlike the disinterested agape, eros desires urgently to be loved, as well as to love. Erotic love is hungry, full of need, and defined by desire, the desire to be fulfilled—and a matching urgent desire to fulfill that which one loves. Eros contains this simultaneous desire: That the good exists and that it *loves*.

The rhetoric of romantic love is filled with expression of this desire, a drive for union with what seems the ultimate good—a union of hearts, of wills, of flesh, and of interests—reverence combined with a wish to be revered, to consume and to be consumed, and thereby to become one substance with the beloved. "I feel as if my being were dissolved, and the idea of you were diffused throughout it," Nathaniel Hawthorne writes to his beloved wife-to-be, Sophia.

This drive for union at the heart of eros explains why the lover is impelled toward the most extraordinary of acts: the vow. As C. S. Lewis noted, "Those who are in love have a natural inclination to bind themselves by promises. Love songs all over the world are full of vows of eternal constancy."[7] Love seeks to rescue itself from its human limitations, change, uncertainty, and the terrible decay of time.

Lust is degraded eros; lust desires possession, not union; lust wishes to debase the beloved into an object, the better to own. Lust takes but does not surrender. In eros, the gift of the beloved's self is matched by the gift of the lover's self. Lover and beloved become confused. What separates eros and lust is reciprocity. The desire to be for the other what the other is for you.

The link between eros and lust has been endlessly discussed in Western history. It has usually been the neediness of eros that caused saints and philosophers to warn us against it. But it is not need, or at least not desire, that makes eros similar to lust. It is the focus on the self.

Agape can be just as self-centered, because it aspires to self-sufficiency—to give and not to need. This desire for self-contained virtue is the secret link between agape and lust.

The priest has (or is supposed to have) agape for his fellow man. The consecrated celibate is freer to do good to mankind in general because he has not promised to love one person in particular. But in another, deeper sense, the married man and the monk are mirror images of one another. The priest is revered because his agape—his disinterested love for mankind—frees his erotic love for God. It is not the absence of desire but the object of his desire that does him honor: He chooses as his beloved the highest Good.

And God. Does he love us disinterestedly, in the classical agape style, without desire? "And God so loved the world that he gave his only begotten Son." Was he self-possessed and even-handed in his love for David? Did he send Abraham and Isaac into the desert, the father to sacrifice the son, out of a disinterested regard for their personal growth?

"It is only infatuation, the unjust disregard for the claims of every existing thing, that does justice to what exists," writes Theodore Adorno. Marriage is the embodiment of infatuation in this sense: It is the unjust disregard for the claim of every other person for our regard. In return we can come as close as human beings are capable of doing "justice" to one human being: to know and to love him. To attempt to love just one other person the way God loves everyone. That is the seal, the aim, the substance of the marriage contract. Marriage is the incarnation of eros, the body of love. It is the psalms and the Song of Songs and it is the Crucifixion, or at least it is our aspiration to all of these things.

A conference of distinguished experts—psychologists, sociologists, therapists. The subject is the collapse of marriage and how to stop it. But each attempt to come up with some concrete solution—in law, economics, or even culture—comes smack up against this wall: "What are we telling people, that happy marriages should stay together? They do."

For a moment we stop stupefied before the bleak picture that emerges from these words: two miserable, bitter people grimly hanging together "for the sake of children." Is this what we advocate? Is this what we want for ourselves, for our children, or for our nation? Is this the image of marriage we are trying to preserve: the grim-faced couple, barely speaking, waiting around for merciful death?

And yet the alternative is bleaker still: to use people until they are no longer useful, to have no ties that bind, no way to make a declaration of enduring love. To have only disposable wives and husbands (followed closely by disposable mothers and fathers and disposable children). For some of us, and perhaps a growing number, no sacrifice is too great to avoid the bleakness of the world we are now busily (in the name of happiness) creating.

But to rebuild marriage, we must recognize that grimly hanging in there "for the sake of the children" will not work, that it has never been enough. For marriage to thrive, and perhaps even to survive, we need to recapture our vision of the undertaking, to reimagine it as worthy for its own sake.

In spite of everything, America remains a marrying society. In the 1980s, despite the rise of divorce, single motherhood, and cohabitation, there were more marriages performed each year than ever before.[8] Each year more than 2 million Americans made it to the altar or the justice of the peace, and made vows to each other, made demands on each other,and went beyond making love to making a marriage. What were they trying to do?

I was raised in a traditional family with untraditional ideas. My mother, particularly, found many of the new ideas of marriage deeply attractive. "People should have choices," she told me.

We settled the argument this way: "When you talk about divorce," I finally told her, "you are thinking about yourself now: whether, having raised your kids, you and Dad should stay together out of duty or choice. When I think about divorce, I am wondering whether the man I marry will feel entitled to walk out whenever he thinks it would further his personal growth, leaving me with three little kids to raise alone."

Though we may never agree, at least we understood each other. For my mother had always known that, whatever happened in their marriage, my father would never abandon her or us. It is precisely that kind of certainty which, for many younger women and men, has fled. For far too many people, living amid the collapse of marriage, marriage no longer represents safety, but danger.

Those who try to avoid the danger by avoiding marriage discover that the dangers are not embedded in the social construction of marriage but in the nature of love itself. To trust is to risk betrayal. To refuse to trust is to refuse to love.

Marriage as an institution frays and falls not when it makes too many demands on people but when it makes too few; not when it is too imperiously and terrifyingly erotic but when it is too risk averse, too accommodating of our timidity. Men and women marry because they long for certainty, for secure love. Not only to have it but to give it, and to give it and have it in a way that becomes indistinguishable. They want to trust and become trustworthy. When marriage fails to deliver this good, the line between marriage and unmarriage blurs. When marriage becomes a contract not worth the piece of paper on which it is written, people begin saying, "Why do we need a piece of paper?"

But because there is no alternative to love, people keep trying to re-create marriage on their own, with or without the piece of paper: It is an attempt doomed to failure.

How do we raise men to be dependable husbands and fathers? Do we raise women to appreciate, in men, those qualities? What kind of legal, cultural, and economic institution will marriage be? No neutrality is possible in answering questions like these. To design an institution of marriage that has all the virtues of free love is to abolish marriage, to throw people entirely on their own individual resources.

A hundred years ago (and for centuries before that) romantics, living in a time when marriage could be taken for granted, imagined that the heroic acts of love must take place outside of marriage. But these wistful romantics were wrong. Today we have learned through a painful process of social experimentation that it is not free love but the vow that is daring. To dare to pledge our whole selves to a single love is the most remarkable thing most of us will ever do.

With the abolition of marriage, that last possibility for heroism has been taken from us.

NOTES

CHAPTER 1

1. David T. Ellwood, *Poor Support: Poverty and the American Family* (New York: Basic Books, 1988), 46.

2. Arlene Skolnick, *Embattled Paradise: The American Family in an Age of Uncertainty* (New York: Basic Books, 1991), 18.

3. Teresa Castro Martin and Larry L. Bumpass, "Recent Trends in Marital Disruption," *Demography* 26 (1989): 37–51.

4. Larry L. Bumpass, "What's Happening to the Family? Interactions Between Demographic and Institutional Change," *Demography* 27, no. 4 (1990): 485.

5. Dennis A. Ahlburg and Carol J. DeVita, "New Realities of the American Family," *Population Bulletin* 47, no. 2 (August 1992): 15.

6. Amara Bachu, *Fertility of American Women: June 1994* (Washington D.C.: Bureau of the Census, September 1995), xix, Table K.

7. Ahlburg and DeVita, "New Realities," 4–12.

8. Bachu, *Fertility of American Women: June 1994*, v.

9. Sara Bonkowski, *Kids Are Non-Divorceable: A Workbook for Divorced Parents and Their Children* (Chicago: Buckley Publications, 1987).

10. Martin King Whyte, *Dating, Mating, and Marriage* (New York: Aldine de Gruyter, 1990), 1.

11. Stephanie Coontz, *The Way We Never Were: American Families and the Nostalgia Trap* (New York: Basic Books, 1992), 15.

12. Arlene S. Skolnick and Jerome H. Skolnick, *Family in Transition* (Boston: Little, Brown and Company, 1986), 6–7.

13. Whyte, *Dating, Mating, and Marriage*, 1.

14. *Rebuilding the Nest: A New Commitment to the American Family*, ed. David Blankenhorn, Steve Bayme, and Jean Bethke Elshtain (Milwaukee, WI: Family Service America, c. 1990), 97–98.

15. Whyte, *Dating, Mating, and Marriage*, 57.

16. Andrew J. Cherlin, *Marriage, Divorce, Remarriage* (Cambridge, Mass.: Harvard University Press, 1981), 129. See also Arland Thornton, "Changing Attitudes Towards Family Issues in the United States," *Journal of Marriage and the Family* 51 (November 1989): 873–893.

17. Frank F. Furstenberg, Jr., and Andrew J. Cherlin, *Divided Families: What Happens to Children When Parents Part* (Cambridge, Mass.: Harvard University Press, 1991), 22.

18. Glenda Riley, *Divorce: An American Tradition* (New York: Oxford University Press, 1991), 6.

19. Bachu, *Fertility of American Women*, xix, Table K.

20. June Axinn, "Japan: A Special Case," in *The Feminization of Poverty: Only in America?* Gertrude Schaffner Goldberg and Eleanor Kremen (New York: Greenwood Press, 1990), 101.

21. Martin and Bumpass, "Recent Trends," 37–51.

22. See Larry L. Bumpass, "What's Happening to the Family: Interactions Between Demographic and Institutional Change," *Demography* 27 (1990): 483–498.

23. See Sara McLanahan and Larry L. Bumpass, "Intergenerational Consequences of Family Disruption," *American Journal of Sociology* 94 (1988): 130ff.

CHAPTER 2

1. Laurence Krasny Brown and Marc Tolon Brown, *Dinosaur's Divorce* (Boston: Atlantic Monthly Press, c. 1986).

2. Edward W. Beal and Gloria Hochman, *Adult Children of Divorce: Breaking the Cycle and Finding Fulfillment in Love, Marriage, and Family* (New York: Delta Books, 1991), 317–319.

3. Lynn Smith, "Building a Family in Steps," *Los Angeles Times*, 6 October 1993.

4. Richard A. Gardner, *The Boys' and Girls' Book About Divorce* (New York: Bantam Books, 1988), xxv–xxvi.

5. See, for example, Beal and Hochman, *Adult Children of Divorce*; Diane Fassel, *Growing Up Divorced: A Road to Healing for Adult Children of Divorce* (New York: Pocket Books, 1991).

6. Marjorie A. Pett, Nancy Long, and Anita Gander, "Late-Life Divorce: Its Impact on Family Rituals," *Journal of Family Issues* 13, no. 4 (December 1992): 526–552.

7. Lyla H. O'Driscoll, "Toward a New Theory of the Family," in *The American Family and the State*, ed. Joseph R. Peden and Fred R. Glahe (San Francisco: Pacific Research Institute for Public Policy, 1986), 81.

8. Judith S. Wallerstein and Sandra Blakeslee, *Second Chances: Men, Women, and Children a Decade After Divorce* (New York: Ticknor & Fields, 1989), 27.

9. Ibid., 52.

10. Sylvie Drapeau and Camil Bouchard, "Support Networks and Adjustment Among 6- to 11-Year-Olds from Maritally Disrupted and Intact Families," *Journal of Divorce and Remarriage* 19 (1993): 75–97.

11. Another study found that, for both black and white women, home life at age fourteen was linked to likelihood of marriage: Women who lived with both parents at the age of fourteen were more likely to marry as young adults than peers who lived in either single-parent or stepfamily homes. Daniel T. Lichter et al., "Race and the Retreat from Marriage: A Shortage of Marriageable Men?" *American Sociological Review* 57 (December 1992): 781–799.

12. Lawrence A. Kurdek, "Predicting Marital Dissolution: A 5-year Prospective Longitudinal Study of Newlywed Couples," *Journal of Personality and Social Psychology* 64, no. 2 (1994): 221–242.

CHAPTER 3

1. Bureau of the Census, *Statistical Abstract of the United States, 1992* (Washington, D.C.: U.S. Government Printing Office), Table 719.

2. David J. Eggebeen and Daniel T. Lichter, "Race, Family Structure, and Changing Poverty Among American Children," *American Sociological Review* 56 (December 1991), 807.

3. National Center for Children in Poverty, School of Public Health, Columbia University, *Five Million Children: A Statistical Profile of Our Poorest Young Citizens* (New York: Columbia University, 1990).

4. Eggebeen and Lichter, "Race, Family Structure," 801.

5. Douglas J. Besharov, "Not All Single Mothers Are Created Equal," *American Enterprise* (September/October 1992): 15.

6. National Center for Children in Poverty, *Five Million Children*, 29, Table 2.

7. Alan Booth and Paul Amato, "Divorce, Residential Change, and Stress," *Journal of Divorce and Remarriage* 18, no. 1/2 (1992): 205–213.

8. Sara McLanahan and Gary Sandefur, *Growing Up with a Single Parent: What Hurts, What Helps* (Cambridge, Mass.: Harvard University Press, 1994), 24.

9. Bureau of the Census, *Statistical Abstract of the United States, 1994* (Washington, D.C.: U.S. Government Printing Office), Table 81. Calculations by the author.

10. Elaine Ciulla Kamarck and William A. Galston, "Progressive Family Policy for the 1990s," in *Mandate for Change*, ed. Will Marshall and Martin Schram (New York: Berkeley Books, 1993), 155.

11. Pamela J. Smock, "The Economic Costs of Marital Disruption for Young Women Over the Past Two Decades," *Demography* 30, no. 3 (August 1993): 353ff.

12. See, for example, Harriet B. Presser, "Can We Make Time for Children? The Economy Work Schedules and Child Care," *Demography* 26, no. 4 (November 1989): 526.

13. For a discussion of this phenomenon see George Gilder, *Men and Marriage* (Gretna, La.: Pelican Publishing, 1986).

14. Edward W. Beal and Gloria Hochman, *Adult Children of Divorce: Breaking the Cycle and Finding Fulfilment in Love, Marriage, and Family* (New York: Delta, 1991), 27–28.

15. Paul R. Amato and Brian Keith, "Parental Divorce and Adult Well-Being: A Metaanalysis," *Journal of Marriage and the Family* 53 (1991): 54. See also, P. R. Amato and B. Keith, "Parental Divorce and the Well-Being of Children: A Meta-Analysis," *Psychological Bulletin* 110 (1991): 26–46.

16. McLanahan and Sandefur, *Growing Up*.

17. Verna M. Keith and Barbara Finlay, "The Impact of Parental Divorce on Children's Educational Attainment, Marital Timing, and Likelihood of Divorce," *Journal of Marriage and the Family* 50 (August 1988): 787–809.

18. Kamarck and Galston, "Progressive Family Policy," 162.

19. Carmen N. Velez, Jim Johnson, and Patricia Cohen, "A Longitudinal Analysis of Selected Risk Factors for Childhood Psychopathology," *Journal of the American Academy of Child and Adolescent Psychiatry* 28 (1989): 861–864.

20. Robert E. Emery, *Marriage, Divorce, and Children's Adjustment* (Newbury Park, Calif.: Sage Publications, 1988), 50–54.

21. David Lester, "Time-Series Versus Regional Correlates of Rates of Personal Violence," *Death Studies* (1993): 529–534.

22. Gregory Stephen Kowalski and Steven Sack, "The Effect of Divorce on Homicide," *Journal of Divorce and Remarriage* 18 (1992): 216–217.

23. "The Price of a Broken Home," *Time*, 53.

24. *Time*, 27 February 1995, 50.

25. Leslie Margolin and John L. Craft, "Child Sexual Abuse by Caretakers," *Family Relations* 38 (1989): 450ff.

26. Martin Daly and Margo Wilson, "Child Abuse and Other Risks of Not Living with Both Parents," *Journal of Ethology and Sociobiology* 6 (1985): 197ff.

27. Diana Russell, *The Secret Trauma: Incest in the Lives of Girls and Women* (New York: Basic Books, 1986), 234.

28. Leslie Margolin, "Child Abuse by Mother's Boyfriends: Why the Overrepresentation?" *Child Abuse and Neglect* 16 (1992): 541–552.

CHAPTER 4

1. Lis Harris, *Rules of Engagement: Four Couples and American Marriage Today* (New York: Simon & Schuster, c. 1995), 17.

2. Ibid., 107.

3. Ibid., 108.

4. Nicholas Eberstadt, "America's Infant Mortality Puzzle," *Public Interest* (fall 1991): 30ff.

5. Ibid.

6. Ibid.

7. Ibid., 37.

8. Judith S. Wallerstein and Sandra Blakeslee, *Second Chances: Men, Women, and Children a Decade After Divorce* (New York: Ticknor & Fields, 1989), 155.

9. Ibid., 156–157.

10. Wallerstein's sample is also not representative in that, as critics have charged, many of the mothers had sought therapy (a not unusual occurrence for educated women going through divorce) and children with chronic emotional disturbance or severe learning disabilities were screened out. At the time of the divorce, the children were all doing well in school and had never been referred for mental health services.

11. Timothy J. Biblarz and Adrian E. Raftery, "The Effects of Family Disruption on Social Mobility," *American Sociological Review* 58 (1993): 97–109.

12. Glenna Spitze, "Adult Children's Divorce and Intergenerational Relationships," *Journal of Marriage and the Family* (May 1994): 279ff.

13. Lynn White, "The Effects of Parental Divorce and Remarriage on Parental Support for Adult Children," *Journal of Family Issues* (June 1992): 234ff. Barbara Grissis, "Effects of Parental Divorce on Children's Financial Support for college." *Journal of Divorce and Remarriage* 22, no. 1/2 (1994): 155ff.

14. George Gilder, *Men and Marriage* (Louisiana: Pelican Publishing, 1986), 65.

15. "Gang Violence Seeps into the Small Cities," *New York Times,* 31 January 1993, 26.

16. "Murder No. 1 Cause of Workplace Death," *New York Newsday,* 29 November 1993.

17. Elaine Ciulla Kamarck and William A. Galston, "A Progressive Family Policy for the 1990s," in *Mandate for Change,* ed. Will Marshall and Martin Schram (New York: Berkeley Books, 1993), 156, Table 1.

18. "Teenage Murders Up," *New York Newsday,* 15 October 1994, A10.

19. James A. Fox and Glenn Pierce, *New York Times,* 31 January 1993.

20. Susan Chira, "Teenagers, In a Poll, Report Worry and Distrust of Adults," *New York Times,* 10 July 1994, 1.

21. "This Crime 'Wave' is Just a Ripple," *New York Post,* 2 May 1994.

22. "Gang Violence Seeps into the Small Cities," *New York Times,* 31 March 1993, 26.

23. Josefina Figueira-McDonough, "Residence, Dropping Out, and Delinquency Rates," *Deviant Behavior* 14 (1993): 109ff.

24. Don Terry, "Killed by Her Friends, Sons of the Heartland," *New York Times,* 18 May 1994, A1.

CHAPTER 5

1. Arlene S. Skolnick and Jerome H. Skolnick, *Family in Transition,* 5th ed. (Boston: Little, Brown and Company, 1986), 371–372.

2. Dr. Morton H. Shaevitz and Marjories Hansen Shaevitz, "How Men Really Feel," *The Superwoman Syndrome* (New York: Warner Books, 1984), 55–56.

3. Nina J. Easton, "Life Without Father," *Los Angeles Times Magazine,* 14 June 1992, 18.

4. Frank F. Furstenberg, Jr., Christine Winquist Nord, James L. Peterson, and Nicholas Zill, "The Life Course of Children of Divorce: Marital Disruption and Parental Contact," *American Sociological Review* 48, no. 5 (October 1983): 663.

5. Frank F. Furstenberg, Jr., and Andrew J. Cherlin, *Divided Families: What Happens to Children When Parents Part* (Cambridge, Mass.: Harvard University Press, 1991), 35–36.

6. Furstenberg, Nord, Peterson, and Zill, "Life Course," 667.

7. Roger A. Wojtkiewicz, "Diversity in Experiences of Parental Structure During Childhood and Adolescence," *Demography* 29, no. 1 (February 1992): 59–67.

8. Susan Chira, "Novel Idea in Welfare Plan: Helping Children by Helping Their Fathers," 30 March 1994, 6. See also, *Young Unwed Fathers: Changing Roles and Emerging Policies,* ed. Robert I. Lerman and Theodora J. Ooms (Philadelphia: Temple University Press, c. 1993).

9. Furstenburg, et al., "The Life Course of Children of Divorce," 663.

10. "The Mainstreaming of Single Motherhood," *San Francisco Chronicle,* 20 July 1993.

11. Frank F. Furstenberg and Christine Winquist Nord, "Parenting Apart: Patterns of Child-Rearing After Marital Disruption," *Journal of Marriage and the Family* 47 (November 1985): 889.

12. Judith S. Wallerstein and Sandra Blakeslee, *Second Chances: Men, Women, and Children a Decade After Divorce* (New York: Ticknor & Fields, 1989), 234.

13. Ibid., 235.

14. See, for example, Furstenberg and Cherlin, *Divided Families*, 22.

15. See, for example, Nicholas Zill and Carolyn Rogers, "Recent Trends in the Well-Being of Children in the United States and Their Implications for Public Policy," in *The Changing American Family and Public Policy*, ed. John L. Palmer and Isabel V. Sawhill (Washington, D.C.: The Urban Institute Press, 1988), 44.

16. Wallerstein and Blakeslee, *Second Chances*, 238.

17. Ibid.

18. Robert E. Emery, *Marriage, Divorce, and Children's Adjustment* (Newbury Park, Calif.: Sage Publications, 1988), 94. For Emery's summary of the literature comparing divorce and death, see pages 57 and 67.

19. Furstenberg and Cherlin, *Divided Families*.

20. James L. Peterson and Nicholas Zill, "Marital Disruption, Parent-Child Relationships, and Behavior Problems in Children," *Journal of Marriage and the Family* 48, no. 2 (May 1986): 295–307.

21. Susan Chira, "Novel Idea in Welfare Plan: Helping Children by Helping Their Fathers," *New York Times*, 30 March 1994, B6.

22. Gary Stern, "Not Much Known About Unwed Dads," *Citizen-Register*, 29 March 1994, 14A.

23. Furstenberg, Nord, Peterson, and Zill, "Life Course," 666.

24. Susan Chira, "Novel Idea in Welfare Plan: Helping Children by Helping Their Fathers," *New York Times*, 30 March 1994, 6.

25. Furstenberg and Cherlin, *Divided Families*, 74.

26. Ibid., 74–75.

27. The literature documenting the negative effects of parental conflict is now large and well-established. For a good summary, see Emery, *Marriage, Divorce*, 94–95.

28. Dorothy Tysse Breen and Margaret Crosbie-Burnett, "Moral Dilemmas of Early Adolescents of Divorced and Intact Families: A Qualitative and Quantitative Analysis," *Journal of Early Adolescence* 13, no. 2 (May 1993): 168–182.

29. Mary-Lou Weisman, "When Parents Are Not in the Best Interests of Their Children," *Atlantic Monthly* 274, no. 1 (July 1994): 56.

CHAPTER 6

1. Dennis A. Ahlburg and Carol J. DeVita, "New Realities of the American Family," *Population Bulletin* 47, no. 2 (August 1992): 17.

2. Frank F. Furstenberg, Jr., and Andrew J. Cherlin, *Divided Families: What Happens to Children When Parents Part* (Cambridge, Mass.: Harvard University Press, 1991), 78.

3. See Ahlburg and DeVita, "New Realities," 6.

4. Stephanie Coontz, *The Way We Never Were: American Families and the Nostalgia Trap* (New York: Basic Books, 1992), 15.

5. Ben Wattenberg, *The First Universal Nation: Leading Indicators and Ideas About the Surge of America in the 1990s* (New York: Free Press, 1991), 86.

6. See, for example, Andrew Cherlin, "Remarriage as an Incomplete Institution," *American Journal of Sociology* 84 (1978): 634ff; Frank F. Furstenberg, Jr., and Graham B. Spanier, *Recycling the Family: Remarriage After Divorce* (Beverly Hills, Calif.: Sage Publications, 1987), 86–90.

7. J. A. Jacobs and Frank F. Furstenberg, Jr., "Changing Places: Conjugal Careers and Women's Marital Mobility," *Social Forces* 64: 714ff.

8. Lynn White, "The Effects of Parental Divorce and Remarriage on Parental Support for Adult Children," *Journal of Family Issues* (June 1992): 234ff. Barbara Grissis, "Effects of Parental Divorce on Children's Financial Support for College," *Journal of Divorce and Remarriage* 22, no. 1–2 (1994): 155ff.

9. Gary D. Sandefur, Sara McLanahan, and Roger A. Wojtkiewicz, "The Effects of Parental Marital Status During Adolescence on High School Graduation," *Social Forces* 71, no. 1 (1992): 103–121.

10. Nicholas Zill and Carolyn C. Rogers, "Recent Trends in the Well-Being of Children in the United States and Their Implications for Public Policy," in *The Changing American Family and Public Policy*, ed. John L. Palmer and Isabel V. Sawhill (Washington, D.C.: The Urban Institute Press, 1988), Table 2.10, 91.

11. Peter Hill, "Recent Advances in Selected Aspects of Adolescent Development," *Journal of Child Psychology and Psychiatry* 34, no. 1 (1993): 69–99.

12. Furstenberg and Cherlin, *Divided Families*, 89.

13. Jiang Hong Li and Roger A. Wojtkiewicz, "A New Look at the Effects of Family Structure on Status Attainment," *Social Science Quarterly* 73 (1992): 581–595.

14. Furstenberg and Cherlin, *Divided Families*, 77.

15. Ibid., 95.

16. Ahlburg and DeVita, "New Realities."

17. Furstenberg, Jr., Nord, Peterson, and Zill, "Life Course," 656–668.

18. Furstenberg and Cherlin, *Divided Families*, 81–82.

19. Ibid.

20. James L. Peterson, "The Effects of Marital Disruptions on Children," *Child Trends* (Washington, D.C., 2 July 1986), 5.

21. Susan Chira, "Struggling to Find Stability When Divorce Is a Pattern," *New York Times*, 19 March 1995, A1.

22. Frank Pittman, *Private Lies: Infidelity and the Betrayal of Intimacy* (New York: W. W. Norton, 1989), 259–267.

23. Peterson and Zill, "Marital Disruption," 295–307.

24. Furstenberg and Cherlin, "Divided Families," 14.

25. Furstenberg, Peterson, Nord, and Zill, "Life Course," 656ff.

26. Peterson, "Marital Disruption," 5.

27. Paul R. Amato and Alan Booth, "Consequences of Parental Divorce and Marital Unhappiness for Adult Well-Being," *Social Forces* 69, no. 3 (March 1991): 895–914.

28. Andrew J. Cherlin, *Marriage, Divorce, Remarriage* (Cambridge, Mass.: Harvard University Press, 1981), 71.

CHAPTER 7

1. Caryn James, "A Baby Boom on TV as Biological Clocks Cruelly Tick Away," *New York Times*, 16 October, 1991 C15.

2. Amy Pagnozzi, "Dan's Coded Message Is Despicable," *New York Post*, 21 May 1993.

3. James, "A Baby Boom," C15.

4. Smith, *Los Angeles Times*, January 1993.

5. Lena Williams, "Pregnant Teen-Agers Are Outcasts No Longer," *New York Times*, 2 December 1993, B13.

6. Jason DeParle, "Big Rise in Births Outside Wedlock," *New York Times*, 14 July 1993, A1.

7. Nicholas Eberstadt, "The Infant-Mortality Puzzle," *Public Interest*, no. 105 (fall 1991): 41.

8. Ahlburg and DeVita, "New Realities," 22.

9. Eberstadt. "Infant-Mortality," 41.

10. Amara Bachu, "Fertility in American Women: June 1992," Census Bureau report, in DeParle, "Big Rise in Births," A1.

11. Ahlburg and DeVita, "New Realities," "In 1960, only 5% of all births were to unmarried mothers."

12. David T. Ellwood, *Poor Support: Poverty in the American Family* (New York: Basic Books, 1988), 63.

13. Tamar Lewin, "Poll of Teen-Agers: Battle of the Sexes on Roles of the Family," *New York Times*, 11 July 1994, A1.

14. Ahlburg and DeVita, "New Realities," 23.

15. "Mothers Go It Alone," *New York Newsday*, 22 July 1993.

16. Ahlburg and DeVita, "New Realities," 23.

17. Amara Bachu, *Fertility of American Women: June 1994* (Washington D.C.: Bureau of the Census, September 1995), xix, Table K.

18. Claude Solnik, "Single With Children: Raising a Child Alone in New York," *NY Perspectives*, 7 December 1990, 12.

19. "Love in the '90s," *Women First* (9 March 1992): 16.

20. Naomi Miller, *Single Parent by Choice: A Growing Trend in Family Life* (New York: Plenum Press, 1992), 38.

21. Ibid., 29–30.

22. Edward H. Thompson, Jr., and Patricia A. Gongla, "Single Parent Families: In the Mainstream of American Society," in *Contemporary Families and Alternative Lifestyles*, ed. Eleanor D. Macklin and Roger H. Rubin, (Beverly Hills, Calif.: Sage Publications), 109–111.

23. Judy Mann, "Helping the Strong," *Washington Post*, 13 March 1987, C3.

24. William R. Mattox, Jr., *Running on Empty: America's Time-Starved Families with Children*, Institute for American Values Working Paper No. WP6 (New York: Institute for American Values, November 1991), 11.

25. Barbara Dafoe Whitehead, *Maryland Focus Group Report on Family Time*, Institute for American Values Working Paper No. WP2 (New York: Institute for American Values, November 1990), 8–10.

26. Janet Lever, and Pepper Schwartz, "Here's How You Feel About Having a Baby on Your Own." *Glamour* (May 1992), 70.

27. *New York Post*, 6 July 1994, 25.

28. Richard Cohen, "Critic at Large: Significant Mothers," *Washington Post*, 30 August 1987, 3.

29. Herbert Stein, "From Bully Pulpit to Pulpit Bully: Why We Conservatives Should Tell Dan Quayle to Shut Up, Please," *Washington Post*, 28 June 1992, C2.

30. Williams, "Pregnant Teen-Agers."

31. "By 1987 over half the children receiving AFDC benefits qualified for the program because their parents were unmarried; their total numbers would account for over nine-tenths of all children for American never-married mothers." Eberstadt, "Infant-Mortality," 42.

32. Ibid., 38, Table II. According to the U.S. Department of Health and Human Services, there were 11.1 deaths per thousand among married women with zero to eight years of education and 18.4 deaths per thousand live births among unmarried women with sixteen or more years of education.

33. Carmen N. Velez, Jim Johnson, and Patricia Cohen, "A Longitudinal Analysis of Selected Risk Factors for Childhood Psychopathology," *Journal of the American Academy of Child and Adolescent Psychiatry* 28 (1989): 861–864.

34. A 1988 University of Illinois study of 2,500 young men and women by Sheila Krein and Andrea H. Beller of the University of Illinois. "Education Attainment of Children from Single Families: Differences by Exposure, Gender, and Race," *Demography* 25 (May 1988): 221–234.

35. Henry B. Biller and Richard Solomon of the University of Rhode Island, *Child Maltreatment and Paternal Deprivation: A Manifesto* (Lexington, MA: Lexington Books, 1986).

CHAPTER 8

1. "Anne Lamott on Raising a Boy by Herself," *San Francisco Chronicle*, 20 July 1993.

2. Sol Gordon and Craig W. Snyder, *A Guidebook to Better Sexual Health* (Boston: Allyn and Bacon, 1989), 184.

3. Judith Stacey, "The New Family Values Crusaders," *The Nation*, 1 August 1994, 119–120.

4. Norval D. Glenn, "The Re-Evaluation of Family Change by American Social Scientists" (1994).

5. "Experts Disagree Over Benefits, Harm, Divorce Can Hold for Kids," *Clarion-Ledger*, 2 September 1992.

6. See also, Peterson and Zill, "Marital Disruption."

7. Peterson and Zill, "Marital Disruption," Table 3.

8. Joseph Hopper, "The Rhetoric of Motives in Divorce," *Journal of Marriage and the Family* 55 (November 1993): 806.

9. In teacher rating of cognitive competence, for example, children from good marriages rated 3.75, children in ideal divorces rated 3.58, and children from angry marriages rated 3.16. But children in high-conflict divorced families rated just 2.46 "Parental Fighting Hurts Even After Divorce," *Washington Post*, 12 November 1986, quoted fron Rex Lloyd Forehand and Robert J. McMhon, *Helping the Noncompliant Child: A Clinicians Guide to Parent Training* (New York: Guildford Press).

10. Wallerstein and Blakeslee, *Second Chances*.

11. Constance Ahrons, *The Good Divorce: Keeping Your Family Together When Your Marriage Comes Apart* (Harper Collins Publications, 1994), 52–59.

12. Wallerstein and Blakeslee, *Second Chances*.

13. See David Finkelhor and Kersti Yllo, *License to Rape: Sexual Abuse of Wives* (New York: The Free Press, 1985), 25.

14. Wallerstein and Blakeslee, *Second Chances*, xviii.

15. Carolyn Webster-Stratton, "The Relationship of Marital Support, Conflict, and Divorce to Parent Perceptions, Behavior, and Childhood Conduct Problems," *Journal of Marriage and the Family* 51 (May 1989): 417–430.

16. Wallerstein and Blakeslee, *Second Chances*, 162–163.

17. Carolyn Webster Stratton, "Marital Support," 417–430.

18. Norval Glenn, "The Social and Cultural Meaning of Marriage," in *The Retreat from Marriage*, ed. Bryce J. Christenses, "Causes and Consequences," 37.

19. Ibid., 38.

20. Glenn, "Re-Evaluation of Family Change," Figures 1 and 2.

21. Norval D. Glenn and Charles N. Weaver, "The Changing Relationship of Marital Status to Reported Happiness," *Journal of Marriage and the Family* 50 (May 1988): 319–320. Single women's reported happiness also increased, but not nearly as dramatically as single men's.

22. Glenn, "The Social and Cultural Meaning of Marriage," 45.

23. Catherine Johnson, *Lucky in Love: The Secrets of Happy Couples & How Their Marriages Thrive* (New York: Penguin Books, 1992), 200–201.

24. John Bradshaw, *Treating Love: The Last Great Stage of Growth* (New York: Bantam Books, 1992), 342.

25. Glenn, *Retreat from Marriage*, 50.

26. John Gottman, in "How to Tell If Your Love Will Last," *Glamour*, February 1994, 147. Mr. Gottman's study has been published in book form: John Gottman, *Why Marriages Succeed or Fail: What You Can Learn From the Breakthrough Research to Make Your Marriage Last* (New York: Simon & Schuster, c. 1994). Also, Gottman and Robert W. Levinson, "Marital Processes Predictive of Later Dissolution: Behaviors, Physiology, and Health," *Journal of Personality and Social Psychology* 63 (August 1992): 221–233.

27. Hopper, "Rhetoric of Motives," *Journal of Marriage and Family* 55 (November 1993): 801–813.

28. Johnson, *Lucky in Love*, 12–13.

29. Johnson, *Lucky in Love*, 263.

CHAPTER 9

1. Robert D. McFadden, "As Children Play, a Flash of Gunfire Takes a Life," *New York Times*, 7 June 1991, B1:2.

2. Alan Guttmacher Institute, *Sex and America's Teenagers* (New York: Alan Guttmacher Institute, 1994), 15.

3. "Blacks Fear for Kids' Future," *New York Newsday*, 27 May 1994.

4. Leland Ropp, et al., "Death in the City: An American Childhood Tragedy," *Journal of the American Medical Association* 267 (1992): 2905ff.

5. David T. Ellwood, *Poor Support: Poverty in the American Family* (New York: Basic Books, 1988), 200.

6. "Blacks Fear for Kids' Future," *New York Newsday*, 27 May 1994.

7. Carl F. Horowitz, "Searching for the Underclass," *National Review* (11 September 1995) 56.

8. Robert D. More and Christopher Winship, "Socioeconomic Change and the Decline of Marriage for Blacks and Whites," in *The Urban Underclass*, ed. Christopher Jenkins and Paul Peterson (Washington, D.C.: The Brookings Institution, 1991), 181.

9. Dennis A. Ahlburg and Carol J. DeVita, "New Realities of the American Family," *Population Bulletin* 47, no. 2 (August 1992): 15.

10. Black women averaged 3.49 children while married, as opposed to 3.45 for white women. Christopher Jencks, "Is the American Underclass Growing," 86, Table 14. In Kencks and Peterson, *Urban Underclass*.

11. Ahlburg and DeVita, "New Realities," 8.

12. Andrew J. Cherlin, *Marriage, Divorce, Remarriage*, rev. and enl. ed., (Cambridge, Mass.: Harvard University Press, 1992), 98–99.

13. Ibid., 110. See also, Herbert G. Gutman, *The Black Family in Slavery and Freedom, 1750–1925* (New York: Pantheon, 1976). For a review of this and similar studies see, Stanley L. Engerman, "Black Fertility and Family Structure in the U.S. 1880–1940," *Journal of Family History* 2 (Summer 1977): 177ff.

14. Data from 1965 to 1979 show that 47 percent of black marriages failed in the first ten years, compared to 28 percent of non-Hispanic whites and 26 percent of Mexican Americans. Cherlin, *Marriage, Divorce, Remarriage*, 95.

15. Cherlin, *Marriage, Divorce, Remarriage*, 95. Another study shows that of all black women who divorced between 1965 and 1984, only one-third had remarried by 1988, compared to almost 60 percent of white women. Kathryn A. London, "Cohabitation, Marriage, Marital Dissolution, and Remarriage; United States, 1988," advance data from *Vital and Health Statistics*, no. 194, (National Center for Health Statistics, 1991), Table 4.

16. Cherlin, *Marriage, Divorce, Remarriage*, 95.

17. More and Winship, "Socioeconomic Change," 176 in *The Urban Underclass*, ed. Christopher Jenks and Paul E. Peterson (Washington, D.C.: The Brookings Institute, 1991), 17. The authors note that their results are similar to those of David Ellwood and David Rodda, who use different data and methods in "The Hazards of Work and Marriage: The Influence of Male Employment on Marriage."

18. Robert D. Mare and Christopher Winship, "Socioeconomic Change and the Decline of Marriage for Blacks and Whites," in *The Urban Underclass*, ed. Christopher Jenks and Paul E. Peterson (Washington, D.C.: The Brookings Institution, 1991), 195.

19. Jencks, "American Underclass," 88.

20. Cherlin, *Marriage, Divorce, Remarriage*, 106.

21. Ellwood, *Poor Support*, 67–68.

22. Ibid.

23. Ibid.

24. Jencks, "American Underclass," 87.

25. Jencks, "American Underclass," 86.

26. Reynolds Forley, "After the Starting Line: Blacks and Women in an Uphill Race," *Demography* 25, no. 4 (November 1988): 487, Figure 6.

27. Ibid., 487.

28. Ibid.

29. Kathleen Gerson, *Hard Choices: How Women Decide About Work, Career, Motherhood* (Berkeley: University of California Press, 1985), 70–74.

30. Mare and Winship, "Socioeconomic Change," 179.

31. Nicholas Zill, "One Million More Children in Poverty: What Are the Reasons?" (testimony before the Subcommittee on Human Resources, Committee on Ways and Means, U.S. House of Representatives, Washington, D.C., 10 September 1992).

32. Sam Roberts, "In Middle-Class Queens, Blacks Pass Whites in Household Income," *New York Times*, 6 June 1994, A1.

33. Ibid.

34. Ibid.

35. See for example Robert E. Emery, "Marriage, Divorce, and Childrens' Adjustment (Newbury Park, Calif.: Sage Publications, 1988), 67–68. Sara McLanahon and Larry L. Bumpass, "Intergenerational Consequences of Family Disruption," *American Journal of Sociology* 94 (July 1988): 120–152.

36. Stephanie Schamess, "The Search for Love: Unmarried Adolescent Mothers' Views of Relationships with Men," *Adolescence* 28 (1993): 425ff. Alan D. Booth, et al., "The Impact of Parental Divorce in Courtship," *Journal of Marriage and the Family* (February 1989): 85–94.

37. Herbert L. Smith, "Current Trends in Non-Marital Fertility and Divorce," *The Retreat from Marriage: Causes and Consequences*, ed. Bryce J. Christensen (Lanham, MD: University Press of America, 1990), 18, Figure 9.

38. Naomi Miller, *Single Parent by Choice: A Growing Trend in Family Life* (New York: Plenum Press, 1992), 37.

39. Jencks, "American Underclass," Table 14, 86.

40. Mare and Winship, "Socioeconomic Change," 175.

41. Cherlin, *Marriage, Divorce, Remarriage*, 95.

42. Reynolds Farley, "After the Starting Line," 1988.

43. "Poll of Teen-Agers Finds Boys Hold More Traditional Views on Family," *New York Times*, 11 July 1994, B7.

44. Paul E. Peterson, "The Urban Underclass and the Poverty Paradox," in Jencks and Peterson, *Urban Underclass*, 19.

45. Ibid.

CHAPTER 10

1. William J. O'Donnell and David A. Jones. *The Law of Marriage and Marital Alternatives* (Lexington, Mass: Lexington Book, 1982), 216, footnote 4.

2. John Noonan, Jr., "The Family and the Supreme Court," *Catholic University Law Review* 23 (1973): 255, 273.

3. *Insight*, 13 September 1993.

4. "Top New Jersey Court Broadens Meaning of 'Family' to Students," *New York Times*, 1 February 1990. The zoning law defined a *family* in a way consistent with the court's prior ruling: "One or more persons occupying a dwelling unit as a single non-profit housekeeping unit, who are living together as a stable and permanent living unit, being a traditional family unit or the functional equivalent thereof."

5. Maggie Gallagher, "Domestic Partnership Is Bad Business," *New York Newsday*.

6. Associated Press, November 12, 1992.

7. See O'Donnell and Jones, *The Law of Marriage*, 112, footnote 3.

8. In Zablocki's case, he had failed to meet court-ordered child-support payments to an illegitimate child then on welfare and sought the right to marry a new girlfriend, who was pregnant with his child.

CHAPTER 11

1. Mary Ann Mason, *The Equality Trap* (New York: Simon and Schuster, 1988) 54–60.

2. Frank F. Furstenberg, Jr., and Andrew J. Cherlin, *Divided Families: What Happens to Children When Parents Part* (Cambridge, Mass.: Harvard University Press, 1991), 6.

3. Willerstein and Blakeslee, "Second Chances," 10.

4. Herbert Jacob, *Silent Revolution: The Transformation of Divorce Law in the United States* (Chicago: University of Chicago Press, 1988), 28.

5. Mary Ann Glendon, *Abortion and Divorce in Western Law: American Failures, European Challenges* (Cambridge, Mass.: Harvard University Press, 1987), 66.

6. Jacobs, *Divorce Revolution*, 154–155.

7. Ibid., 81–82.

8. Thomas B. Marvell, "Divorce Rates and the Fault Requirement," *Law and Society Review* 23 (1989): 557. Martin Zelder, "The Economic Analysis of the Effect of No-Fault Divorce Law on the Divorce Rate," *Harvard Journal of Law and Public Policy* 16, no. 1: 241ff.

9. Ibid., 264.

10. See Gertrude Schaffner Goldberg, "Canada: Bordering on the Feminization of Poverty," in *The Feminization of Poverty: Only in America*, ed. Gertrude Schaffner

Goldberg and Eleanor Kremen (New York: Greenwood Press, 1990), 77.

11. Rev. William Rabior and Vicki Wells Bedard, *Catholics Experiencing Divorce: Grieving, Healing and Learning to Live Again* (Mo.: Ligouri Publications, 1991), 10.

CHAPTER 12

1. In Dennisk Orthner, "The Family in Transition," in *Rebuilding the Nest: A New Commitment to the American Family*, ed. David Blankenhorn, et al., (Milwaukee, Wis: Family Service America, 1990), 102.

2. Ibid.

3. Tad Friend, "Yes," *Esquire*, (February 1994): 49.

4. William H. Masters and Virginia E. Johnson, *The Pleasure Bond: A New Look at Sexuality and Commitment* (Boston: Little, Brown and Company, 1974), 23.

5. Andrea Dworkin, *Intercourse* (New York: Ballantine Publishing Group, 1985), 21.

6. Laurie S. Zabin, et al., "Ages of Physical Maturation and First Intercourse in Black Teenage Males and Females," *Demography* 23 (1986): 181–185.

7. Brent C. Miller and Kristin A. Moore, "Adolescent Sexual Behavior, Pregnancy, and Parenting: Research Through the 1980s," *Journal of Marriage and the Family* 52 (November 1990): 1026.

8. Sanford Dornbusch, et al., "Sexual Development, Age, and Dating: A Comparison of Biological and Social Influences Upon One Set of Behaviors," *Child Development* 52 (1981): 179ff.

9. Miller and Moore, "Adolescent Sexual Behavior," 1026–1027.

10. Dana Mack, "What the Sex Educators Teach," *Commentary* 96, no. 2 (August 1993): 33.

11. John Leo, "Schools to Parents: Keep Out," *U.S. News and World Report* (5 October 1992): 33.

12. "Dear Abby," *New York Post*, 5 August 1993.

13. Brent C. Miller, et al., "Parental Discipline and Control Attempts in Relation to Adolescent Sexual Attitudes and Behavior," *Journal of Marriage and the Family* 48 (August 1986): 503–512.

14. Kristin Moore, M. C. Simms, and C. L. Betsey, *Choice and Circumstance* (New Brunswick, N.J.: Transaction Books, 1986). Kristin A. Moore, et al., "Parental Attitudes and the Occurrence of Early Sexual Activity," *Journal of Marriage and the Family* 48 (November 1986), 777–782.

15. Bryce J. Christensen, "Lost in Translation? The Mexican-American Family," *Family in America* 3, no. 10 (October 1989).

16. Charles Hobart and Frank Grigel, "Cohabitation Among Canadian Students at

the End of the Eighties," *Journal of Comparative Family Studies* 23 (Autumn 1992): 311–336.

17. For a discussion, see Miller and Moore, "Adolescent Sexual Behavior," 1033.

18. Ibid.

19. Mack, "What Do Sex Educators Teach."

20. Ellen Hopkins, "What Kids Really Learn in Sex Ed," *Parents* (1993).

21. William A. Fisher and Deborah M. Roffman, "Adolescence: A Risky Time," in *Independent School: Sexuality Education in the Age of AIDS* (Spring 1992).

22. Mack, "What the Sex Educators Teach," 35.

23. William Leach, *True Love and Perfect Union: The Feminist Reform of Sex and Society* (New York: Basic Books, 1980), 81.

24. Mack, "What the Sex Educators Teach," 36.

25. Heather Little, "Fear of Commitment: It's Not Just a Man's Problem," *Montreal Gazette*, 6 June 1994.

26. Stephanie Schamess, "The Search for Love: Unmarried Adolescent Mothers' Views of, and Relationships with, Men," *Adolescence* 28, no. 110 (1993): 425ff.

27. Dennis A. Ahlburg and Carol J. DeVita, "New Realities of the American Family," *Population Bulletin* 47, no. 2 (August 1992): 10.

28. David Popenoe, *Modern Marriage: Revising the Cultural Script*, Institute for American Values Working Paper No. WP17 (New York: Institute for American Values, August 1992), 4.

29. Ahlburg and DeVita, "New Realities," 10.

30. Sol Gordon and Craig W. Snyder, *A Guidebook to Better Sexual Health* (Boston: Allyn and Bacon, 1989), 357.

31. Ahlburg and DeVita, "New Realities," 10.

32. "Chronicle: Duchess of York Packs Them In," *New York Times*, 8 December 1994, B36.

33. Ahlburg and DeVita, "New Realities," 10.

34. William G. Axinn and Arland Thornton, "The Relationship Between Cohabitation and Divorce: Selectivity or Causal Influence?" *Demography* 29 (1992): 357ff.

35. Larry L. Bumpass and James A. Sweet, "National Estimates of Cohabitation: Cohort Levels and Union Stability," NSFH working paper no. 2 (June 1989), in *Family in America New Research* (September 1989).

36. Ibid.

37. Jan E. Stets, "The Link Between Past and Present Intimate Relationships," *Journal of Family Issues* 14, no. 2 (June 1993): 236–260.

CHAPTER 13

1. Steven Mintz, "The Ties That Bind Have Always Been Elastic," *New York Newsday*, 13 December 1993.

2. Frank F. Furstenberg, Jr., and Andrew J. Cherlin, *Divided Families: What Happens to Children When Parents Part* (Cambridge, Mass.: Harvard University Press, 1991), 6.

3. Dennis A. Ahlburg and Carol J. DeVita, "New Realities of the American Family," *Population Bulletin* 47, no. 2 (August 1992):15.

4. Phillip Blumstein and Pepper Schwartz, *American Couples: Money, Work, Sex* (New York: William and Morrow, 1983), 309

5. Arlene Skolnik, *Embattled Paradise: The American Family in an Age of Uncertainty* (New York: Basic Books, 1991), 13.

6. Ibid.

7. Robert Pear, "Poverty Termed a Divorce Factor," *New York Times*, 15 January 1993, 10.

8. David Popenoe, *Disturbing the Nest: Family Change and Decline in Modern Societies* (New York: Aldine De Gruyter, 1988), 223.

9. Andrew Cherlin, *Marriage, Divorce, Remarriage: Revised and Enlarged Edition* (Cambridge, Mass: Harvard University Press, 1992) 56.

10. Frank F. Furstenberg, Jr., "Good Dads—Bad Dads: Two Faces of Fatherhood," in *The Changing American Family and Public Policy*, ed. Andrew J. Cherlin (Washington, D.C.: The Urban Institute Press, 1988), 195.

11. Anna Quindlen, "Public and Private: Men at Work," *New York Times*, 18 February 1990, 19.

12. For the original and more definitive exploration of the relation between sex and work for men, see George Gilder's *Men and Marriage*, (Gretna, La.: Pelican Publishing Company, 1986).

13. Ibid.

14. Ibid.

15. Sanders D. Korenman and David Newmark, *Does Marriage Really Make Men More Productive?* Finance and Economics Discussion Series, no. 29 (Washington, D.C.: Division of Research and Statistics, Federal Reserve Board, May 1988).

16. Terry Lunn, "The Impact of Divorce on Work," *Personnel Management* (February 1990): 28–31.

17. Bryce J. Christensen, "'Love in the Ruins?' The Future of Marriage in Modern America," *The Retreat of Marriage: Causes and Consequences* (Lanham, MD: University Press of America, 1990), 75–96.

18. Jessie Bernard, *The Future of Marriage* (New York: World Publishing, 1972), 51.

19. Sol Gordon and Craig W. Snyder, *A Guidebook to Better Sexual Health* (Boston: Allyn and Bacon, 1989), 358.

20. Bureau of the Census, "Fertility of American Women: June 1992," in *Star-Ledger*, 14 July 1993.

21. Ibid.

22. Ibid.

23. National Commission on Children, *Speaking of Kids: A National Survey of Children and Parents* (Washington, D.C. National Commission on Children, 1991).

24. Ibid.

25. Family Research Council, "Earners Per-Family Appears to Be Bigger Concern Than Work-Hours Per-Family," *In Focus*.

26. Stephanie Coontz, *The Way We Never Were: American Families and the Nostalgia Trap* (New York: Basic Books, 1992).

27. Bernice Kanner, "Advertisers Take Aim at Women at Home," *New York Times*, 2 January 1995.

28. Catherine Johnson, *Lucky in Love: The Secrets of Happy Couples and How Their Marriages Thrive* (New York: Penguin Books, 1992), 201–202.

29. Ibid., 202.

30. Arlene Skolnick, 210.

31. Ibid.

CHAPTER 14

1. Dan Wechsler Linden, "The Class of '65," *Forbes* (July 1994), 92.

2. Ibid., 95.

3. "Playing Perfect Pattycake," *New York Times*, 13 April 1994, 21.

4. Census Data.

5. Robert D. Mare and Christopher Winship, "Socioeconomic Change and the Decline of Marriage for Blacks and Whites," in *The Urban Underclass*, ed. Christopher Jencks and Paul E. Peterson (Washington, D.C.: The Brookings Institution, 1991), 179.

6. Black women now make slightly more than black men. Over the same period, white women's earning relative to white men's actually fell slightly from 54 percent in 1947 to 50 percent in 1984 (rising to the famous 62 percent among full-time, year-round employees). Reynolds Farley and Suzanne M. Bianchi, "The Growing Racial Difference in Marriage and Family Patterns," research report, April 1987—revised version of paper presented at American Statistical Association meeting, Chicago, August 1986, Table 2. See also, "A Degree's Shrinking Returns: College Educated Men Slipping in Pay," *New York Times*, 5 September 1994, 33.

7. Christopher Jencks, *The Urban Underclass* (Washington, D.C.: Brookings Institute, 1991), 35.

8. Greg J. Duncan and Saul D. Hoffman, "Teenage Underclass Behavior and Subsequent Poverty: Have the Rules Changed?" *The Urban Underclass*, 157.

9. Ibid.

10. Duncan and Hoffman, "Teenage Underclass Behavior," 163.

11. Ibid., 161, Table 3.

12. Bill Carter, "Television: Women Anchors Are on the Rise as Evening Stars," *New York Times*, 12 August 1990.

13. David T. Ellwood, *Poor Support: Poverty in the American Family* (New York: Basic Books, 1988), 52.

14. Frank Levy, *Dollars and Dreams: The Changing American Income Distribution* (New York: Russell Sage Foundation/Basic Books, 1987), 80.

15. *Gender Gap Study* (Veneta Worthington Center for National Policy), 682-1800.

16. "College-Educated Men Slipping in Wages, Study Finds," *New York Times*, 5 September 1994, 34.

17. Mare and Winship, "Socioeconomic Change," 175–196, see Table 1.

18. Ahlburg and DeVita, 14.

19. Mare and Winship, "Socioeconomic Change," 190–191.

20. Ibid.

21. Jane Gross, "More Young Men Hang onto Apron String," *New York Times*, 16 June 1991, A1.

22. Ibid., A1.

23. Christina Duff, "Cool Pad, Fab Food, One Catch: Mom Lives There, Too," *Wall Street Journal*, 12 September 1994.

24. Allan Schnaiberg and Sheldon Goldenberg, "From Empty Nest to Crowded Nest: The Dynamics of Incompletely-Launched Young Adults," *Social Problems* 36, no. 3 (June 1989): 251ff. In 1974 the proportion of young men in their prime marrying years who still lived with their parents was 11 percent. By 1988 the number living with Mama had jumped to 19 percent. In that age group, men are more than twice as likely as women to live at home.

25. Gross, "Apron String."

26. Duff, "Cool Pad."

27. Gross, "Apron String."

28. Ibid.

29. Ibid.

30. Duff, "Cool Pad."

31. Allan Schnaiberg and Sheldon Goldenberg, "From Empty Nest to Crowded Nest: The Dynamics of Incompletely Launched Young Adults," *Social Problems* 36 (1989): 251ff.

32. "Child-Care Licensing Not a Must to Moms," *USA Today*, 1 April 1993, D8.

33. Susan Chira, "Census Data Show Rise in Child Care by Fathers," *New York Times*, 22 September 1993, A20.

34. Bureau of the Census, "Money Income of Households, Families, and Persons in the United States, 1990," *Current Population Reports* 60, no. 174 (August 1991): Table 13.

35. Steven A. Holmes, "The Nation: Day Care Bill Marks a Turn Toward Help for the Poor," *New York Times*, 8 April 1990, 4.

36. "In the guaranteed-minimum-income experiment in the United States..., the main reason for increased marital breakup was the abandonment of the marriage by women who had newfound economic independence." Blumstein and Schwartz, 309ff.

37. Scott Hodge, "Washington Should Turn Bipartisan Talk of Family Tax Cuts into Action," *Heritage Foundation Backgrounder* (27 September 1994), 1-2.

38. Lawrence Kudlow, "Middle-Class Tax Hike," *National Review* (13 June 1994): 25.

CHAPTER 15

1. Jesse Bernard,*The Future of Marriage* (New York: World Publishing, 1972), 92.

2. John Scanzoni, "Families in the 1980s: Time to Refocus Our Thinking," *Journal of Family Issues* 394, no. 4 (December 1987): 394–421. For a more extensive discussion of this trend, see Milton C. Regan, Jr., *Family Law and the Pursuit of Intimacy* (New York: New York University Press, 1993).

3. Barbara Dafoe Whitehead, "The Experts' Story of Marriage," Institute for American Values Working Paper No. WP14 (New York: Institute for American Values, August 1992), 6.

4. Ibid., 16.

5. Bruce M. King, Cameron J. Camp, and Ann M. Downey, *Human Sexuality Today* (Englewood Cliffs, NJ: Prentice Hall, 1991), 240.

6. Sol Gordon and Craig W. Snyder, *Personal Issues in Human Sexuality: A Guidebook for Better Sexual Health* (Boston: Allyn & Bacon, 1989), 78.

7. Ibid., 18.

8. Constance R. Ahrons, *The Good Divorce: Keeping Your Family Together When Your Marriage Comes Apart* (New York: HarperCollins, 1994), 4.

9. Steven Mintz, "The Ties that Bind Have Always been Elastic," *New York Newsday*, 13 December 1993, 4.

10. Melvin Konner, "Everything is Relative," *New York Newsday*, 14 December 1993, 984.

11. Dennis A. Ahlburg and DeVita, "New Realities of the American Family," *Population Bulletin* 47, no. 2 (August 1992), 10.

12. Joyce L. Vedral, *Get Rid of Him* (New York: Warner Books, 1993).

13. Ibid., 147.

14. Arland Thornton, "Changing Attitudes Towards Family Issues in the United States," *Journal of Marriage and the Family* 51 (November 1989): 873–893.

15. Andrew J. Cherlin, *Marriage, Divorce, Remarriage* (Cambridge, Mass.: Harvard University Press, 1992), 45–48.

16. Richard A. Gardner, *The Parents' Book About Divorce*, rev. ed. (New York: Bantam Books, 1991), 11.

17. Sharon Price-Bonham, David W. Wright, and Joe F. Pittman, "Divorce: A Frequent 'Alternative' in the 1970s," in *Contemporary Families and Alternative Lifestyles* (Beverly Hills, Calif.: Sage Publications, 1983), 138.

18. Gardner, *Parents Book*, 4.

19. Anne E. Kazak, et al., "Perception of Normality in Families: Four Samples," *Journal of Family Psychology* 2 (1989): 277ff.

20. Monte Bobele, "A Comparison of Beliefs About Healthy Family Functioning," *Family Therapy* 16 (1989): 21ff.

21. "Experts Disagree Over Benefits, Harm Divorce Can Hold for Kids," *Clarion-Ledger*, 2 September 1993.

22. Ibid.

23. Ibid.

24. Ibid.

25. "Changes in Laws Have Changed Divorce," *Jersey Journal*, 11 June 1987.

26. John Bradshaw, *Creating Love: The Next Great Stage of Growth.* (New York: Bantam Books, 1992), 6.

CHAPTER 16

1. Karen Lystra, *Searching the Heart: Women, Men, and Romantic Love in Nineteenth Century America* (New York: Oxford University Press), 28.

2. Jeannie Ralston, "The Man You'd Leave Him For," *Redbook* (November 1993), 78ff.

3. Betty Radice, trans., *The Letters of Abelard and Heloise* (New York: Penguin Books, 1974), 74.

4. Ibid., 113.

5. William Leach, *True Love and Perfect Union: The Feminist Reform of Sex and Society* (New York: Basic Books, 1980), 144–145.

6. Elaine Tyler May, *Great Expectations: Marriage and Divorce in Post-Victorian America* (Chicago: University of Chicago Press, 1980), 113.

CHAPTER 17

1. John Bradshaw, *Creating Love: The Next Great Stage of Growth* (New York: Bantam Books, 1992), 341.

2. Ibid., xiv.

3. Daphne Rose Kingma, *Coming Apart: Why Relationships End and How to Live Through the End of Yours* (New York: Ballantine Books, 1987), 14–15.

4. Ibid., 35–36.

5. Ibid., 18.

6. Ibid., 9–10.

7. Ibid., 10.

8. Robert N. Bellah, et al., *Habits of the Heart: Individualism and Commitment in American Life* (New York: Harper & Row, 1985), 47.

9. William Leach, *True Love and Perfect Union: The Feminist Reform of Sex and Society* (New York: Basic Books, 1980), 284.

10. Marianne Williamson, *A Return to Love* (New York: HarperCollins, 1993), 107.

11. Ibid., 108.

12. Ibid., 166.

13. Arlene Skolnick, *Embattled Paradise: The American Familyman's Age of Uncertainty* (New York: Basic Books, 1991), 212.

CHAPTER 18

1. William Leach, *True Love and Perfect Union: The Feminist Reform of Sex and Society* (New York: Basic Books, 1980), 10–11.

2. Glenda Riley, *Divorce: An American Tradition* (New York: Oxford University Press, 1991), 121.

3. Leach, *True Love*, 31–32.

4. Ibid., 80.

5. Riley, *Divorce*, 121.

6. Ibid., 38.

7. David Popenoe, *Disturbing the Nest: Family Change & Decline in Modern Societies* (New York: Aldine De Gruyter, 1988), xiii.

8. Asa Murray and Karin Sandovist, "Fathers' Absence and Children's Achievement from Age 13 to 21," *Scandinavian Journal of Education Research* 34, no. 1 (1990): 3–28.

9. Popenoe, *Disturbing the Nest*, xiv–xv.

10. Frank F. Furstenberg, Jr., and Andrew J. Cherlin, *Divided Families: What Happens*

to Children When Parents Part (Cambridge, Mass.: Harvard University Press, 1991), 72–74.

11. Dennis A. Ahlburg and Carol J. DeVita, "New Realities of the American Family" *Population Bulletin* 47, no. 2 (August 1992): 29.

12. Richard Cohen, "Huffington? He's No Worse Than His Party's Program," *New York Post*, 14 October 1994.

CHAPTER 19

1. Douglas J. Besharov and Karen N. Gardiner, "Paternalism and Welfare Reform," *The Public Interest* (Winter 1986): 2.

2. Ibid.

3. Family Research Council, September 1993.

CHAPTER 20

1. Randall Collins, *Sociology of Marriage and the Family: Gender, Love, and Property* (Chicago: Nelson-Hall, 1985), in Andrew J. Cherlin, *Marriage, Divorce, Remarriage* (Cambridge, Mass.: Harvard University Press, 1992), 137.

2. Dennis A. Ahlburg and Carol J. DeVita, "New Realities of the American Family," *Population Bulletin* 47, no. 2 (August 1992): 15.

3. Frank F. Furstenberg, Jr. and Andrew. J. Cherlin, *Divided Families: What Happens to Children When Parents Part* (Cambridge, Mass.: Harvard University Press, 1991), 6.

4. I Corinthians 13: 4–8.

5. Laurel Thatcher Ulrich, *Good Wives: Image and Reality in the Lives of Women in Northern New England 1650–1750* (New York: Oxford University Press, 1983), 121.

6. Joseph J. Ellis, *Passionate Sage: The Character and Legacy of John Adams* (New York: Norton, 1993).

7. C. S. Lewis, *Mere Christianity* (New York: Collier Books, 1960), 97–98.

8 Ahlburg and DeVita, "New Realities," 11.

INDEX

95652